LET ME FINISH

ALSO BY ROGER ANGELL

Game Time

A Pitcher's Story

Once More Around the Park

Season Ticket

Late Innings

Five Seasons

The Summer Game

A Day in the Life of Roger Angell

The Stone Arbor

LET ME FINISH

Roger Angell

Harcourt, Inc.

Orlando   Austin   New York

San Diego   Toronto   London

Library of Congress Cataloging-in-Publication Data
Angell, Roger.
Let me finish/Roger Angell.—1st ed.
p.   cm.
1. Angell, Roger.   2. Sportswriters—United States—Biography.
3. Authors—United States—Biography.   I. Title.
GV742.42.A76 A3   2006
070.4'40796092—dc22   2005033067
ISBN-13: 978-0-15-101350-0   ISBN-10: 0-15-101350-0

Text set in Adobe Garamond
Designed by Scott Piehl

Printed in the United States of America

First edition
K J I H G F E D C B A

CONTENTS

CONTENTS

LET ME FINISH

Introduction

MOST of the true stories in this book were written in the last three years and came as a surprise to me, the author. I'd not planned a memoir, if that's what this is, and never owned a diary or made notes about the passage of the days. "The King of the Forest," a piece of mine about my late father, Ernest Angell, was inspired by a letter I'd received from a woman I didn't know, enclosing a story he'd written for the children's magazine *St. Nicholas,* in 1903, when he was thirteen, which tells a family tragedy in a fresh way. My own piece was well received when it ran in *The New Yorker* but got mixed reviews from others in the family, who shook their heads and told me that I'd pretty much blown my portrait of Father. "He was never like that," they said. "Not with me." Our stories about our own lives are a form of fiction, I began to see, and become more insistent as we grow older, even as we try to make them come out in some other way.

There is a bit of melodrama attached to a golf game I once played in Maine, back in 1940—a turn of events so strange that I tucked it away as something I might write one day. But I never could get it right, couldn't find a form or a tone for it. I even tried to write it as a short story but quickly gave that up as well. I saved one paragraph, a description of the little harborside course and how it looked to us teenagers back then, as a memorandum or preservative, and that found its way intact into the chapter "Getting There," when it sprang to life in my head a year ago and got written in three days.

These old stories we tell ourselves in the middle of the night require no more than a whisper or a street noise to get them whirring again in a fresh production. William Maxwell, in his autobiographical novel "So Long, See You Tomorrow," recalls himself as a small boy with an earache, back at home in Lincoln, Illinois, and his father, bending close, blowing cigar smoke into his ear to make him feel better. My story about my father begins with the perfectly remembered sound of his pen on paper while he writes letters in the evening, in our library on Ninety-third Street, in New York, while the ten- or eleven-year-old me awaits the larger swirl of his signature on the last page of the evening, after which he'll pick up *Oliver Twist*—"Now, where were we?"— and continue our reading aloud. Life is tough and brimming with loss, and the most we can do about it is to glimpse ourselves clear now and then, and find out what we feel about familiar scenes and recurring faces this time around.

What is startling about memory is its willful persistence and its obsession with detail. "Hold on," it says. "Don't lose this." The other day I unexpectedly found myself seeing the shape of the knobs at the top of the low iron posts that stand along the paths of Central Park—a magnolia bud or perhaps an acorn—and then, long before this, the way such posts looked when they were connected by running strands of heavy wire, which were slightly bent into irregularity and almost loose to the touch. Going down a path in those days you could hook the first joints of your forefinger and second finger over the darkly shining wire and feel it slither along under your touch. In winter, you could grab the wire in your gloved or mittened hand and rush along, friction free, and make it bounce or shiver when you reached the next post and had to let go. But what's the point of this, I wonder: what's my mind doing back there? A week or so before my father died, in his eighties, he told me he'd been thinking about a little red shirt that he'd worn when he was four or five years old. "Isn't that strange?" he said.

My stepfather, E. B. White, is in this book as well, and so are my first wife and some car trips and tennis games and, again and again, my mother, but these chapters don't add up to biography. Nor do they evoke a better time. To keep things moving, I have interspersed short entertainments about drinking or sailing or the movies—parts of my life as well, but in here mostly for the fun of it. One chapter, "Early Innings," may be familiar to some readers, but I've revived it because it evokes a different era in sports and continues or fills out what I've written about my father. Another section, "At the Comic Weekly," brings up friends and colleagues of mine at *The New Yorker,* as they once were. I don't yearn for the past—I doubt that I could have written much of this if I did—and my present-day family and friends and the people I see at work don't need to be put down on paper for me to notice and enjoy them.

The title of this book, I should add, isn't about wrapping up a life or a time of life but should only evoke a garrulous gent at the end of the table holding up one hand while he tries to remember the great last line of his monologue.

Romance

ONE spring Saturday when I was seven going on eight, my mother brought me with her on an automobile outing with her young lover and future husband, E. B. White. She took our family car, a slope-nosed Franklin sedan, and we must have met Andy by prearrangement at our garage. He did the driving. We left New York and went up into Westchester County for lunch—this was 1928 and it was still mostly country. On the way back, my mother, who had taken the wheel, stripped the gears while shifting, and we ground to a halt, halfway onto a shoulder of the Bronx River Parkway. Disaster. Andy thumbed a ride to go find a tow truck, and my mother, I now realize, was left to make this into an amusing story to tell my father and my older sister at dinner that evening. She almost never drove—thus the screeching and scraping sounds beneath us and the agonized look on her face when she got lost in mid-shift and we broke down. It was also unusual, an adventure, for me to be alone with her and her office friend Mr. White, as she'd described him. I think I wasn't meant to be there; maybe a Saturday date with a schoolmate had fallen through, and she'd had no recourse but to bring me along. But she never would have taken me off on an outing that would require me to lie about it to my father afterward, so the trip must have been presented to him beforehand as a chance for her to practice her driving, with the reliable Andy White as instructor. I had no idea, of course, that she and I were stranded in a predicament, but I recall sitting beside her on the running board of the ticking, cooling Franklin while we waited, with the pale new shrubs and pastoral grasses of the Parkway around us, and the occasional roadster or touring car (with its occupants swiveling their gaze toward us as they came by) swooshing past. Then a tow truck appeared around the curve behind us, with Andy White standing on the right-hand running board and waving excitedly. Yay, I'm back, we're rescued! My father would never have done that—found a tow so quickly or waved like a kid when he spotted us.

The story stops here. I don't remember that night or anything else about our little trip, but in less than two years my parents were divorced and my mother and Andy married and living on East Eighth Street. They soon had their own car, or cars: they kept changing. The Depression had arrived, but they were a successful *New Yorker* couple—she a fiction editor; he a writer of casuals and poetry and the first-page Comment section—and they loved driving around in an eight-year-old Pierce-Arrow touring car, with a high-bustle trunk, side mirrors, and flapping white roof. After their son was born—my brother Joel—they moved up to a staid seven-passenger Buick sedan. In the mid-thirties, Andy also acquired a secondhand beige-and-black 1928 Plymouth roadster—country wheels, used mostly around their place in Maine. The Buick still mattered to him. Back when it was new, thieves stole it out of a garage on University Place one night and used it in a daring bank stick-up in Yonkers. Andy was upset, but when he read an account of the crime in the newspapers the next day, with a passage that went "and the robbers' powerful getaway car swiftly outdistanced police pursuers," he changed sides. "C'mon, Buick!" he said. "Go!"

Every family has its own car stories, but in another sense we know them all in advance now, regardless of our age. The collective American unconscious is stuffed with old Pontiacs, and fresh reminders are never lacking. Weekend rallies flood the Mendocino or Montpelier back roads with high-roofed Model A's and Chevys, revarnished 1936 Woodies, and thrumming, leaf-tone T-Birds; that same night, back home again or with our feet up at the Hyatt, we click onto TCM and find *The Grapes of Wrath,* or *Bonnie and Clyde,* or *Five Easy Pieces,* or *Thelma & Louise,* waiting to put us out on the narrow, anachronism-free macadam once again. (A friend of mine used to drive around the Village in his 1938 De Soto hearse, except when it was out on lease to still another *Godfather* movie.) Grandchildren, clicking to 50 Cent or Eminem on their iPods in the back seat, sigh and roll their eyes whenever the old highwayman starts up again. Yes, car travel was bumpier and curvier back then, with more traffic lights and billboards, more cows and hillside graveyards, no air-conditioning and almost no interstates, and with tin cans and Nehi signs and red Burma-Shave jingles crowding the narrow roadside. Give us a break.

Still, we drove, and what startles me from this great distance is how often and how far. I was a New York City kid who knew the subways and museums and movie theatres and zoos and ballparks by heart, but in the 1930s also got out of town a lot, mostly by car. I drove (well, was driven) to Bear Mountain and Atlantic City and Gettysburg and Niagara Falls; went repeatedly to Boston and New Hampshire and Maine; drove to a Missouri cattle farm owned by an uncle; drove there during another summer and thence onward to Santa Fe and Tesuque and out to the Arizona Painted Desert. Then back again, to New York. Before this, in March, 1933—it was the week of Franklin Delano Roosevelt's first inaugural—I'd boarded a Greyhound bus to Detroit, along with a Columbia student named Tex Goldschmidt, where we picked up a test-model Terraplane sedan at the factory (courtesy of an advertising friend of my father's who handled the Hudson-Essex account) and drove it back home. A couple of months later, in company with a math teacher named Mr. Burchell or Burkhill and four Lincoln School seventh-grade classmates, I crammed into a buckety old Buick sedan and drove to the Century of Progress Exposition in Chicago; we came back by way of

Niagara Falls, and, because I had been there before and knew the ropes, took time also to visit the Shredded Wheat factory, some tacky mummies, and a terrific fifty-cent roadside exhibition of dented and rusty, candy-wrapper-littered barrels and iron balls in which various over-the-brink daredevils had mostly met their end. With one exception, all of us in our party were still speaking.

If I now hop aboard some of these bygone trips for a mile or two, it is not for the sake of easy nostalgia—the fizz of warm moxie up your nose; the Nabokovian names of roadside tourist cottages; the glint of shattered glass and sheen of blood around a tree-crumpled gray Reo; or the memory of collies and children, unaccustomed to automotion, throwing up beside their hastily parked family vehicles—but in search of some thread or path that links these outings and sometimes puts Canandaigua or Kirksville or Keams Canyon back in my head when I wake up in the middle of the night. Effort can now and then produce a sudden fragment of locality: the car stopped and me waking up with my sweating cheek against the gray plush of the back seat, as I stare at a mystifying message, "VEEDOL," painted on a square of white tin so bright in the sun that it makes me wince. Veedol? Beyond it, against the stucco gas-station wall, is a handmade sign, wavery in the gasoline fumes rising outside my window. Where are we? I want to sit up and ask my father, standing out there in his sneakers, khaki pants, and an old shirt with rolled-up sleeves, who is fishing his thick brown wallet—we're on a long haul to somewhere—out of a hip pocket, but I'm too dazed to speak.

The first day of that 1933 school trip to the Chicago World's Fair went on forever, and it was after dark when we topped a hillside in Ligonier, Pennsylvania, slowed at the vision of Pittsburgh alight in the distance, and felt a little lurch and jolt as the right rear wheel fell off the Buick and rolled gently on ahead for a few yards by itself. I can't remember dinner, but it was past midnight when, rewheeled, we pulled up at the McKeesport YMCA and settled for two double rooms, plus cots. Jerry Tallmer, a surviving member of the party, tells me that a fellow traveler, less suave than the rest of us, confessed to him later that until this moment he'd held a childhood notion that if you weren't in bed by midnight you died. Out in Chicago, we took in the House of Tomorrow and Buckminster Fuller's Dymaxion Car; ogled Sally Rand's "Streets of Paris" but didn't attend; went to the Museum of Natural History; laughed at Chicago's dinky elevated cars; and in our little notebooks wrote down that Depression soup kitchen lines in Chicago looked exactly like the ones in depressed New York. We were smart and serious, and would be expected to report on this trip in Social Studies, come fall. The Century of Progress, we concluded, was mostly about *advertising*. One afternoon, the temperature went down twenty-nine degrees in an hour and a half as a black storm blew in from over Lake Michigan; the next morning we read that the sightseeing plane whose ticket window we'd seen at the Fair had crashed, killing all aboard. Three days later, wheeling south from Niagara Falls, my companions (including the heroic Burkhill or Burchell, who did all the driving) offered to pay me two dollars apiece if I'd just shut up for a change, and not speak another word for the rest of the trip. Unaffronted and short of cash, I agreed, and collected my princely ten bucks while we were passing under the new George Washington Bridge, just about home.

Breakdowns happened all the time. A year earlier, headed for Missouri with my pal Tex Goldschmidt, our car, another family Franklin, quit cold on a hillside in Liberty, New York. Towed to a garage, we learned that the replacement part we needed would arrive by mail in two days. We put up in an adjacent boarding house, where the large brown cookies permanently in place in the center of the dining-room table were just possibly varnished. Sitting on porch rockers that evening, with our feet up on the railing, we were terrified by a Catskill lightning bolt that flew along a grounding wire from the rooftop rod and down a viney column a yard or two from our toes. We sat on, listening to the thrash of night trees and the gurgle of water through the gutter downspouts, when—*bam!*—it happened again: an explosion and a blaze of white down the same path, and the smell of immeasurable voltage in the air around us.

"Well, so much for *that* adage," Tex said, rising. "I'm going to bed."

Arthur Goldschmidt came from San Antonio, and was knowledgeable about cars and roadside stuff. He'd been hired by my father, with whom I lived on weekdays, to come down from Columbia a couple of afternoons a week and spend some time with me when I got home from school, but he was so smart and engaging that he became a fixture. Here, a few months later, he'd been given the family car and the family wise guy to take out West; my father would come along by train a little later, while Tex continued south to see his folks. Driving, Tex smoked Chesterfields and talked about the Scottsboro boys, asked if I thought Babe Ruth wore a girdle, and wondered how much I knew about the corrupt but colorful governor of Texas, Ma Ferguson. We had no radio but stayed alert anyway. Tex was the one to spot the first buzzard aloft and the rare passing North Dakota license plate, and to pick up on roadside or billboard names. ("Sweet Orr Pants," he said, musingly. "Coward Shoes?") He challenged me to recite all the Burma-Shave jingles we'd encountered ("The bearded lady / tried a jar / she's now / a famous movie star / Burma-Shave"; "Rip a fender / off your car / mail it in for / a half-pound jar / Burma-Shave") and make up some of our own. He made me rate the girls in my class for looks and then for character, and said, "If our left front tire is six feet around, how many revolutions will it make by the time we reach Cleveland?" Late in our trip, wheeling down an unpopulated gravel highway west of Edina, Missouri, Tex slowed as we came up to three black sedans, oddly parked crossways on the road at a little distance from each other. As we passed the first one, to our left, the second moved forward from the right to block our path, but Tex spun us hard right, spewing gravel, passed behind him, and floored it up the road and away. Prohibition revenue inspectors, he thought, or maybe a highway stickup. Bonnie Parker and Clyde Barrow were around here somewhere, making do in hard times.

I keep forgetting how hot it was, driving. Two summers along, in late August of 1934, my father replanned the second part of our trip by leaving my uncle's place in Green Castle, Missouri (the same haven Tex and I had been heading for), around noon and driving non-stop to Santa Fe. We'd do Kansas by night and stay cool. Our party—Father, my eighteen-year-old sister Nancy, her Concord Academy classmate Barbara Kidder (the two had just graduated), and I—were experienced car people by now. We hated motels, carried water in our two big thermoses (later, in New Mexico, we bought a waterskin and slung it on a front fender), and favored gas stations with the old-style pumps that were cranked by hand like an ice cream freezer while you watched your Sunoco or Gulf slosh into a glass ten-gallon container up on top, then empty into your tank. We knew how to open a Coke by sticking a silver dollar under the cap and banging the bottle with your fist, and we'd learned to stop wincing or weaving when another languid or headlight-entranced rabbit in the road—ba-bump—went to the great cabbage patch in the sky. The floor in the back of the car filled up with crumpled sections of the Kansas

City *Star* or the St. Joseph *News-Press* that we'd picked up at the last diner.

Nancy was driving by now, and could spell my father for two-hour stretches. She was a better driver than he was. Her hair was tied up with a string of red yarn, keeping it off her ears; at the wheel, she'd fire up a cigarette with the dashboard lighter, then hold it in the air in her long fingers, a ring of scarlet lipstick around the nearer end. Too classy for Bryn Mawr, I thought. I liked Barbara Kidder, who wore a blue neck bandanna and shorts, and had a nice store of rattlesnake and Gila-monster stories; her parents were archeologists—she was joining them later at a dig in Nevada. My father overcorrected while driving and favored long silences, but he was a soldier, a *commandante,* at the wheel, good for a five-hour bore through the blazing Indiana afternoon while we dozed and told dumb jokes. He didn't go in for jokes, but laughed out loud when we imitated him trying to order his breakfast café au lait from a waitress at our creaky small-hotel dining room. This always started our day. "I want a glass of milk," he began, speaking loudly and fashioning the shape of a glass in the air. "*Cold* milk, in a glass. Then, and in addition, I'd like a cup of coffee"—his hands moved to one side, forming an invisible cup with a saucer underneath—"and with it a pitcher of *hot* milk, to put into the coffee. Now, again: cold milk, please, in a glass"—he poured it and pushed it carefully to the side—"coffee, hot coffee"—he made a happy sniffing sound, at the Maxwell Houseness of it—"and over here our hot milk"—little finger waves to show heat rising—"to put into the hot coffee. Is that clear?" But of course it wasn't.

The waitress, bewildered by this mixture of mime and command and terrified by the lawyerly glare in his dark eyes, had long since paused with her pencil. What Father got was generally coffee with cold milk in the pitcher, or coffee and boiling water, or, at least once, iced coffee. It never came out right. We shook our heads helplessly, knowing that he wasn't cruel or unfeeling: he just liked things nice.

That night, in Kansas, Father held to course, upright at the wheel through the eight- or ten-mile straightaways, with the bright headlights forming—for me, in back—an outlined silhouette of his ears and bald head and strong forearms. I would fall asleep, and when I woke again it would be Nancy driving and smoking, with Father asleep on the right-hand seat and Barbara asleep beside me in back. The night air rushed in about us through the tilted wind portals at the front of the front windows and the smaller ones in back (we were in the zippy Terraplane that Tex and I had brought from Detroit), and with it the hot, flat scent of tall corn; a sudden tang of skunk come and gone; the smell of tar when the dirt roads stopped, fainter now with the hot sun gone; and, over a rare pond or creek as the tire noise went deeper, something rich and dank, with cowflop and dead fish mixing with the sweet-water weeds. I had a Texaco road map with me in back, and when we came through a little town or stopped at a ringing railroad crossing I got out my flashlight and tried to follow the thin blue line of our passage: Chapman and WaKeeney, Winona, and now—we must have turned south a bit—Sharon Springs. I fell asleep again. Sometime in the night, my hand found Barbara's hand and held on. When I awoke with the first sun behind us, we'd climbed out of the heat, and the field dirt around us had a redder hue. "Colorado," Father said softly. I lay back in my nest and Barbara's hand came out from under her thin Mexican blanket and took mine once again. That morning, we went through La Junta and Trinidad and over the Raton Pass into New Mexico. (We'd stopped earlier at a lookout where four different states were visible, surely, in the haze to the east and south.) The Sangre de Cristos came into view and the first soft-cornered adobe houses, and that night we ate at La Fonda with my Aunt Elsie, who worked for the Indian Bureau, and had Hopi snake dances and San Ildefonso pottery-makers and Mabel Dodge Luhan in store for us in the coming weeks. Almost the best part was still ahead.

I learned how to drive early, and in June of 1936 sent five dollars to the Bureau of Motor Vehicles in Augusta, Maine, along with a note saying, "I am fifteen. Please send my license in enclosed envelope." That was all it took. I appropriated the Whites' yellowy old Plymouth roadster, with its splayed fenders, wooden-spoke wheels, cracked leather front seat, and leaky ragtop roof. (I carried a thick roll of Johnson & Johnson adhesive tape under the seat, for rainy-day patch-ups.) There was a little hole in the floorboards, near the brake pedal, and if you glanced down there on a daytime errand you could see the grainy macadam streaming by under your foot. Soon I was taking girls to the movies on Tuesday or Saturday nights, upstairs at the Town Hall in Blue Hill, or to the Grand, in Ellsworth. I kept my headlights on low beam on foggy nights, suavely navigating through sudden thick blankets of damp, and found quiet places to park in East Blue Hill or out on Naskeag Point. I had become Andy Hardy. Making out in parked cars puts me into the movies or into a thousand cartoons, but what memory presents about these chilly long-gone summer evenings is the first five minutes under way, with my hands at ease on the nubbly wheel, and with the white highway ahead and the gleam from the looped roadside power wires giving back tanned knees, a sweet nose and strong chin, just there to my right. Intimacy.

Late on a Sunday afternoon in February, 1938, somebody called up the stairs of my boarding school dormitory, "Angell, there are three women from Smith down here to see you." We were in the hilly northeast corner of Connecticut, far into the dreary winter-term stretches of my senior year, with spring vacation still six weeks away. A gag of some sort. Muttering, I came down and found Cynthia Coggan's blue Ford phaeton waiting by the door, and her tickled smile behind the snap-on winter side window—a friend from Maine, with crinkly blond hair and her own low, late-model white-wall speedster, the snazziest wheels I knew. She was about my age, but a year and a light-year ahead. Now, with two classmates for company, she'd driven seventy or eighty miles from Northampton on impulse, to press a surprise Sunday call. I rushed upstairs for a coat and permission, and in another minute was turning around from the cozy front seat to meet the new ladies in back as we sped away, delightfully in motion. I only had an hour—time enough for tea and cake at an inn in the next village, it turned out—and they got me back barely before compulsory evening Vespers. Walking into the chapel, I knew that every eye was on me and that my school clout had just taken a gigantic upward leap. I didn't have to tell anybody that Cynthia was a friend, not a girlfriend, or that the difference didn't matter to me. All I could think about was the ride and the compliment.

Driving nowadays is nothing like it was. Mostly, it's a time of day: where we are before the mall, or around nine and six and—thank you, God—not later. On longer reaches, noise and wind rustle have been abolished, traffic-free stretches appear only late at night or in the moments when a red light has swept the road clean and our power-laden machines provide an airliner sort of lift that does away with inertia and topography. We move in ceaseless company, each of us wrapped in cold air and an expensive and imperturbable anonymity. Only now and then, easing at seventy-six miles per hour past the Audi going seventy-two, do we throw a glance at our neighbors three feet to the right and are startled—it nearly makes you jump—by pure genre: two or three young men gesturing and laughing at something in there, or an older woman holding up her book and reading out loud to her driver husband. Driving, for all its drags and trouble, puts us together—I'm amazed that its immense advertising never quite gets this right—and on some trips delivers a complicated fresh sense of ourselves. I think that pause with my mother on the Bronx River Parkway first stuck in my memory as an adventure but later on because she and I almost never had something happen just to the two of us. And if she thought back to that outing it could have been to see Andy

White—perhaps they were not quite lovers yet—finding a boyish and confident joy in the unexpected. My Lincoln school classmates didn't hate me for my non-stop blather in our crowded Buick; they craved a little quiet, and bet that perhaps I'd enjoy it, too, given a chance. It was a long shot, but maybe I'd find, along about Poughkeepsie, that I didn't have to be on all the time to stay alive. Tex Goldschmidt never looked at his watch in the day and a half we hung out together in Liberty, New York, waiting for that distributor part, while my father would have seen the mishap as a test of some kind, and gone all stern and strong in response. But Father trusted Tex because he'd seen what his jokes and sweet spirit did for us; there was something easy and silly there that he longed for. I don't know what Barbara Kidder made of our holding hands like that. She was almost a woman that night and I still almost a boy, and I can't say why I'm so sure she never mentioned it to anyone.

There's a famous story by John Updike called "The Happiest I've Been," which ends in a long car trip. In it, the narrator, John, a college sophomore, is driving back to Chicago after a Christmas visit home in the middle of Pennsylvania. The trip back is a seventeen-hour haul and he shares a car with a friend named Neil (it's his father's car). Before heading west, they stop at a drunken party, and late that night John holds a girl in his arms on a sofa, mostly because they're both so cold. He kisses her a little and she falls asleep. Dawn is coming when the trip begins at last (the girls are gone), and Neil unexpectedly lets John drive the car. Then Neil falls asleep, too. As I read this story for the first time, in 1959, when it came out in *The New*

Yorker, my mind went back, as if on radar, to Barbara Kidder.

"When we came into tunnel country"—the last passage goes—"the flicker and hollow amplification stirred Neil awake. He sat up, the mackinaw dropping to his lap, and lit a cigarette. A second after the scratch of his match the moment occurred of which each following moment was a slight diminution, as we made the long irregular descent toward Pittsburgh. There were many reasons for my feeling so happy. We were on our way. I had seen a dawn. This far, Neil could appreciate, I had brought us safely. Ahead, a girl waited who, if I asked, would marry me, but first there was a long trip; many hours and towns interceded between me and that encounter.... And there was knowing that twice since midnight a person had trusted me enough to fall asleep beside me."

Movie Kid

TRACKING shot, please, of a twelve-year-old boy running north on Lexington Avenue as a 1933 twilight begins to fall. He is sprinting for home, on Ninety-third Street, and guilt makes him fly. He must be there in time to get a little homework under his belt before his old man arrives from the office, and in time to assume the bored, everyday look of a kid just back from his school's afternoon rec program, instead of from "King Kong" at the RKO 86th Street, where he has really been. Panting, he lets himself in the front door, checks out the mail for a *Popular Mechanics*, checks out the dog, grabs a banana, falls on his bed, opens a math book, and gives himself over to thoughts of Robert Armstrong, Bruce Cabot, Fay Wray (Fay Wray!), jungle drums, aerial machine-gun fire, and the remembered velvety dark of a movie theatre in the afternoon. The thought *Lucky again* crosses his mind, and in time he may actually find a pencil and begin to write down fractions. The boy (he is me) went on being lucky. No one at home or at school ever twigged to his stolen movie afternoons, and for the rest of that school year, as in the year before, he made it down to the Eighty-sixth Street casbah a couple of times a week, where there were five theatres to choose from, each offering a double feature, to deepen his budget of guilt and joy, make critical inroads on his allowance, and hook him, once and for good, on the movies. Afternoon ticket prices stood at an invariable fifteen cents, and another nickel covered a Milky Way, a Hershey's Almond, or a tube of chalky Necco Wafers, from which I discarded the licorice layers in advance. Now and then, one of these palaces would decide to enforce the city's "No Unaccompanied Minors" ordinance, whereupon I would hold out my sweaty dime and nickel to the nearest approaching pervert or dope fiend, and say, "Take me in, Mister?" as was the convention. "The kid's wit' me," he would say to the woman in the booth, as was also the convention, and we would walk in as family and wordlessly part forever.

What I saw on those stolen afternoons (and, on the up and up, sometimes on weekends) was a cross-section of early-thirties Hollywood, which was just then coming into high gear. Paul Muni in Howard Hawks' *Scarface* and *I Am a Fugitive from a Chain Gang* slip into view, as do Cecil B. De Mille's *The Sign of the Cross* (with Claudette Colbert as a Roman temptress bathing in ass's milk), the Barrymores in *Rasputin and the Empress,* Dick Powell in another Busby Berkeley musical, the Marx Brothers (with the dopey Zeppo singing "Everyone Says I Love You" to Thelma Todd), the vine-borne Johnny Weissmuller, Jimmy Cagney shot dead

in his pin-striped suit in *The Public Enemy,* and Laurel and
Hardy forced to share their bed with a chimp and a flea circus. One afternoon, I found myself alone in the dark with
Bela Lugosi's pallid, orally fixated Count Dracula, and real-
izing, even as I stared, that I wouldn't be able to call out for
help that night, when he returned, in his cape and slippery
hair, to break in on my sleep.

Mostly, I would turn up at the Orpheum or the 86th
Street Garden while the second feature was in progress—a
low-budget murder or a B-musical starring Lupe Velez, say,
or a Wheeler & Woolsey comedy, or Leo Carillo's carefree
gaucho act—and then wish for its ending to hurry along (as
I tilted my wristwatch toward the screen), so that I might
squeeze in a full main feature before my deadline. The better movies ran long, though, and I don't think I ever did
learn the foredoomed end of Garbo's *Mata Hari*—although
the moment when she leans over and blows out John Gilbert's
bedside icon candle has stayed with me. I didn't know what
this meant but zowie! Walking into the middle of movies
was the common American thing during the double-feature
era, and if one stayed the course, only minimal mental splic-
ing was required to reconnect the characters and the plot of
the initial feature when it rolled around again. The demise
of the double bill has done away with this knack and has
also expunged "I think this is where we came in" from the
language—a better phrase, all in all, than "déjà vu," and easier to pronounce.

Quality was not much of a factor in my afternoon
choices, but I had already noticed that although the flicks
were clearly wasting my mind, as my father would have put

it, they were richly nutritious to some other side of me. One bathed in this scummy Ganges and arose refreshed, with surprising memories. Most of my friends still go to the movies, but not many of them are movie-goers in this sense, and while I sometimes wonder at the thousands of hours I have spent in the popcorned dark, there was an avid, darting kind of selection one learned there—a process at once ironic and romantic which plucks up scenes and faces, attitudes and moments to save from the rush of events—that felt like a saving knack of some sort, and passkey for later times.

When I moved along to high school and then college, I found movie-permeated friends waiting for me. Big-screen dialogue and scenes filled our talk and if one of us unexpectedly held up an invisible lorgnette, like the dandified eighteenth-century spy Leslie Howard, and began, "They seek him here, they seek him there / Those Frenchies seek him everywhere. / Is he in Heaven," the rest of us in the room would join in: "Is he in—" (*lorgnette points downward*) / "That demned elusive Pimpern*el*?" I graduated and went into the Air Force and eventually off to the Pacific. At Hickam Field, in Hawaii, we'd check out the post theatre in the evening and, if we didn't like what was on, slip through a hole in the fence into adjoining Pearl Harbor and walk to the sector of docks where five or six destroyer escorts were tied up side by side. (The Navy always had the latest releases, for some reason.) Sailors on board would tip us about which ship had the best feature that night, and we'd step over—saluting the con as we came aboard—and settle down with the crew on the fantail, just in time for the Mickey. One night, late in 1944, while I lay under the stars and watched Gene Kelly and Rita Hayworth dancing to Jerome Kern tunes in *Cover Girl,* it came to me that this war might end some day, and there would be more life and movies to come.

Before that, much earlier in my time in the service, I had joined a reluctant audience in a sunstruck Army shack one afternoon, where we enlisted men had been assembled to watch another morale booster or sex hygiene film. The compulsory sex one-reelers had once been grisly, military-produced affairs, whose main effect was to breed some lifelong sexual repressives among their captive audiences of young farm boys and dropouts, but now Hollywood had got into the production end, with professional crews and actors. This time, the lights came down and on the screen a colonel looked up from his desk to talk to us about the Articles of War. "Men," he began in a manly, authoritative way, when he was drowned out by our shouts and clapping. "Hey, it's Mister Dithers!" we yelled. "Look—it's Dithers, the old fart got *drafted!*" The man up here on the screen—narrow face, pointed nose, fussy manner—was the character actor Jonathan Hale, here recognized in a flash as Mister Dithers, Dagwood Bumstead's boss in all those Blondie movies, back in peacetime. We talked it over afterward and said it was great casting. Dagwood—he was Arthur Lake, of course—would have beaten the draft, because of his kids and his dumbness, but Mister Dithers, with his chickenshit ways, was pure officer material. The movie had built our morale after all.

When I click on an old movie nowadays, on TCM or some middle-of-the-night back channel—it isn't the stars who keep me awake but a dazzling pack of supporting actors: Frank Morgan, Patsy Kelly, Alan Hale. William Demarest, Billie Burke, and Douglass Dumbrille; C. Aubrey Smith, Andy Devine, and Edna Mae Oliver. "Hey," I murmur, "it's Roscoe Karns. And here's Lynn Overman again." These were all broad types, to be sure, notable for their quirks and reliable charm, and as soon as I name one, others leap to mind. Here's a heart-of-gold Claire Trevor—and Glenda Farrell and Una Merkel. Here are the bumbling Guy Kibbee and Eugene Pallette—and Raymond Walburn. If this is Spring Byington, can Fay Bainter be far behind? And here I recall a later moment, recounted to me by my *New Yorker* colleague Burton Bernstein, about the night when his brother Leonard Bernstein brought their mother along to a big Hollywood party on a Saturday night in the 1950s, and there introduced her to the blonde Anita Louise, an established second-level star. "Anita Louise! Anita Louise!" Mrs. Bernstein cried. "Why, I named my daughter Shirley after you!" Lenny understood his mom's mix-up in a flash, just as I did when the tale was told to me. She was thinking of Ann Shirley, of course, a different reliable blonde in another bunch of movies.

I had a family of my own, back in my movie-sneaking youth, but the addition of so many vivid and confidently eccentric faces and mannerisms to my store of adults was a comfort to me. Sig Rumann, Ann Revere, Jack Oakie, Franklin Pangborn, Eduardo Cianelli, and Porter Hall are still neighbors or perhaps cousins of mine: folks you can count on. I liked it when some of these friends began to turn up in larger roles: they'd made good and done us proud. Mischa Auer, for instance, played the moody Balkan free-loader in the splendid *My Man Godfrey*, and then attained a unique niche of reference when Fred Astaire, singing to Joan Leslie in *The Sky's the Limit*, comes to the last verse of the Johnny Mercer lyric to Harold Arlen's classic "My Shining Hour":

> *This will be my shining hour,*
> *Lonely though it may be,*
> *Like the face of Mischa Auer*
> *On a Music Hall marquee.*

I began sneaking off to movies just when the successive earthquakes of the Depression and the Second World War were coming along, and there was a yearning for a broader and more sophisticated set of attitudes in this country. The movies did it for us; they were just the ticket. The great cresting tide of late-thirties and early-forties Hollywood—an Augustan era, when the studios were cranking out five hundred films each year—swept over us and changed us forever: Astaire and Rogers, Bogart, Judy Garland, Olivier, Cary Grant (wrestling with Irene Dunne's fox terrier, which has his—well, not his, it turns out—derby in its mouth); Gable and Tracy; the Joads and Rupert of Hentzau and Aunt Pittypat; Miss Froy's name drawn on the fogged train window, and David Niven, under fire in his Spad, wiping a spray of engine oil from his aviator goggles. Grant and Hepburn step into a waltz as the old year dies, von Stroheim snips his geranium, and spoiled heiress Bette Davis has this brain tumor that brings about a brief, strange happiness with her brain surgeon husband George Brent.

Anyone who was the wrong age or in the wrong place for this stuff—my parents and my children, for instance, and even those who picked it up later from videos and American-studies classes—never quite caught up. We were the lucky ones, we first citizens of film, and we trusted the movies for the rest of our lives. We sat down in our Loew's or Bijou or Pantages as strangers to each other but together absorbed fresh gestures, new tones of voice, and different tones of mind and style, as taught by the dashing, elegant, or stricken figures up on the screen: the same wished-for, uniting experience that sends us out to the movies today but too often without reward. I still go to the movies, of course, and one of the overcrowded plexes I frequent—with their squalid queues and deafening trailers—is the same Orpheum, sans stage and soaring balconies, that I used to emerge from, guilty and entranced, into the speckled shade of the Third Avenue El.

The King of the Forest

EVERY night when I was a boy, I sat and read in our living room, listening to my father writing letters. He wrote on his lap in longhand, with the letter paper backed by one of his long yellow legal pads, and the scratch and swirl of his black Waterman pen across the page sounded like the scrabblings of a creature in the underbrush. There were no pauses or crossings out, and in time I realized that I could even identify the swash of a below-the-line "g" leaping diagonally upward into an "h" and the crossing double zag of an ensuing "t," and, soon after, the blip of a period. When he reached the bottom of the page, the sheet was turned over and smoothed down in a single, back-of-the-hand gesture, and the rush of writing and pages went on, while I waited for the declarative final "E" or "Ernest"—the loudest sound of all—that told me the letter was done. When the envelope had been addressed, licked, and sealed with a postmasterish thump of his fist, he would pluck a Lucky

Strike out of its green pack and whack it violently four times against his thumbnail, like a man hammering a spike, then damply tongue the other end before lighting up. By the time the first deep drag appeared as a pale upward jet of smoke, another letter was in progress. I went back to my book. Sooner or later, the letters would be over, and he would be ready to read aloud to me. "Finished," he would announce, picking up *Oliver Twist*. "Now, where were we?"

Friends my age—I am past my seventies—tell me that they, too, often find themselves caught up in details of their childhood, but I wonder if they ever find, as I do, that they are reliving a parent's life as well as their own. My father, a New York lawyer, was lean and tall, with long fingers, brown eyes, and an air of energy about him. One of his great-grandmothers was a Seneca Indian—the Angell family had come from western New York State—and his high forehead, strong nose, and long upper lip affixed an Iroquois solemnity to his expression that he did not always feel. Handsome and dashing in the flattering, tightly cut suits and jackets of the 1930s (like Gary Cooper, he remained unstuffy in a vest), he strode swiftly, banged doors behind him, and swarmed up stairs, appearing always on the verge of some outdoor errand or expedition. Bravura came naturally to him. In Snedens Landing, a hillside enclave twenty miles upriver from New York where we sometimes passed our summers, there is a small waterfall made by a brook that splashes steeply down into a mossy and perpetually shadowed woodland pool. When I was a child, there were always large Sunday picnics there, in an adjoining pergola that looked out on the Hudson, and my father, on the slightest urging and sometimes with no urging at all, would climb up to a scary, almost invisible niche in the cliff face, nearly thirty feet above the water. He would stand there interminably—a bald, narrow Tarzan in floppy bathing trunks—and then at last launch himself out over the boulders in an elegant swan dive into the exact center of the tiny pool. I can still see the waves sloshing over the spillway as he came up, spouting and triumphant. It was a parlor trick, of a kind, and, like all parlor tricks, perhaps insufferable— except to a small son of the diver.

We stopped going to Snedens when my parents were divorced, but I remember returning to the pool with Father once when I was in my teens. He climbed up the cliff again and poised and dived, but this time I tried to talk him out of it; I was embarrassed by the whole dangerous performance. The truth was, of course, that I didn't have the nerve to try it myself, and I lacked the spirit that made it all so important to him.

It was this spirit, brought to mountain climbing, to figure skating, to tap dancing, to tennis and trout fishing, to skiing and canoeing and gardening and so forth, that sometimes inspired us in the family to call him the King of the Forest. His tennis game was thunderous but erratic, and it took years for me to realize that his real physical grace was non-suburban. He could flick a Royal Coachman fly again and again into a backwater beneath an alder thicket twenty yards away; he knew how to carve an axe handle; and he swam, otterlike, with an oily smoothness that left no ripples. He was a terrible tap dancer, by contrast, but undauntable. Late one night in Paris (he was in his sixties), while in company with his friends the British writer V. S. Pritchett and his wife, he broke into a creaky, Gene Kelly-ish spatter of kicks and taps across the sidewalk and up against the store shutters of a steep little side street in Montmartre. I was appalled when the Pritchetts told me about it later, but they didn't agree. "No, no," they said, laughing. "It was simply extraordinary."

Where this élan came from is a mystery, for he was not a trivial sort of person, not an entertainer. He didn't get it from his father, a slight, almost frail man, who had been crippled by childhood polio. My father didn't know him for long, in any case. Elgin Adelbert Angell was aboard the French liner *La Bourgogne*—one of the last North Atlantic blue-ribbon ships with masts as well as steam—which sank, en route to France, on July 4, 1898, off Sable Island, southeast of Nova Scotia, after a dawn collision with a British merchant vessel, Cromartyshire, with the loss of five hundred and forty-nine lives. It was a famous marine disaster of its day. My grandfather, a Cleveland lawyer, had embarked the day before, and was looking forward to a reunion with his wife and daughter—my father's younger sister, Hildegarde—who had been in Europe for six months. The story behind this is that my grandmother had exhausted herself nursing my father through a long bout of typhoid, and had been sent abroad, on doctor's advice, to recover her health. My father, who had just turned nine, had been booked aboard *La Bourgogne* as well, but he came down with chicken pox and had to be left behind. Fortuitously, my grandmother's brother, Frederick Curtis, was the head of a small school for boys in Brookfield, Connecticut; my father had been enrolled there during his mother's absence, and there the disappointed patient had to remain, while his father went on alone. My father never said much about this episode in his life, but he did once tell me that his Uncle Fred, who had a long beard, used to make the rounds in his nightshirt, carrying a candle, to kiss each of the boys good night. I don't know when my father got word about La Bourgogne or how many weeks or months went by before he was reunited with his mother and sister, but this Dickensian scene is what comes to mind when I try to imagine the moment: the wavering candle held by his approaching, sadly murmuring uncle, who wakes him up for the bad news.

Ernest Angell (school friends sometimes called him Sincere Cupid) grew up in Cleveland, did well at the private University School there, and was sent off to Paris and Munich for a year of studies before entering Harvard, in 1907. A photograph of him at the time shows the stiff collar, upright carriage, and chin-up, serious gaze that we have come to associate with the optimism of those times. He took six subjects in his freshman year, including physics, German 4 (a Goethe course), Latin composition, and Greek. Somewhere along the line, he had taught himself trigonometry. He took a cold shower at seven-thirty each morning, and resolved to "make a hard try for ØBK"—a successful one, it turned out—and strove even harder, I think, to find friends. He went out for and failed to make the *Crimson* and the freshman baseball team but got over it. He attended sermons and concerts and galleries and operas (he heard Caruso in "Il Trovatore" at the Boston Theatre); performed in a German play with the Deutsche Verein; went to dinners and dances and football games; frequently called on a Cambridge girl named Evelyn Bolles and her family; and berated himself for a generally wasted year. "Outside of regular work I've done nothing that counts for anything," he writes in his diary on May 23, 1908. He passed his summers at Chocorua, in the midst of the White Mountains of New Hampshire, as he had since boyhood, and here, I think, his insatiable energy brought him more happiness. He became an accomplished woodsman, bushing out new trails along the Sandwich Range, camping for days at a time along the Albany Intervale, and canoeing and fishing with the other young summer people; there are snapshots of him there in winter as well, grinning in bear-paw snowshoes. It was in Chocorua that he met my mother, Katharine Sergeant, whom he married after he got out of Harvard Law School, in 1913. "Ernest was easily our leading spirit," a lifelong friend of his, Stuart Chase, said many years later. "Sometimes we called him 'the Great Man.'" One summer, there was a tragedy at Chocorua, when two young Irishwomen, immigrant domestics with one of the visiting families, got into a canoe on their day off and disappeared. When they were discovered in the lake, a day or two later, my father was the one who dived down and brought up the bodies; what he remembered about it, he told me once, was that the turtles had been at them.

On one or perhaps two of those college summers, he sailed north in a schooner from Boston with Sir Wilfred Grenfell's mission to the Eskimos and fishermen along the outer Labrador coast: an odd journey, for him. I think he was impelled more by the adventure of it than by the good works. He took along a huge .45-90 rifle that I was sometimes allowed to heft when I was a kid; he'd wanted to bag a polar bear, he said, but never got off a shot. Only lately has it dawned on me that these summers may have had a purpose that he himself didn't wholly understand, and that the voyages out and back must have brought him close to the foggy cold waters where he had lost his father.

I want to bring back this sad, formidable man as he was in the early nineteen-thirties, when he and I and my older sister, Nancy, were living together in a narrow brownstone on East Ninety-third Street, with the steep front stoop of its time. We are comfortable enough there, God knows, with a succession of governesses to keep an eye on us kids, and a delightful French couple, Joseph and Edmonde Petrognani, living in the basement. Joseph does the cooking, while Edmonde, thin and beautiful, keeps house and waits on us at dinner. These are hard times, all the same. The Great Depression is deepening, and some of Father's friends who come for dinner have lost their jobs and are silent with anxiety; now and then we take in a frayed banker or architect friend for a week or two, a man who has lost his house or apartment and his savings as well, and has sent his family off somewhere while he stays in the city and looks for work. New York has taken on a shriveled appearance; nothing is painted or shined, and the people one passes on the sidewalk move slowly, with a stunned look on their face. Our house is mortgaged, and the time comes when Father tells Edmonde and Joseph that he's sorry, but he can no longer keep them on. They have no place to go, though, and so they stay on and, for the time being, agree to work for nothing. (Later on, he paid them back.) Our mother, Nancy's and mine, has been gone some years since. There has been a bitter divorce—in love with another man, the young writer E. B. White, she went off to Reno. My father's pride was injured, and he fought her hard, wore her down, until he won an agreement for joint custody of his children that would keep them under his roof, not hers; he swore that he would take her to court and shame her unless she agreed. A mistake all around: neither of them ever talks about this deadlock, and no wonder. Nancy and I don't talk about it, either. We go off to school together each morning on the double-decker No. 3 Fifth Avenue bus, to the lively, faintly cuckoo Lincoln School, up near Columbia; we can hardly wait for the weekends, when we visit our mother and Andy White in their happy, sunlit apartment down on Eighth Street. They have a Scottie named Daisy and a new baby, our brother Joel; there is a Ping-Pong table in one room, and the place is full of laughing, chain-smoking young writers and artists from *The New Yorker*, where they all work.

It doesn't occur to me to blame anybody for this setup, but it is plain that something has gone wrong. Nancy, graver now and more grown up, goes off to boarding school outside Boston. I am living on the top floor at Ninety-third Street, where the bathroom connects via an odd skylight airshaft to my father's bathroom, directly below, and sometimes in the morning I silently unlatch the little window there and listen to my father talking to himself while he shaves. He mutters and exclaims under his breath. *What!* I hear, and *No, I won't!* There is a harsh, mumbled discourse— I can't make it out—and then a quieter trailing off: perhaps a more complicated thought about some law case of his. Things aren't going well down at his office, I know that much. Then I hear an *If she thinks...* that's almost shouted: he's back on my mother again. My name turns up, too, some days: *Rog-er,* with the syllables broken in half like a stick, or *Why can't he ever...* I close the window.

This stuff scared me, not just because of its severity and barely suppressed anger but because Father and I were in this together now, and he was suffering in spirit. I didn't put it to myself that way, but I sensed we were in danger. I knew I was letting him down in school, where I had stopped working. My notebooks were in a hopeless mess, and I was always in trouble, often being turned in to the principal's office. I broke windows and lab objects, slid off to afternoon movies, and skipped gym. One day, I dropped some pistol cartridges from a high window onto the sidewalk below, to see if they'd go off; a couple of other times I was found in the crawl space under the auditorium, where I had smoked vile messages on the ceiling with a candle. Father was angry when news of my school malfeasances came home; veins stood out on his forehead and he shouted. Bad manners also set him off. He never whacked me but sometimes I wished he would. Instead, he sat me down and flailed me with long, lawyerly arguments about my shortcomings. "Where is your sense of responsibility?" he said. "I see no signs of it, young man. There has been no progress whatsoever." On and on he went, for twenty minutes at a stretch. He appeared barely able to contain his disappointment in me or his fears for my future. I sat in silence, waiting for it to be over, and secretly counted the detested "young man" appellations. At times these courtroom dramas took me to tears. One night, it became too much for me. "You make me want to be dead!" I burst out, and saw the shock of it turn him pale. He stopped at once, and then it was a long time before the next lecture.

He wasn't cruel: he was scared to death. Not much was going right with him, his money was running low, and he had to borrow from his sister, Hildegarde, to keep things going; my mother, who was doing well at *The New Yorker*, paid an increasing share of the school bills for Nancy and me—a bitter blow for him. He had taken on the burdens of being a single parent—both parents, actually—with little talent for the work and no firsthand example or memory to draw upon. He had no idea what kids were like. He was winging it there for a couple of years, and it amazes me sometimes that we came through at all.

He held on. He never gave in, never succumbed to languor or self-pity, never failed to go off to work, and, except for those morning groans and curses to himself, never said a word to anyone about his fears. He sustained a formidable social life, going to dinners or a dance two or three times each week, joining friends for weekend hikes or gallery visits, and entertaining at home, where he liked to serve the illicit, Prohibition-era wine he had fermented and aged in the cellar—Château Quatre-Vingts Treize. Father was good company and attracted lively friends—among them the playwright Sidney Howard, Walter Lippmann, and the Sam Lewisohns, whose house on Fifth Avenue was stuffed with Seurats and Renoirs and Cézannes. In that smaller New York of the thirties, people saw each other often, with an intimacy not much distracted by celebrity or wealth; in the Depression particularly, they needed the comfort of talk and laughter. I couldn't take my eyes off the women, with their shining hair and glittering dresses. My father loved women, too, and sometimes one of his lady friends would still be there at the house in the morning, having coffee at the breakfast table with us before I went off to school. I wanted him to marry again; for a long time he was in love with a beautiful divorcée, with three terrific daughters, but she could never quite get over her failed marriage. Another one of his girls, Jean Simon, came up to my room with him one evening and kissed me good night after he did. He was lonely, but said so only to his sister Hildegarde—in some of those swiftly scrawled letters I saw him turn out—a writer who was living in Mexico. She was his confidante, and in those letters, which have somehow come down to me, he is less cheerful. "Lost my big case." "I'm tired as I can be—the difficulties with K, worry about finances, etc." I am in there, too: he is thinking of sending me to military school.

There is a misapprehension here, a dark crosscurrent, that still startles me. I wasn't a bad kid—I missed my mother, and I had guessed that somehow he was to blame for that, and I was lazy and careless and sometimes silly in return—but the struggle that he couldn't win or shake free of was his failed marriage, not his children. The divorce was off limits for us all, and his expression grew taut and wary if Nancy or I went on about our weekends or vacations with Mother and Andy. My mother, for her part, waited some years and then told us that it was our father's love affairs that had destroyed the marriage. He had been an intelligence officer in France in the war, and had come back after three years abroad with different ideas about sex and marriage. He had even encouraged her to try an affair of her own: they would be a modern couple. This was what had done them in, but my mother could never bring herself to say that she had left us kids behind, along with the marriage, in order to join Andy White. Her tale stopped at that point, for all her life. Family memoirists, caught somewhere between feelings of disloyalty and the chic contemporary mode that demands that we tell all and affix damages, don't take this stuff lightly. Neither could the principals. Why else do I remember a day in the 1960s when I was having lunch with my mother at the Algonquin and she introduced me to Groucho Marx, who had stopped by our table to say hello? "A son named *Angell*?" Groucho said at once. "How did that happen?"

"Well," my mother began, "it's a long story—"

"And a sordid one, I'll wager," Groucho said. Waggling his eyebrows, he departed.

What a marriage that must have been—hers and my father's, I mean—stuffed with sex and brilliance and psychic murder, and imparting a lasting unease. Get hold of Groucho again: it's time to sweep up these bodies. Tales like this were not uncommon for people of my generation, to be sure, and have grown into cliché; what perhaps makes mine different is that the central figure, the king, for all his destructiveness and ferocity and self-doubt, turned out to be an exceptional father, with heroic energies. "Parenting" in its contemporary sense was not a concept most fathers would have understood back then, but if it was pride that first made him fight to keep his children, he then plunged right ahead with fatherhood, striding up its trail at full charge. I can scarcely remember a weekend when he and I were not off tobogganing, or taking the ferry to Staten Island, or hurrying to see the latest Diego Rivera murals, or climbing in Inwood Park, or working on my new curveball (I blew out my arm early), or stitching costumes for a marionette show I was preparing to put on, or catching the new Ed Wynn show at a matinée, or, one late-November Saturday, getting up early to drive to the Yale Bowl for a famous Barry Wood–Albie Booth Harvard-Yale game. (On the way, with other friends aboard, he stopped the car unexpectedly in the middle of a covered bridge in Connecticut—there were no parkways then—forcing us all to expel the hold-your-breath wishes we were making about the game's outcome. Red-faced, we at last let go and glared at him. He laughed, but when he started up again he said, "To hell with Yale!" and then we all shouted it together.)

Summers were no different, and in his half of our vacations—we went to Maine and the Whites in August—he took Nancy and me to a ranch in Montana; to the oil fields and semi-jungles around Tampico, Mexico; to Nantucket and Chocorua; to New Mexico and the Painted Desert of Arizona; to a cattle farm in Missouri. These were inventive, unpackaged vacations, more adventurous than anything my school friends seemed to be doing in their summers, and he was our driver and guide and keeper.

In Montana one day—it was the summer I was ten—he and Nancy and I tied up our horses when the canyon trail we were descending grew too steep for them to carry us closer to the stream at the bottom we wanted to fish. Fly rods held high, we went the rest of the way on foot or sliding on the seat of our jeans. We ran down the steep last yards laughing, with dirt and stones pattering around us, and when we landed on the flat bank at the bottom, with the sunlight from the water in our eyes, we were abruptly surrounded with an electric sound that came from no one place yet was urgently close at hand.

"Stand exactly where you are!" Father said in a voice I'd not heard before. "No talking."

He took a slow backward step, then another; he looked like a player in Still Pond, No More Moving. "I think—" he said, and, bending low, nudged a frond of bush aside with the tip of his rod. There, staid in the shadows, awaited the thrilling celebrity profile—the yellow eye, the thick, poised head retracted above the topmost bend of heavy coils, with dust blurring the curves and patterns below. Not our first Diamondback of that month but easily the biggest and nearest. "See him watching us?" Father whispered. "He'll be moving along any minute now." And the great snake, as if listening, went silent and unhurriedly but all at once slid away.

In Tampico, we took a trip down the brackish Laguna de Tamiahua, south of the port, hooking passage on an ancient, lifeboat-size ferry that was towed all through the memorable second night behind a larger vessel loaded with pigs. Another day, Father and I got aboard a narrow-gauge, gasoline-powered train that putted us twenty-five miles inland to Pánuco, an oil town that dated back to Cortés's time. A couple of armed soldiers lounged on the platform of our crowded car, protecting us against bandits; it was the rainy season, and for most of the distance we swished our way through a lake of drowned trees, leaving a widening wake astern. That night, I saw a corpse being carried along on a shutter, just across the street, and went to my first prizefight, up onstage at the local theatre. When "The Treasure of the Sierra Madre" came along, seventeen years later, I knew they'd got the local stuff right.

Every book I read back then, and every sudden passion I developed, elicited Father's curiosity and support. After I determined that I would become a naturalist when I grew up, our house filled up with fish tanks and snakes and horned toads, mice (to feed the snakes), a coatimundi that we picked up on the trip to Mexico, and then a fiercely biting macaque given to me by my mother's friend Emily Hahn. "Interesting. Let's see," my father said of each proposed further addition, and that night or the next he would sit down with me as I pored over the catalogue from the Ross Allen Reptile Institute, in Silver Springs, Florida, while, counting up my allowance, I selected the next specimen. Then he would go downstairs to prepare Joseph and Edmonde for another creature under our roof.

What lightened us up for good was that sudden notion of Father's, in the autumn of 1931, of finding a young Columbia student to come by late in the afternoons to provide me with some company until he got home from the office. (At eleven, I had outlasted the final governess.) As I've mentioned before, Arthur (Tex) Goldschmidt turned up for the job—a slight, smiling political-economy major from San Antonio, with a slant of blond hair across his forehead, and fingers stained yellow by his incessant Chesterfields, and after Father caught my eye he asked him to stay on for dinner. This was a good thing, Tex confessed later, because he was flat broke. Soon Tex's hours had expanded to four nights a week; and within weeks he moved in with us for good. Tex taught me a rackety, blindfolded, down-on-your-knees game called Calf Rope, in which you bashed your opponents with a rolled-up newspaper. He asked me about my school girl-friends and named one of them Betty Boop. He got me reading *The New Republic* and *New Masses,* and took me to see grainy Sergei Eisenstein films, on Fourteenth Street. Observing the pantings and fartings of our old Boston terrier Tunney one day, he proposed that the federal government should fund a plan like the Passamaquoddy Bay project that would put all this energy to some use. When word came back from Lincoln that I was being viewed as the worst head of student government in the history of the elementary school (the job was handed out by rote, not merit), Tex said, "Wow, and you weren't even trying!"

Tex saved my life, and perhaps he did more than that for Father. The product of a family of idealistic German intellectuals, Tex fired up my father's rather distant liberalism, brought professors and journalists he knew to dinner, and got us talking about Tammany Hall and the Reichstag fire, the Scottsboro boys and subsistence gardens for the unemployed. Tex was a leader of a Columbia student strike over the university's expulsion of the editor of the *Spectator,* and the next day at breakfast we excitedly passed around the *Herald Tribune,* with a heroic photograph of him addressing a crowd from the base of the Alma Mater statue while being pelted with eggs. He insisted that I take part in all this fervor and discussion, and within weeks had converted me into the junior op-ed voice at the dinner table, and a major pain in the neck. When Tex came back from a week's visit to the bloody mine strike in Harlan County, Kentucky, my father gave him a watch and a dinner party. He and my father shaved together each morning, after I'd gone to school, and talked politics and ideas and books, which is to say that Father had stopped talking to himself, except on weekends. He trusted Tex in everything, and let him take me along in our old Franklin sedan for local and long-distance trips. When Tex and I went to Detroit by bus in March of 1933 to pick up that new Hudson Terraplane that Father had wangled at a very low price from an advertising friend, we found that all the banks had closed down and the city was running on scrip, not U.S. currency. The New Deal was at hand.

Evenings at Ninety-third Street have kept their zing. The candles are lit, people are here for dinner, and Tex has once again brought along his friend and mentor Joseph D. McGoldrick—a rotund, pink-haired professor of government, with glasses slipping down his nose, who would soon become New York City Comptroller under Fiorello

LaGuardia. Joseph (the other Joseph) has given us crêpes Suzette for dessert, and after dinner, up in the library—where my four-and-a-half-foot king snake Humphrey, the very Mona Lisa of my collection, is oozing his way contentedly along behind the blue Conrad volumes—we'll play the new game that's all the rage with university faculties. Like everyone else just then, Tex and I have laid out our own board on easel paper, with ruled-in squares, made-up corporate names, and hand-scissored strips of money, and tonight, as before, Joe McGoldrick will be the first player in the room to go broke. Maybe this game, Monopoly, as yet unpatented, will catch on someday.

I'm not sure if Tex was at the house on a snowy night in the winter of 1933 when my father asked a few men friends in for drinks before a Roman Revel masquerade party at the Century Association. Observing that each of them had managed no more than the predictable bed-sheet toga and paper-laurel crown, I said to Father, "Why don't you dress up like Cleopatra and take Humphrey along with you?" The suggestion came halfway into the second round of martinis and was acted upon at once. Lady friends of my father were consulted by telephone, and quickly rallied round with filmy garments and makeup. I remember gilding the paternal toes with poster paint. In no time, the startling drag was complete, and Father, wrapping my long king snake around one arm, slipped into his overcoat and departed for Rome with his entourage. He had a thin time of it there, it turned out, discovering to his amazement that not many fellow-members among the distinguished group shared his interest in partying in first-class reptilian com-

pany. " 'My God, it's alive!' " he said the next morning, imitating, for my delight, his clubmates' squeamish noises and
unherpetological departing scuttle.

After Tex finished his graduate work at Columbia, and
got married and went off to work for the New Deal—
he became a noted Department of the Interior specialist
in water development and environmental protection—he
told friends of his that it was my father's trust and fairness
of mind that had probably kept him from joining the
Communist Party in those anxious times. And my father,
in a letter to Tex's parents, said that he liked him better
than any young person he knew and had come to think of
him as a combination son and brother. Tex, laughing with
me years later, said, "Of course, it was just like him not to
tell *me* that he'd done such a thing."

This account, a boy's view, has not offered much about
my father's other self—his politics, say, which he took
seriously. He busied himself within the American Civil
Liberties Union and the Foreign Policy Association, and
sopped up all the weightier weekly and quarterly journals.
(Well, almost all: unopened copies of the weekly *Manches-
ter Guardian,* in their yellowish wrappers, tended to pile up
under a table in the living room and would only later be
taken out, ripped open, and absorbed over a giant weekend
cram course.) Father voted for the Socialist Norman Thomas
in 1932 as a protest against the hopeless Hoover and the
lightweight Franklin Delano Roosevelt, then underwent
something of a conversion to the New Deal. But F.D.R.'s
maneuverings with the Constitution meant another crisis

of principles for my old man, and a second Norman Thomas gesture in 1936. His real affiliation was for fairness. As a member of the liberal Willard Straight Post, which unsurprisingly got itself thrown out of the American Legion after much public opposition to that staid body's patriotic and isolationist lobbyings, he happily led a legal battle that went to the New York State Supreme Court and brought vindication and reinstatement. I'm not sure he ever went to another meeting.

I have slighted my mother, whose professional and emotional attachment to *The New Yorker* drew me inexorably toward writing and editing and, in time, to the magazine itself. The choice was an easy one for me, because my father never murmured or hinted that I had let him down in some fashion by joining the Whites' family firm. It was quite the contrary. In 1950, I wrote a story called "Tennis," a work of fiction, thinly veiled, that drew heavily on the struggles I was still experiencing in beating Father at singles. In the story, the narrator, a man named Minot, is rebuked by his wife for pouting and carrying on when his more spectacular father takes him again, on his court in New Jersey. Later in the story, the senior player suffers a courtside heart attack but survives, leaving the two men to wonder what they've been doing to the game all this time. I ran this effort past my father, in manuscript, who saw the connection, of course, but insisted that it should be submitted unchanged. When it came out in *The New Yorker,* he called to tell me how proud he was, and added that a few friends of his had already been in touch with him to protest my perfidy. "I can't believe it," he said. "Can't they see it's a *story*? Can't they see how good it is?" Four or five years after this, almost inevitably, after my father and I had been playing Sunday doubles together at his friend Stuart Chase's court in Redding, he complained in the car of a heaviness and some twinges in his chest: a full-blown coronary, it turned out. When we got home to his weekend place in Newtown, I called his doctor, who said he'd send over a local man he knew and that he was ordering an ambulance from Danbury. My father waited calmly enough, lying out on an old Victorian sofa in his tennis whites, and at last I said, "This is weird, isn't it?"

"I've been thinking that, too," he said, with a little gleam of pleasure.

"Just remember the script," I said. "If you die now, I'll never forgive you."

"O.K.," he said, "I won't die." And he didn't—not for a long time.

I have passed over most of the second half of my father's life, which brought him a happy second marriage, financial and social comfort, a twin son and daughter, and some honors at the end. (He was, among other things, an almost perpetual chairman of the board of the A.C.L.U., and served as well at International Commission of Jurists meetings in Athens and New Delhi.) None of Father's other children share the view of him that I have offered. Nancy found it harder to forgive the harsh terms of that long-ago divorce and the worrying sort of love that came from our guilt-worn mother. The twins, Abby and Christopher, recall a father who was too old for the job—he was fifty-five when they were born—and too willing to hand the work over to others. Quite by chance, I had the best of him, and it was by luck that I had final word of him in the early '90s, almost a quarter century after his death, when a woman I didn't know sent me a clipping from the August, 1903, issue of *St. Nicholas* magazine. Both of my parents had grown up reading this famous children's monthly, and both of them had been contributors to the "St. Nicholas League," a popular feature that ran poems and stories and drawings and photographs by young subscribers. The clip that was marked for me—I have no idea how my correspondent knew the connection—was called "Polly's Fourth (A True Story)," with the byline "by Ernest Angell (Age 13)." It begins briskly: "One 29th of June found Polly Stewart and her parents in the city of Montreal. Late that evening they took a steamer en route for England, sailing early the next morning." The story goes on, in unadorned prose, to describe the wonders of the "ever-widening St. Lawrence" and the option that liners had in summertime of steaming north of Newfoundland, instead of taking the longer southern route. Polly's vessel goes north, and passes the Strait of Belle Isle. But "when Polly awoke the next morning the engines were still and silence reigned....The steamer was inclosed by ice stretching as far as the eye could reach, tumbled, irregular, of a pale green color!" The vessel lies motionless in this dangerous situation, "save when the ice parted a little around the boat, showing the black water....Of course the weather was bitterly cold." The next day, the ship moves more freely, drawing clear of the floes, although it is learned that during the night it grazed a large iceberg. "The rest of the voyage was uneventful, and the

Stewarts arrived in due time at Liverpool. But that Fourth in the ice Polly will never forget."

Neither had my father forgotten, for the journey he writes, with its proper date, takes his father's boat north of Newfoundland, rather than on the fatal course to the south, and he steers its passengers and crew safely home at last. I can't get this brusque tale out of my mind, or account for the audacity of its author. He has rewritten the worst moments of his life, and, at whatever price, put them behind him. At thirteen, he is on his own, and ready for all of us who await him eagerly up the line.

Twice Christmas

THE black dog of Christmas jumps in the window, right on schedule, around eleven in the morning, or maybe sneaks in the front door you've just opened to admit the granddaughter who's here on time, after all—her cheek cold from outdoors—before the serious present-opening. It's still skulking around a little later when you make a tour of the room to pick up the ribbons and bright ripped-off wrappings and the cards (well, save the cards) and walk back to stuff them deep into the big kitchen wastebasket. Come on, this is Christmas, so brighten up, can't you? Listen to them, out there. Smile. Back before this one—on Christmas Day, 1931, let's say—the day began for my sister Nancy and me and our father with the stockings. Our narrow brownstone-house living room had a mantelpiece made of some dark oaky wood, with carved wreaths on the flankings, on either side of the fireplace: exactly the right thing, I noticed again, for this one day of the year. Then the tree, then the presents, then the lonely aunt and weird old cousins arriving to be cheered up on this special day. The goose, well carved by Father. The plum pudding, with bits of burnt matches floating in the brandy that at last takes light. The hard sauce. Now Nancy and I exchange a glance and get up and leave the others; upstairs we take our stuffed shopping bags and tiptoe back down and grab our coats. Goodbye, goodbye. Merry Christmas, everybody.

Out on the empty, sunlit street, there's a stripy blue taxi just coming by. We jump in and fly downtown. There's no Christmas tree at Rockefeller Plaza, because there's no Rockefeller Plaza yet—no Radio City at all. Maybe there's a tree at the far end of Madison Square, but it's not lit up or anything. Never mind. I look at Nancy—she's just turned fifteen—whose brown eyes are glittering, the way they do when she's excited. Yay, Christmas!

Back to our own tree, earlier that day. My father had kept the Victorian ornaments of his childhood—the fragile and now tarnished brownish-crimson or dark-green balls, the glass icicles, a bent-velvet Santa with an ancient bit of rippled peppermint candy undetachably stuck inside his pack. Also the snap-on candleholders, which we fitted with fresh little candles and affixed carefully to the outer balsam branches, pinching the springy snap until the thing stood upright on the swaying branch, with nothing above it to catch fire and bring on disaster and the Fire Department. Three or four of the candles had interesting counterweights below and could be hooked over the smaller branches, where they balanced magically upright, staunch against the swayings of your touch. Father had filled a white enamel kitchen pail with water and put it down, with the invariable short-handled dish mop beside it, next to the tree. Then we lit the candles, one by one. We started opening presents, but soon my father broke off to pick up the little mop and begin putting out the candles, one by one, as they burned low. Already, I thought—I *think* I thought—he looked grave at what was to come.

Downtown, a left onto Eighth Street and ring the bell. Christmas is starting all over again—my mother and step-father's Christmas, in their little apartment looking down (from the back) onto Washington Mews. There are more presents here than uptown, and they're better wrapped. This tree has lights, not candles. Everything is new and young, even the Christmas-tree balls: I can't get over that. There's the Scottie named Daisy. A one-year-old brother, Joe, just up from his nap. The rubber plant named Hattie. My stepfather, Andy, mixing a Manhattan and offering one to Joe's slim young nurse, Eleanor McCluskey, who laughs and blushes at the idea. Happy Christmas, everyone. Shall we start the presents?

When it was over, after our second Christmas and second Christmas dinner, Nancy and I drove back uptown to Ninety-third Street in mid-evening—this was the plan: it was all written into the divorce agreement—in another cab, with our different presents in other shopping bags propped on the seat beside us, and by the time we hit Park Avenue, with only the low ranks of green and red traffic lights up ahead for decoration, we'd fallen silent at the thought of Father again, and the quiet house waiting, and the put-aside stories about our Eighth Street Christmas, which we'd learned not to talk about, ever. Nancy had Father's long face, with a natural shadowing under her brown eyes, and at times like this, I later came to realize, she bore the look of a chorus member from a Greek play; because she was older I studied her expression with care and wondered if my own face would some day carry this important seriousness.

This, in one form or another, is a particularly American sort of Christmas for perhaps millions of us—right up there with Clement C. Moore and "It's a Wonderful Life." Even then, well before I'd grown up, I swore to myself that such a thing would never be done to my own kids, when they came along. Only it was.

Is it this cut-rate Dickens tale that makes me glum in the middle of Christmas every year? No, not really. Is it the Christmas deodorant and electric-razor commercials, or the eighteen-hundred-dollar Christmas scarves, or the "God Rest Ye"s coming at us from Vienna and La Jolla and Baghdad and Nazareth, PA? No. Is it because I don't wake up that morning anymore and think, Christmas! No, but we're getting close: it's because I do still think that, at least for the first second or two. Just about the way I used to when I was eleven, except that back on that 1931 morning I still thought you could grab onto Christmas as it began to happen and more or less throw it to the floor. Was that the sound of an odd, early holiday train slithering along half empty toward Grand Central on the tracks under Park Avenue? Was there somebody walking by, across the street? There they went, and goodbye to this day, too, already a goner by the time Father rattled a box of matches and tossed it invitingly over to me, then fished for his cigarette lighter in the lower-right pocket of his vest as he stepped up to the tree. Shading the white triangle of flame behind his hand, he brought it up to the first candle, on its bending branch, and said, "Well, here we go. Christmas again."

Early Innings

I was born in 1920, and became an addicted reader at a precocious age. Peeling back the leaves of memory, I discover a peculiar mulch of names. Steerforth, Tuan Jim, Moon Mullins, Colonel Sebastian Moran. Sunny Jim Bottomley, Dazzy Vance, Goose Goslin. Bob La Follette, Carter Glass, Rexford Guy Tugwell. Robert Benchley, A. E. Housman, Erich Maria Remarque. Hack Wilson, Riggs Stephenson. Senator Pat Harrison and Representative Sol Bloom. Pie Traynor and Harry Hopkins. Kenesaw Mountain Landis and Benjamin Cardozo. Pepper Martin. George F. Babbitt. The Scottsboro Boys. Franklin Delano Roosevelt. Babe Ruth. In my early teens, I knew the Detroit Tigers' batting order and F.D.R.'s first Cabinet, both by heart. Mel Ott's swing, Jimmy Foxx's upper arms, and Senator Borah's eyebrows were clear in my mind's eye. Baseball, which was late in its first golden age, meant a lot to me, but it didn't come first, because I seem to have been a fan of everything at that age—a born pain in the neck. A city kid, I read John Kieran, Walter Lippmann, Richards Vidmer, Heywood Broun, and Dan Daniel just about every day, and what I read stuck. By the time I'd turned twelve, my favorite authors included Conan Doyle, Charles Dickens, Will James on cowboys, Joseph A. Altsheler on Indians, and Dr. Raymond L. Ditmars on reptiles. Another batting order I could have run off for you would have presented some prime species among the Elapidae—a family that includes cobras, coral snakes, kraits, and mambas, and is cousin to the deadly sea snakes of the China Sea.

Back then, baseball and politics were not the strange mix that they would appear to be today, because they were both plainly where the action lay. I grew up in New York and attended Lincoln School of Teachers College (old Lincoln, in Manhattan parlance), a font of progressive education where we were encouraged to follow our interests with avidity; no Lincoln parent was ever known to have said, "Shut up, kid." In classic pattern, it was my father who started me in baseball. He had grown up in Cleveland in the Nap Lajoie–Addie Joss era, but he was too smart to try to interpose his passion for the Indians on his son's idolatrous attachment to the Yankees and the Giants, any more than he would have allowed himself to smile at the four or five Roosevelt-Garner buttons I kept affixed to my windbreaker (above my knickers) in the weeks before Election Day in 1932.

The early- to mid-1930s were tough times in the United States, but palmy days for a boy-Democrat baseball fan in New York. Carl Hubbell, gravely bowing twice from the

waist before each delivery, was throwing his magical screwball for the Giants, and Joe DiMaggio, arriving from San
Francisco in '36 amid vast heraldings, took up his spread-
legged stance at the Stadium, and batted .323 and .346 in
his first two years in the Bronx. He was the first celebrated
rookie to come up to either team after I had attained full
baseball awareness: my Joe DiMaggio. My other team, the
New Deal, also kept winning. Every week in 1933, it seemed,
the White House gave birth to another progressive, society-
shaking national agency (the A.A.A., the N.R.A., the C.C.C.,
the T.V.A.), which Congress would enact into law by a huge
majority. In my city, Fiorello LaGuardia led the Fusion
Party, routed the forces of Tammany Hall, and, as mayor,
cleared slums, wrote a new city charter, and turned up at
five alarmers wearing a fire chief's helmet. (I interviewed
the Little Flower for my high-school paper later in the
decade, after sitting for seven hours in his waiting room. I
can't remember anything he said, but I can still see his feet,
under the mayoral swivel chair, not quite touching the
floor.) Terrible things were going on in Ethiopia and Spain
and Germany, to be sure, but at home almost everything I
wanted to happen seemed to come to pass within a few
weeks or months—most of all in baseball. The Yankees and
the Giants between them captured eight pennants in the
thirties, and even played against each other in a subway series in 1936 (hello, ambivalence) and again in 1937. The
Yankees won both times; indeed, they captured all five of
their World Series engagements in the decade, losing only
three games in the process. Their 12-1 October won-lost to-
tals against the Giants, Cubs, and Reds in '37, '38, and '39

made me sense at last that winning wasn't everything it was cracked up to be; my later defection to the Red Sox, and toward the pain-pleasure principle had begun.

There are more holes than fabric in my earliest baseball recollections. My father began taking me and my four-years-older sister to games at some point in the latter twenties, but no first-ever view of Babe Ruth or of the green barn of the Polo Grounds remains in mind. We must have attended with some regularity, because I'm sure I saw the Babe and Lou Gehrig hit back-to-back home runs on more than one occasion. Mel Ott's stumpy, cow-tail swing is still before me, and so are Gehrig's thick calves and Ruth's debutante ankles. Baseball caps were different back then: smaller and flatter than today's constructions—more like the workmen's caps that one saw on every street. Some of the visiting players—the Cardinals, for instance—wore their caps cheerfully askew or tipped back on their heads, but never the Yankees. Gloves were much smaller, too, and the outfielders left theirs on the grass, in the shallow parts of the field, when their side came in to bat; I wondered why a batted ball wouldn't strike them on the fly or on the bounce someday, but it never happened. John McGraw, for one, wouldn't have permitted such a thing. He was managing the Giants, with his arms folded across his vest (he wore a suit some days and a uniform on others), and kept his tough, thick chin aimed at the umpires. I would look for him— along with Ott and Bill Terry and Travis Jackson—the minute we arrived at our seats in the Polo Grounds.

I liked it best when we came into the place from up top, rather than through the gates down at the foot of the lower-right-field stand. You reached the upper-deck turnstiles by walking down a steep, short ramp from the Speedway, the broad avenue that swept down from Coogan's Bluff and along the Harlem River, and once you got inside, the long field within the horseshoe of decked stands seemed to stretch away forever below you, toward the bleachers and the clubhouse pavilion in center. My father made me notice how often Terry, a terrific straightaway slugger, would launch an extra-base hit into that bottomless countryside ("a homer in any other park" was the accompanying refrain), and, sure enough, now and then Terry would reaffirm the parable by hammering still another triple into the pigeoned distance. Everything about the Polo Grounds was special, right down to the looped iron chains that separated each sector of box seats from its neighbor and could burn your bare arm on a summer afternoon if you weren't careful. Far along each outfield wall, a sloping mini-roof projected outward, imparting a thin wedge of shadow for the bullpen crews sitting there: they looked like cows sheltering beside a pasture shed in August.

Across the river, the view when you arrived was different but equally delectable: a panorama of svelte infield and steep, filigree-topped inner battlements that was offered and then snatched away as one's straw-seat I.R.T. train rumbled into the elevated station at 161st Street. If the Polo Grounds felt pastoral, Yankee Stadium was Metropole, the big city personified. For some reason, we always walked around it along the right-field side, never the other way, and each time I would wonder about the oddly arrayed ticket kiosks (General Admission fifty-five cents; Reserved Grandstand a dollar ten) that stood off at such a distance from the gates. Something about security, I decided; one of these days, they'll demand to see passports there. Inside, up the pleasing ramps, I would stop and bend over, peering through the horizontal slot between the dark, overhanging mezzanine and the descending sweep of grandstand seats which led one's entranced eye to the sunlit green of the field and the players on it. Then I'd look for the Babe. The first Yankee manager I can remember in residence was Bob Shawkey, which means 1930. I was nine years old.

I can't seem to put my hand on any one particular game I went to with my father back then; it's strange. But I went often, and soon came to know the difference between intimate afternoon games at the Stadium (play started at 3:15 P.M.), when a handful of boys and night workers and layabouts and late arriving businessmen (with vests and straw hats) would cluster together in the stands close to home plate or down in the lower rows of the bleachers, and the sold-out, roaring, seventy-thousand-plus Sunday doubleheaders against the Tigers or the Indians or the Senators (the famous rivalry with the Bosox is missing in memory), when I would eat, cheer, and groan my way grandly toward the distant horizon of evening, while the Yankees, most of the time, would win and then win again. The handsome Wes Ferrell always started the first Sunday game for the Indians, and proved a tough nut to crack. But why, I wonder, do I think of Bill Dickey's ears? In any case, I know I was in the Stadium on Monday, May 5, 1930, when Lefty

Gomez, a twitchy rookie southpaw, pitched his very first game for the Yankees, and beat Red Faber and the White Sox, 4-1, striking out his first three batters in succession. I talked about the day and the game with Gomez many years later, and he told me that he had looked up in the stands before the first inning and realized that the ticket-holders there easily outnumbered the population of his home town, Rodeo, California, and perhaps his home county as well.

I attended the Gomez inaugural not with my father but with a pink-checked lady named Mrs. Baker, who was— well, she was my governess. Groans and derisive laughter are all very well, but Mrs. Baker (who had a very brief tenure, alas) was a companion any boy would cherish. She had proposed the trip to Yankee Stadium, and she was the one who first noticed a new name out on the mound that afternoon, and made me see how hard the kid was throwing and what he might mean for the Yanks in the future. "Remember the day," she said, and I did.

Baseball memories are seductive, tempting us always toward sweetness and undercomplexity. It should not be inferred (I remind myself) that the game was a unique bond between my father and me, or always near the top of my own distracted interests. If forced to rank the preoccupying family passions in my home at that time, I would put reading at the top of the list, closely followed by conversation and opinions, politics, loneliness (my father had not yet remarried, and I missed my mother), friends, jokes, exercises and active sports, animals (see below), theatre and the movies, professional and college sports, museums, and a very large Misc. Even before my teens, I thought of myself as a full participant, and my fair-minded old man did not patronize me at the dinner table or elsewhere

Baseball (to get back on track here) had the longest run each year, but other sports also got my full attention. September meant Forest Hills, with Tilden and Vines, Don Budge and Fred Perry. Ivy League football still mattered in those times, and I saw Harvard's immortal Barry Wood and Yale's ditto Albie Booth go at each other more than once; we also caught Chick Meehan's N.Y.U. Violets, and even some City College games, up at Lewisohn Stadium. Winter brought the thrilling Rangers (Frank Boucher, Ching Johnson, and the Cook brothers) and the bespangled old Americans; there was wire netting atop the boards, instead of Plexiglas, and Madison Square Garden was blue with cigarette and cigar smoke above the painted ice. I went there on weekends, never on school nights, usually in company with my mother and stepfather, who were red-hot hockey fans. Twice a year, they took me to the six-day bicycle races at the Garden (Reggie McNamara, Alfred Letourner, Franco Georgetti, Torchy Peden), and, in midwinter, to track events there, with Glenn Cunningham and Gene Venzke trying and again failing to break the four-minute mile at the Millrose Games. Looking back, I wonder how I got through school at all. My mother, I should explain, had been a Red Sox fan while growing up in Boston, but her attachment to the game did not revive until the mid-nineteen-forties, when she fetched up at Presbyterian Hospital for a minor surgical procedure; a fellow patient across the hall at Harkness Pavilion was Walker Cooper, the incumbent Giants catcher, drydocked for knee repairs, who kept in touch by listening to the Giants' game broadcasts every day. My mother turned her radio on, too, and was hooked.

Sports were different in my youth—a series of events to look forward to and then to turn over in memory, rather than a huge, omnipresent industry, with its own economics and politics and crushing public relations. How it felt to be a young baseball fan in the thirties can be appreciated only if I can bring back this lighter and fresher atmosphere. Attending a game meant a lot, to adults as well as to a boy, because it was the only way you could encounter athletes and watch what they did. There was no television, no instant replay, no evening highlights. We saw the players' faces in newspaper photographs, or in the pages of *Baseball,* an engrossing monthly with an invariable red cover, to which I subscribed, and here and there in an advertisement. (I think Lou Gehrig plugged Fleischmann's Yeast, a health remedy said to be good for the complexion.) We never heard athletes' voices or became aware of their "image." Pedro Martinez and Barry Bonds and Michael Jordan were light-years away. Baseball by radio was a rarity, confined for the most part to the World Series; the three New York teams in fact, banned radio coverage of their regular-season games between 1934 and 1938, on the theory that daily broadcasts would damage attendance. Following baseball always required a visit to the players' place of business, and, once there, you watched them with attention, undistracted by Diamond Vision or blasting rock music or game promotions. Seeing the players in action on the field, always at a little distance, gave them a heroic tinge. (The only player

I can remember encountering on the street, one day on the West Side, was the Babe, in retirement by then, swathed in his familiar camel-hair coat with matching cap.)

We kept up by reading baseball. Four daily newspapers arrived at my house every day—the *Times* and the *Herald Tribune* by breakfast time, and the *Sun* and the *World-Telegram* folded under my father's arm when he got home from the office. The games were played by daylight, and, with all sixteen teams situated inside two time zones, we never went to bed without knowledge of that day's baseball. Line scores were on the front page of the afternoon dailies, scrupulously updated edition by edition, with black squares off to the right indicating latter innings, as yet unplayed, in Wrigley Field or Sportsman's Park. I soon came to know all the bylines—John Drebinger, James P. Dawson, and Roscoe McGowen in the *Times* (John Kieran was the columnist); Rud Rennie and Richards Vidmer in the *Trib;* Dan Daniel, Joe Williams, and Tom Meany in the *World-Telly* (along with Willard Mullin's vigorous sports cartoons); Frank Graham in the *Sun;* and, now and then, Bill Corum in the *Sunday American,* a paper I sometimes acquired for its terrific comics.

Richards Vidmer, if memory is to be trusted, was my favorite scribe, but before that, back when I was nine or ten years old, what I loved best in the sports pages were box scores and, above all, names. I knew the names of a few dozen friends and teachers at school, of course, and of family members and family friends, but only in baseball could I encounter anyone like Mel Ott. One of the Yankee pitchers was named George Pipgras, and Earle Combs played center. Connie Mack, a skinny old gent, managed the Athletics and was in fact Cornelius McGillicuddy. Jimmy Foxx was his prime slugger. I had a double letter in my name, too, but it didn't match up to a Foxx or an Ott. Or to Joe Stripp. I read on, day after day, and found rafts of names that prickled or sang in one's mind. Eppa Rixey, Goose Goslin, Firpo Marberry, Jack Rothrock, Eldon Auker, Luke Appling, Mule Hass, Adolfo Luque (for years I thought it was pronounced "Lyoo-kyoo")—Dickens couldn't have done better. Paul Derringer was exciting: a man named for a pistol! I lingered over Heinie Manush (sort of like sitting on a cereal) and Van Lingle Mungo, the Dodger ace. When I exchanged baseball celebrities with pals at school, we used last names, to show a suave familiarity, but no one ever just said "Mungo," or even "Van Mungo." When he came up in conversation, it was obligatory to roll out the full name, as if it were a royal title, and everyone in the group would join in at the end, in chorus: "Van Lin-gle MUN-go!"

Heading for Fifth Avenue and Ninety-fourth Street each morning, where I picked up the No. 3 uptown bus to school, I sometimes encountered Colonel Jacob Ruppert, the owner of the Yankees, on the way to work at his brewery on Third Avenue. He had pink cheeks and shiny, shoe-button eyes, and wore an invariable bow tie. If our encounter came in the spring and if I was carrying my baseball glove back uptown after some weekend ball, I would give the mitt a whack with my fist as we passed, and shoot the Colonel a burning look. Nothing happened, but the next time, surely, he would stop me and ask my name, fish his calling card out of his vest pocket, and deliver the awaited invitation: "My boy take this up to the Stadium and tell them I want you to have a tryout. Use my name. And good luck to you, young fellow."

By every measure, this was a bewitching time for a kid to discover baseball. The rabbit ball had got loose in both leagues in 1930 (I wasn't aware of it)—a season in which Bill Terry batted .401 and the Giants hit .319 as a team. I can't say for sure that I knew about Hack Wilson's astounding hundred and ninety R.B.I.s for the Cubs, but Babe Herman's .393 for the Dodgers must have made an impression. (The lowly Dodgers. As I should have said before, the Dodgers—or Robins, as they were called in tabloid headlines—were just another team in the National League to me back then; I don't think I set foot in Ebbets Field until the 1941 World Series. But they became the enemy in 1934, when they knocked the Giants out of a pennant in September.) The batters in both leagues were reined in a bit after 1930, but the game didn't exactly become dull. Lefty Grove had a 31-4 season for the A's in 1931, and Dizzy Dean's 30-7 helped win a pennant for the Gas House Gang Cardinals in 1934. That was Babe Ruth's last summer in the Bronx, but I think I was paying more attention to Gehrig just then, what with his triple-crown .363, forty-nine homers, and hundred and sixty-five runs batted in. I became more aware of other teams as the thirties (and my teens) wore along, and eventually came to think of them as personalities—sixteen different but familiar faces ranged around a large dinner table, as it were. To this day, I still feel a little stir of fear inside me when I think about the Tigers, because of the mighty Detroit teams of 1934 and 1935, which two years running shouldered the Yankees out of a pennant. I hated Charlie Gehringer's pale face and deadly stroke. One day in '34, I read that a Yankee bench player had taunted Gehringer, only to be silenced by Yankee manager Joe McCarthy. "Shut up," Marse Joe said. "He's hitting .360—get him mad and he'll bat .500." Gehringer played second in the same infield with Hank Greenberg, Billy Rogell, and Marv Owen; that summer, the four of them drove in four hundred and sixty-two runs.

I was living in the sports pages by 1932, when the mighty Yankees blew away the Cubs in a four-game series, blasting eight home runs. It troubled me in later years that I seemed to have no clear recollection of what came to be that Series' most famous moment, when Babe Ruth did or did not call his home run against Charlie Root in the fifth inning of the third game, out at Wrigley Field. What I remembered about that game was that Ruth and Gehrig had each smacked two homers. A recent investigation of the microfilm files of the *Times* seems to clear up the mystery, since John Drebinger's story for that date makes no mention of the Ruthian feat in its lead, or, indeed, until the thirty-fourth paragraph, when he hints that Ruth did gesture toward the bleachers ("in no mistaken motions the Babe notified the crowd that the nature of his retaliation would be a wallop right out the confines of the park"), after taking some guff from the hometown rooters as he stepped up to the plate, but then Drebinger seems to veer toward the other interpretation, which is that Ruth's gesture was simply to show that he knew the count ("Ruth signaled with his fingers after each pitch to let the spectators know exactly how the situation stood. Then the mightiest blow of all fell"). The next-mightiest blow came on the ensuing pitch, by the way: a home run by Lou Gehrig.

I remember 1933 even better. Tex and I were in the lower stands behind third base at the Stadium on Saturday, April 29th, when the Yankees lost a game to the ominous Senators on a play I have never seen duplicated—lost, as Drebinger put it, "to the utter consternation of a crowd of 36,000." With the Yanks trailing by 6-2 in the ninth, Ruth and then Gehrig singled, and Sammy Byrd (a pinch-runner for the portly Ruth) came home on a single by Dixie Walker. Tony Lazzeri now launched a drive to deep right center. Gehrig hesitated at second base, but Walker, at first, did not, and when the ball went over Goslin's head the two runners came around third in tandem, separated by a single stride. The relay—Goslin to Joe Cronin to catcher Luke Sewell—arrived at the same instant with the onrushing Gehrig, and Sewell, whirling in the dust, tagged out both runners with one sweeping gesture, each on a different side of the plate. I was aghast—and remembered the wound all summer, as the Senators went on to win the A.L. pennant, seven games in front of the Yanks.

It's always useful to have two teams to care about, as I had already learned. My other sweethearts, the Giants, moved into first place in their league on June 13th and were never dislodged. Needless to say, I had no ticket for the big Fourth of July doubleheader against the Cardinals at the Polo Grounds, but I'm positive I read John Drebinger the next morning: "Pitching of a superman variety that dazzled a crowd of 50,000 and bewildered the Cardinals gave the Giants two throbbing victories at the Polo Grounds yesterday over a stretch of six hours. Carl Hubbell, master lefthander of Bill Terrry's amazing hurling corps, blazed the trail by firing away for eighteen scoreless innings to win the opening game from the Cards, 1 to 0.... Then the broadshouldered Roy Parmelee strode to the mound and through semi-darkness and finally a drizzling rain, blanked the St. Louisans in a nine-inning nightcap, 1 to 0. A homer in the fourth inning by Johnny Vergez decided this battle."

Trumpet arias at this glorious level require no footnotes, and I would add only that Tex Carleton, the Cardinal starter in the first game, threw sixteen scoreless innings himself before giving way to a reliever. He was pitching on two days' rest, and Dizzy Dean, the starter and eventual loser of the afterpiece, on one. The first game got its eighteen innings over with in four hours and three minutes, by the way, and the nightcap was done in an hour and twenty-five.

The Giants went the distance in 1933, as I have said, and took the World Series as well, beating the Senators by four games to one. Hubbell, who had wound up the regular season with an earned-run average of 1.66 (he was voted Most Valuable Player in his league), won two games, and Ott drove in the winning runs in the opener with a home run, and wrapped matters up with a tenth-inning shot in the finale. I had pleaded with my father to get us some seats for one of the games at the Polo Grounds, but he didn't come through. I attended the games by a different means— radio. Five different New York stations carried the Series that year, and I listened either to Ted Husing, on WABC, or to the old NBC warhorse, Graham McNamee, over at WEAF or WJZ. I knew how to keep score by this time, and I rushed home from school—for the four weekday games, that is—turned on the big RCA or Stromberg-Carlson (with its glowing Bakelite dial), and kept track, inning by inning, on scorecards I drew on one of my father's yellow legal pads. When my father got home, I sat him down and ran through it all, almost pitch by pitch, telling him the baseball.

I was playing ball myself all this time—or trying to, despite the handicaps of living in the city and of a modestly muscled physique. But I kept my mitt in top shape with neat's foot oil, and possessed a couple of Louisville Slugger bats and three or four baseballs, one so heavily wrapped in friction tape that making contact with it with a bat felt like hitting a frying pan. (One of the bats, as I recall, bore lifelong scars after a game of one-o'-cat played with a rock.) Neat's foot oil was a magical yellow elixir made from cattle bones and skin—and also a password, unknown to girls. "What's a neat?" every true American boy must have asked himself at some point or other, imagining some frightful amputation made necessary by the demands of the pastime.

What skills I owned had been coached by my father from an early age. Yes, reader: we threw the old pill around, and although it did not provide me with an instant ticket to the major leagues, it was endlessly pleasurable. I imagined myself a pitcher, and my old man and I put in long hours of pitch and catch, with a rickety shed (magically

known as the Bull Pen) as backstop; this was at a little summer colony on the west bank of the Hudson, where we
rented. My father had several gloves of his own, including
an antique catcher's mitt that resembled a hatbox or a
round dictionary. Wearing this, he would squat down again
and again, putting up a target, and then fire the ball back
(or fetch it from the weeds somewhere), gravely snapping
the ball from behind his ear like Mickey Cochrane. Once
in a while, there would be a satisfying pop as the ball hit
the pocket, and he would nod silently and then flip the pill
back again. His pitching lexicon was from his own boyhood: "inshoot," "hook," "hard one," and "drop." My own
drop dropped to earth so often that I hated the pitch and
began to shake him off.

I kept at it, in season and out, and, when I finally began
to get some growth, developed a pleasing roundhouse curve
that sometimes sailed over a corner of the plate (or a cap
or newspaper), to the amazement of my school friends.
Encouraged, I began to work on a screwball, and eventually could throw something that infinitesimally broke the
wrong way, although always too high to invite a swing; I
began walking around school corridors with my pitching
hand turned palm outward, like Carl Hubbell's, but nobody noticed. Working on the screwball one cold March
afternoon (I was thirteen, I think), on a covered but windy
rooftop playground at Lincoln, I ruined my arm for good.
I continued pitching on into high school (mine was a boarding school in northern Connecticut), but I didn't make the
big team; by that time, the batters I faced were smarter and

did frightful things to my trusty roundhouse. I fanned a batter here and there, but took up smoking and irony in self-defense. A short career.

When I began writing this part of my past, I was surprised to find how often its trail circled back to my father. If I continue now with his baseball story, instead of my own, it's because the two are intertwined and continuous. Born in 1889, he grew up in a time when there were diamonds and pickup nines in every hamlet in America. He played first base and pitched, and in his late teens joined a village team, the Tamworth Tigers, that played in the White Mountain valleys of New Hampshire, where he and his mother and sister went on their vacations. Years later, he told me about the time he and some of the other Tamworth stars—Ned Johnson, Paul Twitchell, Lincoln and Dana Steele—formed a team of their own and took a train up into Canada, where they played in a regional tournament; he pitched the only game they got to play, against a much better club (semi-pros, he suspected), and got his ears knocked off. The trip back (he said, still smiling at the pain) was a long one.

Long after this, on a car trip when he was in his seventies, my father found himself near the mountains he knew so well and made a swing over to Chocorua and Tamworth to check out the scenes of his youth. He found the Remick Bros. General Store still in business, and when he went in, the man at the counter, behind the postcards and the little birchbark canoes, was Wadsworth Remick, who had played with him on the Tigers long ago. Waddy Remick. There were no signs of recognition, however, and my old man, perhaps uncomfortable in the role of visiting big-city slicker, didn't press the matter. He bought a pack of gum or something, and was just going out the door when he heard, "Played any first base lately, Ernest?"

I think people gave up with reluctance in olden days. My father sailed through Harvard in three years, but failed to attain his great goal of making the varsity in baseball, and had to settle for playing on a class team. Most men would call it a day after that, but not my father. He went to law school, got married, went off to the war in France, came back and moved from Cleveland to New York and joined a law firm—and played ball. I think my very first recollection of him—I was a small child—is of standing beside him in a little downstairs bathroom of our summer place while he washed dirt off his face and arms after a ballgame. Rivers of brown earth ran into the sink. Later that same summer, I was with my mother on the sidelines when my father, pitching for some Rockland County nine, conked a batter on the top of his head with an errant fastball. The man fell over backward and lay still for a moment or two, and my mother said, "Oh, God—he's done it!" The batter recovered, he and my father shook hands, and the game went on, but the moment, like its predecessor, stayed with me. Jung would appreciate such tableaux.

Years passed. In the summer of 1937, I worked on a small combined ranch and farm in northern Missouri, owned by an aunt and uncle who were raising purebred white-faced Herefords. I drove cattle to their water holes on horseback, cleaned chicken coops, and shot marauding evening jackrabbits in the vegetable garden. It was a drought year, and the temperature would go well over a hundred degrees every afternoon; white dust lay on the trees. I was sixteen. Both the Giants and the Yankees were rushing toward another pennant in New York (it was the DiMaggio, Henrich, Rolfe, Crosetti Yankees by now); but I had a hard time finding news of them in the austere, photoless columns of the Kansas City *Star*. All I could pick up on the radio was Franc Laux doing Cardinals games over KMOX.

My father arrived for a visit, and soon discovered that there would be a local ballgame the next Sunday, with some of the hands on the ranch representing our nearby town. Somehow, he cajoled his way onto the team (he was close to fifty but looked much younger); he played first base, and got a single in a losing cause. Late in the game, I was sent up to pinch-hit for somebody. The pitcher, a large and unpleasant-looking young man, must have felt distaste at the sight of a scared sixteen-year-old dude standing in, because he dismissed me with two fiery fastballs and then a curve that I waved at without hope, without a chance. I sat down again. My father said nothing at the time, but later on in the day, perhaps riding back to supper, he murmured, "What'd he throw you—two hard ones and a hook?" I nodded, my ears burning. There was a pause, and Father said, "The curveball away can be very tough." It was late afternoon, but the view from my side of the car suddenly grew brighter.

It is hard to hear stories like this now without an accompanying inner smirk. We are wary of sentiment and obsessively knowing, and we feel obliged to put a spin of psychology or economic determinism or bored contempt on all clear-color memories. I suppose someone could say that my father was a privileged Wasp, who was able to pursue some adolescent, rustic yearnings far too late in life. But that would miss the point. My father was knowing, too; he was a New York sophisticate who spurned cynicism. He had only limited financial success as a Wall Street lawyer, but that work allowed him to put in great amounts of time with the American Civil Liberties Union. Most of his life, I heard him talk about the latest issues or cases involving censorship, Jim Crow laws, voting rights, freedom of speech, racial and sexual discrimination, and threats to the Constitution; these struggles continue to this day, God knows, but the difference back then was that men and women like my father always sounded as if such battles would be won in the end. The news was always harsh, and fresh threats to freedom immediate, but every problem was capable of solution somewhere down the line. We don't hold such ideas anymore—about our freedoms or about anything else. My father looked on baseball the same way; he would never be a big-league player, or even a college player, but whenever he found a game he jumped at the chance to play and to win.

If this sounds like a romantic or foolish impulse to us today, it is because most of American life, including baseball, no longer feels feasible. We know everything about the game now, thanks to instant replay and computerized stats, and what we seem to have concluded is that almost none of us are good enough to play it. Thanks to television and sports journalism, we also know everything about the skills and financial worth and private lives of the enormous young men we have hired to play baseball for us, but we don't seem to know how to keep their salaries or their personalities within human proportions. We don't like them as much as we once did, and we don't like ourselves as much, either. Baseball becomes feasible from time to time, not much more, and we fans must make prodigious efforts to rearrange our profoundly ironic contemporary psyches in order to allow its old pleasures to reach us. My father wasn't naive; he was lucky.

One more thing. American men don't think about baseball as much as they used to, but such thoughts once went deep. In my middle thirties, I still followed the Yankees and the Giants in the standings, but my own playing days were long forgotten; I had not yet tried writing about the sport. I was living in the suburbs, and one night I had a vivid dream, in which I arose from my bed (it was almost a movie dream), went downstairs, and walked outdoors in the dark. I continued down our little patch of lawn and crossed the tiny bridge at the foot of our property, and there, within a tangle of underbrush, discovered a single gravestone. I leaned forward (I absolutely guarantee all this) and found my own name inscribed there and, below it, the dates of my birth and of the present year, the dream time: "1920–1955." The dream scared me, needless to say, but providentially I was making periodic visits to a shrink at the time. I took the dream to our next session like a trophy but, having recounted it, had no idea what it might mean.

"What does it suggest to you?" the goodly man said, in predictable fashion.

"It's sort of like those monuments out by the flagpole in deep center field at the Stadium," I said. Then I stopped and cried, "Oh... Oh," because of course it had suddenly come clear. My dreams of becoming a major-league ballplayer had died at last.

Consultation

WHEN I was growing up, the top floor layout of our East Side brownstone had some features of interest for a young boy. The bathroom was halfway between the front and back of the house—between my sister's better and larger bedroom facing Ninety-third Street and my own narrower chamber, with only one window as against her three. My window faced some discouraged-looking back yards with tall, laundry-line-bearing poles. (For some reason, Ninety-fourth Street between Park and Madison was run down, more like the blocks east of Lexington.) Sometimes I brooded about the unfairness of my room assignment, even though I knew that my backyard vista, with its closely adjacent tenement windows and noises—conversations and music and sometimes yellings and curses—was preferable to the staid street stuff on Ninety-third Street. Just below my window and to my right, I looked down on the jutting oblong roof over our own lower setback, with its second-floor pantry and, below that, a ground floor laundry room with stone tubs and slabs of yellow laundry soap. My father slept in the back, underneath me. One of his windows opened out onto that tarred half-roof; winter and summer, he left the window half open at night, so that our Boston terrier Tunney could go out there whenever he needed to, then hop back in and go back to sleep on his green cushion. There was a tall, full-scale mirror on one wall of Father's bedroom, and on Monday mornings I'd stop by there and find my allowance waiting on its narrow counter— fifty cents is what I remember but it must have been lower than this at some point and then more—and, lined up neatly next to it, ten dimes: my fare on the Fifth Avenue bus to school (on 123rd Street and Morningside Park) and back, for the week. The dimes would be swallowed up, one by one, in the conductor's portable receiver, which he proffered to each boarding passenger. There was an angled trough in the middle of it, and when you slipped your dime sensuously into the center slot the conductor would depress a key in the middle of his gismo and ring up your fare: *Tring!* Only Fifth Avenue busses, which ran both ways on the avenue then, cost a dime; everything else—trolleys, other busses, the subways, and the El—were a nickel.

When I went down into the subways or up to the Third Avenue or Second Avenue Els the nickel I dropped into the receiver box went clunking down, then stopped in a little illuminated box or gallery, with a window on its entering side. The window was a curved lens, which enlarged the image of the contained coin—an Indian chief on one side; a buffalo on the other—so that the IRT change-maker, facing out from his locked cage, could check out the latest deposit from across the entrance space and make sure it wasn't made of tin or wood. The coin, particularly the Indian-head profile, stood out in there with startling clarity, with the shadows and highlights of bas-relief imparting a museum like purity to the object. Even then, in my boyhood, I understood that the mad-inventor cleverness of this rig, though in daily use in thousands of subway stations across the city, belonged to the ornate and whimsical past, and would not survive modernization. Then, sure enough, when the clean and zippy brand-new IND subway system opened in 1933, the light boxes were gone. This is probably why I associate the illuminated coin receiver in memory with El stations, not subways, and with the intriguing advertising signs that you studied on the risers of the iron stairs you climbed to reach platform level—alternating metal strips with the message "Ipana for the Smile of Beauty" in bright red, and "Sal Hepatica for the Smile of Health" in blue. Ipana was a toothpaste and Sal Hepatica (I guess) a laxative. In wintertime when you arrived, panting, at your station and opened the door, there would be the hot, close smell of the potbellied coal stove or kerosene stove that stood in one corner, and, waiting beside your turnstile, the lit-up latest nickel.

Something else was special to me about the dimes you needed for the Fifth Avenue bus. A dime was exactly the right width to fit the screws that held the enameled metal advertising strips across the width of the seat-back in front of you. The signs, a shiny white or blue, advertised Marlborough Cigarettes—still with that elegant "-ough" ending, back then—and also a sample from the Marlborough's "Distinguished Handwriting Contest," an upscale advertising campaign of its day. Heavier and classier than the lowly Ipana-Sal Hepatica boards, they were an object to cherish—and sometimes collect. On afternoons in winter when you were alone or almost alone on the upper deck on the homeward run, you could slip a dime into one of those screws and, with a slight effort, begin to unscrew it from the seat before you. There were eight screws, all told, and if you did this right, you could keep the treasure loosely in place until about 104th Street (I got off at Ninety-fourth), then swiftly finish the job, drop the screws in your pocket while holding the plate in place with your free hand, and, rising to depart, slip the narrow, three-foot prize under your coat. This was a winter caper: in summer even Bulldog Drummond would not have found a way to pull off the heist.

A particular Saturday morning's trip on the New York subways in the spring of 1933 finds me on a swaying, noisy northbound IRT Lexington Avenue Local with my school friend Kimmy Atwood. We are headed for the Bronx Zoo early in the day—there are kids and parents sitting on the straw seats around us with the same destination almost surely in mind—and Kim and I are silent with purpose. On my lap is a green steamer rug, carefully folded, and within it is Humphrey, my king snake, who lies comfortably enough within his cocoon. The primo reptile in my home collection of snakes, turtles, newts, fish, and mice— Tunney and our couple of kitchen cats don't count—he lives in a grocery box cage in the cellar, with wire screening on the top and a pair of smoothly sliding glass panels in front, a design conceived and carried out by me. Inside, there's a water dish, a twisted small tree branch without bark, and a temporary brick, put there to help Humphrey rub free of his old skin at shedding time. This comes along two or three times a year, and leaves the creature with a shining new exterior, in place of his dim and dusty-looking old one. When the process is completed each tan or black or yellow-brown scale gleams clear, as though buffed with wax; it's as if Humphrey has traded himself in for a new Studebaker. This time, though, there's been a hitch. Each time Humphrey gets ready to shed his eyes become covered with a thick, semi-transparent protective skin or scale. This normally comes away with the shed, and can be seen interestingly in place in the wispy-dry inside-out remnants of old skin he's left in the corner of his box, but this time one of the scales is still in place, leaving him with a piratelike appearance. I test him with a waving finger and find he is almost blind on that side. Then I try gently to pry the scale loose but stop almost at once, fearing I'll damage the eye. It's time for professional help.

Kim Atwood was my snakiest friend at Lincoln School, a progressive temple where oddball student interests almost outweighed the curriculum. Any time I put my hand up in class and said that I needed a time to run a mouse trip over to Amsterdam Avenue, Mr. Tibbetts or Miss Barnes would smile and say O.K., fine, because they knew that this was part of Roger's naturalist thing. Forty-five minutes later I'd be back at my desk carrying a small cardboard half-pint ice-cream container by its handle, with Humphrey's bi-weekly dinner scrabbling around inside. Kim had some snakes and salamanders of his own, and we were both customers of the Ross Allen Reptile Institute, in Silver Springs, Florida. One winter morning Kim and I did a Snake Assembly in the Lincoln School auditorium, with live specimens. I recall holding up my midsize, unreliable Brown Water Snake (which had ridged, dull scales, just like a Rattlesnake or Water Moccasin) and saying, "This shy semi-aquatic snake, native to the swamps or lakes of our southeastern United States, is non-poisonous but in captivity is known to display habitual—*Ow!*"

In a class replete with young double-domes, self-assured eleven-year-old artists, and the offspring of Socialists or professors of economics, Kim was our absent-minded professor. On the occasional mornings in fourth and fifth grade when he didn't turned up for class we'd wait in happy anticipation—and then sometimes, sure enough, yell and clap our hands affectionately when the word came that, yes, he'd been nailed or grazed by another car. He had the habit of stepping out into the street from between parked cars while intensely absorbed in a comic book or a science magazine and—*smacko!* I don't recall that he ever broke anything or ended up in the hospital. Smiling sheepishly, he'd turn up again in a day or two with a lump on his forehead or a bandaged knee. The Atwoods had money—his father, Kimball Atwood, Sr., or grandfather was a Florida grapefruit king—and for a week or two after the latest mishap Kimmy would be dropped off at school in the family town car, driven by a chauffeur named Norman, whom I later got to know as a chain smoker and repository of dirty jokes. Kim and I became good pals, frequently visiting back and forth at our houses on weekends. I was invited out to the Atwoods' place in Islip, Long Island, and when I went away to Maine on vacation after fifth grade, the Atwoods took on my monkey, a Javanese Macaque named Mac, for the whole summer. A day or two after the transfer Mac escaped from the Atwoods' house and put in a lively afternoon scampering in and out of apartment houses and delicatessens near Amsterdam Avenue before being recaptured in a boarding house. Kim mailed me a little news clip about the adventure, cut out of a back section of the *Herald-Tribune,* with an attached note that read "Fame!"

Kim and I were alone in the Atwoods' big Upper West Side house after school one afternoon when he came out of his parents' bedroom with a small oblong box in his hand. "Take a look," he said in an odd tone, and I looked and saw a strange, rubbery pink igloo, lightly dusted with powder. "You know what it is, don't you?" he said, and I nodded casually, although I didn't have a clue. "It's for—you know, for sex," he said—and at that instant we heard a key in the front door lock and Kim's mother's cheerful "Hello, anybody home?" He looked frantically this way and that and then dropped the thing, box and all, into the big wastebasket at the side of the magazine-table.

"Why, hello, Roger," she said, coming in to the room, with the day's mail in her hand. "How very nice to see you." I liked her—she was tall and always stylishly dressed—but felt at this instant as if our long and cheerful relationship was suddenly poised above an abyss, with vultures lining up on the cliff face. Glancing through her mail, turning the odd envelope over to read the other side, she abstractedly and relentlessly advanced toward the fatal wastebasket, let drop some envelopes and advertisements there, and, pausing infinitesimally with her gaze on her own diaphragm, here in the living-room wastebasket, continued across the room without pause or fuss and asked if I wouldn't like some lemonade or milk or maybe iced tea, to go with Oreos.

I'm not sure if I yet knew the phrase *sang froid* at the time (I might have), but if I didn't it's a certainty that the first time I read it or had it explained the image of Kim Atwood's mother would have sprung shining into view in my mind: the Queen of Self-Possession, the helmeted goddess of cool.

Arrived in the Bronx, Kim and I hurried up the steps of the East Tremont Avenue subway station with our parcel, and walked quickly along Boston Road to the zoo entrance. I believe admission was free for school kids back then, but one way or another we were swiftly inside and headed for our destination. We knew the Bronx Zoo layout and most of the creatures in it by heart—just as we pretty much knew every floor and exhibit and vitrine at the Natural History Museum—but this time paid no attention to the tatty mountain goats, the motionless bison, and sleeping brown bears along our path. Arrived at the Reptile House, we gave not a glance to its stone crocodile and snake-head cornices and pointedly walked past the front door. Entering there, we knew, one first encountered the babyish preliminary ponds full of turtles, lily pads and torpid minor alligators. The main room, inside, featured a large central cage, within which lay an enormous, always immobile African Rock Python—a palace-sized, rolled-up beige-and-tan carpet, representing the largest reptile species of all, even bigger than the black Giant Anaconda, from South America, which (in a universally-remembered factoid) could constrict and ingest a one-hundred-pound tapir for its semi-annual dinner. No one had to wonder what the zoo's own Rock Python would look like if unwrapped and dekinked to its thirty-four or -five foot length, thanks to an ancient photograph, familiar to every school kid in the greater New York area, that hung near its cage (or perhaps by the front door) and depicted a row of fifteen or twenty uniformed zoo employees staggering under the weight of the great, pulled-out specimen clasped in their arms. Within the perimeter of the snake house, Kim and I also knew, each exhibit had its own little crowd of fans, with the larger numbers always convened before the rattlesnakes, the bushmaster, the sleek and cold-looking black mamba, or the venom-smeared glass of some spitting cobras.

Passing up these pleasures, Kim and I proceeded in businesslike fashion to the employees' entrance, around to the right in back, where I rapped on the door. In memory, the door opens and I now ask "Is Dr. Ditmars in?" but second thought has led me to believe that I would never have been this naïve. Dr. Raymond L. Ditmars, the zoo's Curator of Reptiles, had become a naturalist superstar of his era, almost as famous as Dr. William Beebe, the Aquarium's ubiquitous fish guy. I'd heard Ditmars lecture once, and

had shaken his hand, but could not claim intimate acquaintance. I consoled myself with the reminder that a man
of such importance, up to his ears with his expeditions and
interviews, could not be expected to hang around the office
all the time. In any case, I owned and had just about memorized his *Reptiles of the World,* a glorious, profusely illus-
trated essential text: the boy snake-owner's Koran and
Talmud and Deuteronomy, rolled into one. Kim had his
own copy, of course, and our frequent and extended snake
conversations consisted largely of exchanged texts and photo-
captions that we'd put to mind from this marvelous book,
with heavy emphasis on the more lethal-looking or sound-
ing species: the fer de lance; the eyelash viper; the rear-
fanged African boomslang, which sometimes manifested in
bright green; the Gaboon viper, with the longest fangs on
record and pale-tan leaf-pattern markings that cunningly
mimicked the jungle floor of its equatorial Africa habitat;
the unpleasant tic-polonga, of Ceylon; and of course our
own diamond-backed rattlesnake, whose species name, *Cro-
talus horribilis,* popped up repeatedly in our chats.

The keeper I asked for, I believe, was Ditmars' first assistant, John Toomey, whom I actually had engaged in a few
Sunday afternoon conversations as he stood with folded
arms beside the door to his sanctum. But no, Mr. Toomey
wasn't in today, Kim and I were told. We must have looked
stricken because the man at the door, a youngish fellow
with an Irish air to him, now opened the door wider and
waved us in. "What've you got in the blanket?" he asked.
Within minutes, Humphrey was stretched out on a white-
topped metal table and the young keeper, bending close,

had plucked off the offending eye-scale with a pair of tweezers and dropped it into my palm. "There you go," he said. "Good idea you came." He asked about Humphrey's age and feeding habits, and made sure that there was always a water dish in his cage. "Excellent specimen," he said, and with our permission eased Humphrey into a snowy white cotton collecting bag and knotted the neck. "Come again" he said, shaking our hands.

Outside, Kim and I reverted in three seconds from boy scientists to boys, shrieking and cavorting down the paths, dancing past the camels and cassowaries, and whirling Humphrey (in his bag) in circles around our heads. This continued through our homeward bound trip on the subway, where we told the story of our scientific errand again and again to ourselves, laughing in the half-empty train. We were so full of it all that we almost missed our stop at Ninety-sixth Street and only at the last second remembered—somebody yelled after us as the doors were beginning to close—oops, to nip back and grab Humphrey and the family steamer rug, side by side on our seat in the car.

Kim and Roger stop short here in memory, as such unbidden tales often do. With a bit of effort I can look back on these eager, irony-deprived boys—my bygone self and my long-ago school friend—without an attached moral, but still sometimes wonder how these afternoons would play out in a modern production. Quickly it can be seen that any plan for a present day Kim 'n' Rog series—on daytime HBO, say—would run into script difficulties. The Adventure of the Purloined Diaphragm goes into turn-around when Research reminds us that today's boys would have zero interest in Mrs. Atwood's medicine cabinet, having learned all that stuff in a Third Grade Responsible Reproduction Class, with an accompanying instructive video. The ailing snake still holds promise, but the IRT subway scenes are gone, made superfluous by the Net. The two smart kids talk to each other as much as ever but it's by Live Chat or Instant Messaging. They Google up the passing pit viper or anaconda in full color on *whozoo.org*, with accompanying lengthy texts (perhaps even including passages from Dr. Raymond L. Ditmars), and when Roger, still at home, reports that Humphrey has eye issues, Kim is back in three minutes with the email address of a herpetologist hotline in California, plus another site offering harm-free, environmentally O.K. plans and dimensions for the caging of unthreatened native constrictor species. The story's the same but where's the action?

We Are Fam-ilee

"WE are fam-ilee," the great old Sister Sledge single went, and then the 1979 Pittsburgh Pirates swiped it and made it their own, riding that beat all the way into the World Series and winning with it, of course. Anyone who was there still can see the Pirate player wives, in their full-length October furs and coats, kicking and boogeying together to the song, arm-in-arm on the home-team dugout roof. Who doesn't want to be fam-ilee? Let's start counting, just for fun. There is mine and yours and also the Kennedys and the Cosbys, the Cabots, the Bushes, the bin Ladens, the Roosevelts, the Alous, the Osbournes, the Barrymores, the Brontës, the Marx Brothers, the Jameses (William and Henry), and the Jameses (Jesse and Frank). Also the Gambinos, the Medicis, the Adamses, and the Addamses. The Guermantes. The Bachs, the Windsors, the Wallendas. Oliver Wendell Holmes, Sr. and Jr.; Sherlock and Mycroft

Holmes. Saltonstalls and Pallisers, Fondas and Stuarts. The Bobbseys, the Romanoffs, and die Strausses Johann the Elder, Johann the Younger, Richard, and Levi. The Capets and the Capulets and, yes, the Carters. Jimmy and Rosalynn and Amy and Billy Carter; A. P., June, Maybelle, Helen, and Anita Carter; Gary Carter. Andrew Jackson. Michael, Jermaine, Jackie, Marlon, Tito, La Toya, and Janet Jackson. Stonewall Jackson. Reggie Jackson. Donald Duck; Huey, Dewey & Louie Duck. The Sopranos.

In my early teens, I was startled to learn that a new friend of mine, Fred Parson, had five brothers, and that his father, Ken, whom I also knew, had also grown up as one of six brothers. Now there's a *family*, I thought. I had started with zero brothers and one lone sister. My divorced parents weren't much better off, with my mother being the youngest of three sisters, and my father having had to make do with one younger sister. Thin pickings. True, my mother and stepfather had a son now, Joel, who was still too young to be much fun but would perhaps become a brother down the line. I was dying for relations. For me, aunts and uncles were like the secondary characters you looked for in a good book or a movie: you wanted plenty of them, for color and action and to represent the full spectrum of oddity. A woman I know has told me that a departed great aunt of hers on East Sixty-second Street had been the long-term mistress of the celebrated Metropolitan Opera tenor Giovanni Martinelli—exactly the kind of news my family lacked. With the self-pity of the young, I had observed the slim branches on my tree and seen a poplar. But I was wrong. I hadn't appreciated the relatives I'd been given, and I was not yet aware of the generative powers of American divorce.

Looking at my family now, I note that there have been eleven (or sixteen, counting another way) divorces, spread across three generations—more than enough for a soap, and not what its members would have invented for themselves as children. But we cannot now unimagine the new fathers and step-aunts and half-brothers or sisters and half-grandnieces that sit around the family tables on a Thanksgiving, or wish a life for ourselves that did not include unexpected attachments. In this story, a man is approached by a man he has known for forty years, who says, "Guess what. We have the same father—I'm your brother. No wonder I could always beat you at singles." On another day, a new baby, a wonderful son, is baptized simultaneously in ten or eleven different rites, including the Yoruba. Four years later, the friend who thought of this caper, a minister, and pulled it off is killed in a homophobic murder. Years after this, a blond granddaughter acquires a coffee-colored sister, from Colombia. Much later, a niece writes a daring master's thesis about recent research into the terrible disease ALS, and its inexorable progress in one particular victim, her mother. Long before this, in the fall of 1944, a stepfather sits down in his West Eleventh Street apartment and resumes the abandoned draft of his first children's book, tentatively called *Stuart Little.* Back still farther, in 1918, a bluestocking aunt, now long gone, is wounded on the Western Front, where she'd ventured as a correspondent for *The New Republic.* More recently, a pair

of middle-aged half-brothers—this is me and Joel: "Joe," to
me—smile as they agree that they have never found a way
to express the love they have for each other; now the survivor, sailing over the bit of Jericho Bay where his brother's
ashes were gently sunk, feels that they did close the gap
after all.

I also count in Aunt Olive—my father's second wife's
aunt, Olive Higgins Prouty, the wife of a staid Massachusetts businessman and the redoubtable author of *Stella Dal-
las, Now Voyager,* and eight other weepy best-selling novels.
One day around 1950, she approached me for professional
help. "Now, Roger, you know New York," she began. She
went on to explain that in the novel she was then writing—
it was called *Fabia*—her heroine had moved out on her
husband in Boston and come to New York to live with an
artist. She had them sharing a little apartment on the West
Side, maybe in West Seventy-seventh Street. It was early in
the 1920s. Would that be right?

"That sounds exactly right, Aunt Olive," I said. Needless to say, I waited impatiently for the book's arrival, and
when I read it there they were, almost in sin in the West
Seventies. He never laid a hand on her.

This is my own family. Amazingly, I am its patriarch—
though only one of us, a nephew, seems to see me that way,
thank God. My attachments and affections within it run
every which way, leaping from my children and grandchildren and nieces and nephews to my twin half-brother and
half-sister to my divorced and deceased first wife's nearest
sister, whom I've known for sixty-seven years ("Of course I
live in denial," she says. "It's the perfect place for me"); to

a different ex-sister-in-law, who's a judge in California; to a niece, the single mother of two grown sons, who's an intensive-care nurse in Vermont and trains enormous jumping horses in her off time; and to all and each (well, just about) in between.

What comes back to me these days often begins with an insistent detail, a sunken branch sticking up from a stream which has snagged a mat of memory. When I was a kid I loved our once- or twice-a-year visits to my Aunt Rosie and Uncle John Newberry's house on steep, red-bricked Beacon Hill in Boston. The place had a living-room oddly stuffed down into the basement—you could peek in there through little sidewalk-level windows beside the front steps—and featured a waist-high Stromberg-Carlson phonograph that amazingly played both sides of a regular ten- or twelve-inch 78 rpm record in succession. When your Brunswick or Victor Red Label selection was done a shiny metal apparatus moved magisterially into place, gently plucked up the record, rotated it in midair, and lowered it back into place; almost bowing, it withdrew as the record spun round again and the arm lowered itself toward the new tune. (This was ten or fifteen years before jukeboxes developed the same capability, dealing more briskly with the biscuit-like 45s of the day.) None of my school friends in New York had anything as fancy, but what kept me riveted next to the Newberrys' machine wasn't just "Rosalie" coming after "Valencia," or the "Moonlight Sonata" in two full parts but the machine's delicious fallibility. Now and then—you'd have to wait while twenty or thirty faultless flips and plays went by—the shiny armature would produce a tremble or speed up in mid-transfer and then silently and insanely smash its precious load to bits. "It did it again!" my cousin Jack and I would yell excitedly, and Uncle John, muttering, would tromp down the red-carpeted stairs to inspect the wreckage.

The Newberrys had money—he'd inherited a cement manufacturing business in Ohio, though I don't remember that he ever worked at it or went there—and because Uncle John was a mild eccentric, I conjoined big bucks and weirdness in my young mind. One day when I was about six he parked the Newberry car, a snappy beige Marmon, on the steep little road outside our rented summer house in Snedens Landing, but forgot to engage the hand brake. We were eating lunch when a cry from out there brought us to the windows just in time to see the Marmon slip into the adjacent Hudson River, where it came to a halt with its nose and front wheels buried in the muddy flow. "Oh, dear," said my uncle.

Uncle John, who was silent by nature, had pink cheeks and brown hair that stuck up in spikes behind, and arrives in memory accompanied by a nagging, minatory call from his wife: "John." ... "John?" In later summers, the Newberrys put up at Breezemere Farm, a rustic main house with adjacent cabins in South Brooksville, Maine, about twenty miles away from my mother and stepfather's place in North Brooklin. There were picnics or lunches, back and forth, a couple of them every summer, and whenever there was going to be some swimming I looked forward to watching Uncle John's getaway. Strong and broad-chested above his dark bathing trunks, he stepped his way gingerly down the stony beach, lowered himself into the icy Penobscot waters, and swam away. His progress, in a churning late-Victorian breast-stroke, was slow but cumulatively awesome; ten minutes later, then twenty, you'd see his dark head still bobbing up and away, first the size of an apple, then a distant dot. "John!" Aunt Rose called after him. *"John!"* It was even better when this happened at the Newberrys' picnic place at the western end of Eggemoggin Reach, because Uncle John's swim soon took him out of sight, beyond the point that separated us from Buck Harbor, though even this did not silence her cries. Sometimes he stayed out so long that I too began to imagine that a cramp or a passing Chris Craft had taken him down at last, but then the dot would reappear and surge slowly back to us. "Oh, John," Aunt Rosie said reproachfully as he emerged, with his body scarlet and drops spangling the hair on his chest. He'd wait until he'd found his towel before making his declaration, "Nine hundred and twenty-three!"—the strokes of today's swim. The number varied but never the glow.

Some years later, Uncle John broke his silence with another announcement, the appearance of a book, *The Rainbow Bridge,* a scholarly study of the Sanskrit Antakaranha, a journey to higher awareness and the sources of creation, which he'd been writing and thinking about all along, it turned out. Somewhere I have a snapshot of him and Aunt Rosie standing on the beach with me at Sarasota, where I am visiting in the mid-1950s. They are old now, but Uncle John's hair still sticks up behind. Aunt Rosie is talking, one hand in the air, but Uncle John, who is leaning slightly forward, can't get away this time. One hand is tucked into the pocket of his summer jacket and the other, his right, is oddly angled across his waist: Parkinson's.

My mother's oldest sister, Aunt Elsie, administered one of the shocks of my young life when, on a spring Saturday in 1930, she invited me to pay a call at her apartment near Gramercy Square, where an Indian friend of hers was visiting. An American Indian, she said: the real thing. I grabbed a downtown bus—I was nine—rang the bell and looked eagerly about.

"Mr. Luhan will be right out," Aunt Elsie said. "He's washing his hair."

And out he came in due course—a plump brown gent with a towel on his shoulders and long damp locks smelling of Conti's Castile. Elsie, who was well along in her fifties and had never married, didn't see my consternation—and if she had she'd have told me to forget about Cochise and Crazy Horse, this was Tony Luhan, the Taos Indian husband of Mabel Dodge Luhan, the writer who was so close to D. H. and Frieda Lawrence. You know—Lawrence the novelist. Elsie was implacably literary.

She was the *New Republic* war correspondent aunt who'd gotten herself blown up in 1918, while visiting an abandoned and supposedly safe sector of captured trenches, with a young French officer as guide. Another journalist in the party at Mont Bligny, a Frenchwoman, idly picked up a German potato-masher grenade, which exploded. The woman died, the officer lost an arm, and Elsie, with two smashed ankles, ended up in the French military hospital at Neuilly, to begin a long recovery. She got a book, *Shadow*

Shapes, and a slight limp out of the accident, which never quite fitted the rest of her life story. Thick bodied and slow-moving, eleven years older than my mother, Elizabeth Shepley Sergeant had written for *McClure's* early in the century, had known Willa Cather and Robert Frost (she wrote a memoir of the first and a biography of the second) and Eugene O'Neill, and had been a student or an analysand of Carl Jung's in Zurich. Before this, she'd lived and studied in France and Italy, and had attended the Sorbonne. I have a dim photograph of her standing in a crown and a sweeping robe before a costume party in Sicily in 1904. Her six books were respectfully reviewed, but feel stilted and airless whenever I take down a volume now. One of them, a 1927 collection of literary essays, has a riveting title: *Fire Under the Andes.* She had genuine intellectual credentials. She had translated Giraudoux and other avant-garde French writers. She visited Jung for some weeks in 1930 and was a participant with him in a seminar, "Interpretation of Visions." In a lengthy portrait she wrote for the May, 1931 *Harpers,* she finds him washing out his blue jeans outside his tower, near the Zurichsee. "Dr. C. G. Jung," she begins, "is the only European thinker I know who belongs to the earth people."

I was impressed with Aunt Elsie when my father and Nancy and I stayed with her in 1934, in Tesuque, New Mexico, where she was working for the U.S. Indian Bureau. She was friends with John Collier, the Commissioner of Indian Affairs, and also seemed close to many pueblo children and aspiring students. She knew the mountain back roads, and kept in touch with the outer pueblos. She

told us to keep an eye out for the black pottery at San Ildefonso, and directed us to one of the mesa-top villages in
Arizona on the right day for one of their semi-secret Snake
Dances. Other meetings with her, back east, became strained
because she'd spotted me as an active young reader and
wished to lure me to the higher intellectual ground. At tea
or lunch in New York, she'd ask what I was reading and if
I said Sherlock Holmes or Stevenson she'd bring up Yeats
and Pound and Eliot, all still strangers to me. When I was
about twelve, she invited me to a midweek afternoon event
at the Ninety-second Street YMHA—a lecture on Greek
archaeology, perhaps, or something about Navajo folk songs.
While she was chatting with an acquaintance during the intermission, I recalled that my dog Tunney and perhaps the
new issue of *Baseball* were waiting for me at home, a bare
two blocks away, and when Aunt Elsie wasn't looking I
skimmed out a side door. This was big trouble, of course.
Elsie, fearing kidnappers, had called my father at his office,
and he lit into me lengthily that night. Then my mother
weighed in, by the telephone. In both parental tirades, however, I also detected a gleam of wonder, even admiration—
"You mean you just *walked away?*" Maybe they'd wanted to
stick a pin into Elsie once in a while, too.

The strain between my mother and Elsie was more than
an everyday family tangle. Elsie, lit'ry and sociable, always
looked down on Mother's successful career and busy life
at *The New Yorker*—"that vulgar magazine," she'd once let
slip—and perhaps her marriages as well, but she could never
forget that it was the magazine's success and Mother's hard
work that kept her afloat with privately arranged allowances

and a nice extra check at Christmas. Mother was loyal to Elsie all her life but could not bring herself to say warm things about her writing. She never mentioned her sister's financial dependency or the emotional strain it exacted on both sides, but worried about Elsie's health and living arrangements, even while she was being driven wild by her vagueness and intellectual hauteur. Andy White believed that Mother was secretly afraid of her, for reasons that went back to their childhood, but it may also be that Bryn Mawr was in play between them all along. Elsie had graduated in 1900, eight years before my mother entered the demanding and exalting Bryn Mawr of President M. Carey Thomas's time. The high shrine required four languages, prodigious reading, and a permanent engagement with the classics and a life of the mind. My mother did well there—she graduated fourth in her class—but two decades later, when she'd become the most significant woman editor in New York, was editing Mary McCarthy and Vladimir Nabokov and John O'Hara and Elizabeth Bishop, and week by week having a hand in every aspect of the *New Yorker,* she may have also crazily believed that she'd abandoned the groves of Spenser and Goethe and Kant, where Elsie strolled every day. The two met now and then, but were not capable of the offhand joke or passing embrace that would have blown all this away. My mother found a life-saving lightness in Andy White, but Elsie had no such resource—which inexorably caused my mother further guilt, and added that fresh twinge to the others.

Elsie never wavered. Toward the end of her life, she went resolutely back each summer to MacDowell, the writers' colony in New Hampshire, even in seasons when she'd not been invited to return, again occupying one of the cottages where lunch was left silently at the door in a little basket, and then joining the other artists and poets for jolly dinners and interesting conversations each evening. I happily remember her in her seventies, when she was a neighbor of mine in Rockland County, upriver from New York. She had a tiny house tucked behind a stone wall in the village of Piermont, a cottage so bijou that you had to grab a banister rope while ascending the steep circular staircase to the second floor. Here on a summer Sunday, Elsie would have me and my family to tea on her terrace, a bare few yards from the pallid Hudson. Appearing with her thick braid coiled on her head and wearing amber or ivory beads, a Navajo bracelet, and a white lawn dress that dated back to 1908 or 1910, she would pour tea into thin family China cups, and have me pass round the slivers of cinnamon toast while she talked affectionately with my wife, Evelyn, and our daughters. Roaring outboards sometimes made for a pause in our conversation, and my daughter Alice would slip away from the table to keep watch on the saucer of milk that Elsie had put down for the garter snake said to live in the wall. Elsie, resuming, would mention her neighbor Horace Gregory, the poet, her archaeologist friend Hetty Goldman, and her good friend Thornton Wilder, the playwright. "You've read *The Bridge of San Luis Rey*?" she asked Callie, who was then about ten. "No? Well, one day *soon,* I'm sure." A little before this time, when my brother Joe White and Allene Messer were getting married and preparing to get into the boat-building line of work,

Elsie picked out a nice book for their wedding present: *The Life of Nietzsche.*

Ill and old, she ended up in a retirement home in Westchester County, with her books and a few sticks of her own furniture. Visiting New York one day, at eighty-three, she died at the Cosmopolitan Club, with a check from her publisher in her pocket-book—an advance, issued that day, against her next book. Way to go out, Elsie!

Two more glimpses of Aunt Elsie have surfaced, arriving within three weeks of each other last spring. Dr. Marilyn Norcini, a cultural anthropologist whom I encountered by chance while on a visit to the University of Pennsylvania, turned out to be a wellspring of knowledge about Elsie's days in New Mexico in the 1920s and '30s. She mailed me a packet of my aunt's writings and records, which center on her efforts to appreciate and preserve the expiring culture of the Pueblo lands and people, and to fight for them a little on the political front. In 1935 she appears to have been instrumental in the adoption of a constitution by the Santa Clara Pueblo, which brought claims by various tribal groups into accord. It was signed on one of those iron-cold January mornings in the Southwest: a photograph shows Elsie standing in the snow amid several bundled-up sachems and elders, one whom is wearing an eagle-feather bonnet. There is also further documentation of her studies with Jung, and, most touching to me, a bibliography which lists eighty-three articles she wrote for national periodicals between 1910 and 1963—the steadiest flow is in the teens and twenties—for magazines like *The Nation, The Saturday*

Review, Dial, and *The Atlantic.* It begins with "Toilers of the Tenements," for *McClure's* in July 1910, and includes "Must Great Women Be Ruthless?" in the *Ladies Home Journal* for February, 1928, and "New Deal for the Indian" in the June 15, 1939, *New Republic.* A nice body of work, if never quite a livelihood.

And then, right after the Elsie trove, here came a little packet of letters written by my mother in the 1950s and '60s to a garden or garden-and-literature correspondent of hers in New York named Ambrose Flack. These had lately been unearthed in the attic of a cottage on Fire Island by a renter who didn't know Flack or Katharine S. White but somehow remembered my name and connection, and sent them along. Most of these are about generiads and slipper gloxinias, and the like. But in March 1965, my mother responds at length to an inquiry from Flack about Elsie's book, *Willa Cather: A Memoir,* beginning with the news that when she herself was in college Elsie had taken her on more than one occasion to visit the novelist at her New York apartment on Bank Street. Then, in May 1921, the three meet again at the Central Park Casino, "...where the hanging violet-blue wisteria clusters seemed part of the Victorian age." The lines are from Elsie's memoir, which goes on about her subject to say, "Her way of delivering herself completely to the situation of a little party she was giving and making a friend feel welcomed was most charming. The warm, assertive, direct outgoing side of her nature still came up from the depths of her distance to meet the occasion."

Here is my mother, on the same moment: "My report on the day when Miss Cather, my sister, and I met for tea under the wisteria vine in Central Park would have been very different from the one in my sister's book! It was a matter of two writers, each obsessed with their own books in process, and each hardly allowing the other to get a word in. Miss Cather won. My sister had been wounded and was just back from a long and dreadful experience (of which she wrote or was writing in *Shadow Shapes,* her wartime French diary) and she trustingly thought that Miss Cather was there as a friend to hear about her, Elizabeth's, ordeal. It soon became evident to *me* that Miss Cather was there for another reason—to get factual detail and background for her own novel in progress, since she had not been in France at all and was writing *One of Ours.* (It turned out to be her poorest novel.) I resented this at the time, though my sister did not, and I probably still do."

One more aunt. My father's sister, Hildegarde Angell, three years younger, had the same long face and grave look as he but much larger brown eyes; there was something exotic and thrilling about her, for me. When I was quite young she told me about a day the summer before when she'd taken her bathing suit off while at the beach in Provincetown, and, seeing no one else about, had gone for a walk along the shore without a towel. If another woman hove into view in the distance it wouldn't matter, she told herself, and if the figure turned out to be a man she would reverse course and stroll back to her towel and *maillot.* In time a tiny figure did appear up ahead, and by the time she could make out that it was a man she saw that he, too, was naked. She forged ahead, telling herself not to be the first to bail out. They approached each other, exchanged nods and friendly "Good afternoons," and went on by. I made her tell this to me all over again.

Another reason Aunt Hildegarde still holds a bit of glamour is that I don't know enough about her. She graduated from Wellesley but I don't remember what her work was after that. Now there's no one left for me to ask about this. She passed extended times in Mexico and South America, and in 1930 Norton published a serious, well-regarded biography of hers, *Simon Bolivar*. It's my belief, uncorroborated, that she went through an extended, never-resolved love affair with a married man. She was often around on weekends after my parents were divorced and came skating or hiking with us and friends of Father's, sitting out in the open with sandwiches and hard boiled eggs on their laps afterward, with everyone smoking and talking heatedly about books and plays and painters and politics. She joined Nancy and Father and me in the middle of a vacation at a small ranch in Montana in 1930, and on hot afternoons on the trails above the Little Big Horn would sometimes take off her shirt and ride along ahead of me in jeans and bra. One day, I rode up beside her while she was reading a letter that had just come in the mail, and announced what I saw at the top of the page " 'Darling Hildegarde—' "

She screeched and slashed her hat at me, but the news held up. Later that year she married the letter-writer, Granville Smith—wonderful, delightful Granville, another man in the family at last and a pal for life. He must have been in his late forties then: a lively bow-legged man out of Kansas City and Yale. He was bald, with a round jaw, crinkly narrow eyes, and a Roman nose that shot down from his high forehead. He knew Mexico, too, and the very next summer Nancy and Father and I joined the brand-new Smiths in the Gulf Coast refinery town of Tampico, where we all lived in the mayor's house—actually, *El Calde* lived upstairs, so there was always a cop in a sombrero on guard or asleep at the foot of the steps. One day, at siesta time, there was a loud report outside our windows, where the guard of the moment had fired his rifle at a kid trying to steal my sister's bathing suit off the line, but missed. Each afternoon, Granville came home from his job at the oil camp covered with smudges of creosote—some of it came off on Hildegarde—which he wiped away with a cloth dipped in gasoline before heading off for his bath. He was an oil man but perhaps closer to roustabout than tycoon.

I hung about near Granville, who laughed at my jokes and kid ways. One day we all bundled aboard a narrow, outboard-powered local banana boat—though bigger, it had the same shape and configuration as the *African Queen*—and took that memorable day-and-night's run down the Laguna de Tamiahua, a brackish long lagoon paralleling the Gulf—in company with numerous locals and dogs and goats, and a raffish friend of Granville's named Boo-Hoo. There was no cabin or head, and when necessity called, Nancy and Aunt Hildegarde stepped decorously into a long rowboat astern, and took turns holding up a serape as a bathroom screen. That night, I was told, I almost rolled overboard in my sleep from our part of the rooftop deck, close to some stacked crab traps, but Granville stuck out an arm and grabbed me back. The next morning, we'd arrived at a banana plantation, where the light fell greenly through low leaves; just across the stream there were taller trees bunched into near-jungle, with iguanas and staring small monkeys everywhere. Boo-Hoo handed me a shovel and said "Dig anyplace," and in ten minutes I'd come up with some fragments of painted pots and a stone whistle stoppered with loam. This was old country.

Within a year, Hildegarde and Granville had gone into hock and bought a farm in northern Missouri—Spring Creek Ranch, in Green Castle—and were raising sheep and chickens and seventy-odd white-faced Herefords, of a prime strain they'd found through their rancher friends Ted and Haydee Yates, in Montana. Wild with impatience until vacation rolled around again, I joined Granville on horseback this time, and helped the hands drive the critters to water and back each day, or to a fresh pasture. I learned to ride with my stirrups long and my back straight above the supporting curve of the saddle, the way they did, and in time got the tilt of my hat exactly right. Riding alongside the plodding heifers, I touched up my horse toward the next fence, dismounted in a single motion, and coolly unhooked the barbed-wire gate loop with my shoulder and gloved hand. On drenching day, I wrestled heavy, terrified sheep off their feet and lay panting on top of them, while outsized metal syringes full of copper sulphate were stuffed down their throats; I was the smudge man, marking each woolly head with a chunk of blue chalk, to avoid a fatal repeat dose. Each night, there was shoptalk around the kitchen table about salt licks and brush-whacker tractors, the pick-up times at Milan for next week's cattle-trucks headed for Kirksville or Saint Joe, the damage done to a famous cottonwood that had just been whacked by lightning; and, again and again, the drought and the dropping water levels in the cattle cisterns. Hildegarde and Granville knew all the Herefords—which one had a damaged horn or a hind hoof that needed tarring and which calves would be best to cut out and saved for breeding. In the broiling afternoons, Granville let me steer his ancient Ford station wagon on the dusty dirt roads, and in time let me drive it, too, though I had to reach for the pedals with my toes. What was different about him was he had a terrible heart— he'd damaged it years earlier—and in the midst of these ranch exertions would sometimes gasp and throw his head back and struggle for breath, his body flung back against a railing or the hood of the Ford. Although his shirt went half unbuttoned most of the time he was never tan, and at times like this you could see his heart bumping and thrumming in his white chest. Then he'd draw a breath, smile wanly, and put his dinky straw Stetson back on and resume his tasks. Every day after lunch—or dinner, as it was called—he went to bed again, like clockwork, under the covers for an hour-and-a-quarter siesta.

We went back to this entrancing place the next summer, and I returned alone two summers after that, when I was fifteen, and worked there through August until Father came out, near the end, for some vacation. One day I came down off a barn roof we were patching and stood uneasily by the storm cellar doors, along with everybody else, until a massive gray-green line storm changed its mind at the last moment and went moaning and crackling up the next val-

ley. All was the same, except that this last year, 1936, Granville's wife wasn't Aunt Hildegarde anymore, but Hildegarde's best friend, Evelyn Dewey, the daughter of the
educator John Dewey. Hildegarde had died after two or
barely three years of her happy marriage—it was a breast
cancer, and took her quickly—and Granville, unable to
bear it, had found Evelyn. She missed Hildegarde almost as
much as he did, and with the ranch and its urgent needs
waiting, the two married within months of her death and
went on without her, saving each other from too much
grieving. Evelyn Dewey wore pince-nez and was not beautiful, but she had a serious laugh and didn't let me get away
with anything. I got used to them, though it wasn't quite
the same, but it took Father longer to get over this turn of
events. Nancy and I were growing up and becoming ourselves, and he had not yet married again. Hildegarde was
the companion of his bosom, and she'd become the part of
the family where there was plenty of hope and laughter.

An earlier moment between me and Aunt Hildegarde
remains, a happening so slight that its presence in memory
is a puzzle. One afternoon in my boyhood—I was ten or
eleven, I think—Hildegarde turned up at our house on
Ninety-third Street in the afternoon, after I'd come home
from school. I don't recall the occasion; maybe she was expected for dinner and thought she'd drop in on me beforehand. I was alone in the library when the front doorbell
rang downstairs and when Joseph, our cook, opened the
door I heard her voice and felt a start of pleasure at this
surprise. She was halfway up the stairs when on sudden

impulse I slipped behind one of the long curtains beside one of the windows looking out onto the street. Barely breathing, taking care not to stir the folds of heavy curtain, I peeked out and watched her come into the room. She made a little sound of disappointment, then looked about and sat down in the low armchair facing me. She found a magazine on the table before her and sat back and began to leaf through it, with her legs crossed. Savoring the surprise to come, I took in her stylish dress and saw her long, elegant face as she turned idly from page to page, and was struck, bang, by something previously unknown to me: an intimation or shift of view so strange that it made me jump out almost before I was ready, and run over to share her surprise and laughter and get a hug. Seeing Hildegarde unaware for an instant—alone, or so she thought—in a shadowed room was something I'd not experienced before with her or with any grown-up, and a powerful sense of loneliness and separation overtook me by surprise. She wasn't just Aunt Hildegarde but also simply someone alone in an empty room at that moment, and I was now the possessor of two thoughts, or two shots at the idea of this scene: what it was like to be Hildegarde, and what it was like to be me, watching her and knowing all this. The voyeur's sadness, which infects the watcher and the watched equally, was too much for me—it still is now—and I burst out: "Boo!" to make the day begin again and go on as before.

Andy

LATELY I have been missing my stepfather, Andy White, who keeps excusing himself while he steps out of the room to get something from his study or heads out the back kitchen door, on his way to the barn again. He'll be right back. I can hear the sound of that gray door—the steps there lead down into the fragrant connecting woodshed—as the lift-latch clicks shut. E. B. White died in 1985—twenty years ago, and more—and by "missing" I don't mean yearning for him so much as not being able to keep hold of him for a bit of conversation or even a tone of voice. In my mind, this is at his place in North Brooklin, Maine, and he's almost still around. I see his plaid button-down shirt and tweed jacket, and his good evening moccasins. One hand is holding a cigarette tentatively—he'll smoke it half-way down and then stub it out—and he turns in his chair to put his martini back on the Swedish side table to his right. It must be about dinnertime. What were we talking about, just now? We were close for almost sixty years, and you'd think that a little back-and-forth—something more than a joke or part of an anecdote—would survive, but no. What's impossible to write down, soon afterward, is a conversation that comes easily.

Here we are, instead, on a frigid December day in 1929, walking up a steep stretch of Pinckney Street, on Beacon Hill, in Boston. The narrow brick sidewalk is snowy in places, and the going is harder for Andy than it is for me, because he's wearing ice skates. He's been complaining— who can blame him—and finally he sits down on somebody's front stoop to pull off the skates, and goes on, snow or no snow, in his socks. We've been here on a family visit from New York to the Newberrys' house at 87 Myrtle Street—my Aunt Rosie and Uncle John's place—and Andy and I brought our skates along, just in case. Christmas is two or three days away, and on a clear and cold afternoon he and I head down to Charles Street and then over to the frozen lake in the Public Garden. There may be a red-ball sign standing out on the ice, telling us it's safe to skate, but there's no place you can go to buy a ticket, and no shack with a stove inside, where you could keep warm while you lace up your skates. We find a park bench instead. Andy hides our shoes under a bush and we step down an embankment and sail away. Other skaters are here already— some of the men are in overcoats, along with kids in striped scarves and big mittens—but it's as if we had the place to ourselves. There are wintry trees and park lampposts with a different shape than the ones in Central Park, and though the sense of Boston is close at hand, we could almost be in the country. Wind has cleared patches and paths through snow for us to skate on. The ice is rough, with frozen ripples here and there to trip you up, but Andy and I are good skaters, and we laugh when we come to a curved bridge and, bending low, shoot under and out the other side. It's a great afternoon—right up to the moment when we come back to our bush and see that Andy's shoes are gone. I don't recall that we made a fuss or much of a search; this was hard times, the onset of the Depression, and even a poorly fitting pair of shoes was better than a handout or a hot meal for a lot of men just then.

Andy was shy and self-conscious—he was a slight man, never one to bluster his way through things—and I could see him turn his head away in embarrassment as people coming toward us down Beacon Street began to smile when they saw him tiptoeing along on his hockey skates. Sometimes after they'd gone by he stopped and bent half-double, laughing at himself. "'The Skater,'" he said, shaking his head. It was a relief for me to laugh, too. What came to me later—I was nine but prone to thought—was that this adventure would not have happened with my father. I'd done more skating with him, on rivers and ponds everywhere—he'd started me when I was small—but he'd have taken us home when we found there was no place to check our shoes. Or if he had lost his shoes somehow he'd have found a cab or made a phone call before ever walking a dozen blocks in his skates. Andy was ten years his junior, and younger than my mother, too. He was a grownup, but there was a readiness for play in him that lasted all his life. Luckily, I didn't need another father and that freed us up.

Andy makes light of the lost shoes in a tiny Notes and Comment piece he wrote for *The New Yorker* afterward, and I've remembered the day for boyish reasons—it was an adventure and it put me alone with someone I loved but didn't see all that much. Actually, the story is right up his alley. In *One Man's Meat*, the celebrated collection of his essays published in 1942, he recalls his dreamy seventeen-year-old self at home in Mount Vernon, New York, in 1917, just before he entered Cornell as a freshman. He was thinking of a girl he had skated with the winter before, when "the air grew still and the pond cracked and creaked under our skates," and "the trails of ice led off into the woods, and the little fires burned along the shore. It was enough, that spring, to remember what a girl's hand felt like, suddenly ungloved in winter." The shift from the winter general to the sudden particular of the girl's hand is a White special, as is the self-deprecation. And pegging along on a sidewalk in skates was an embarrassment that he would have made more of in a piece later on and played out with relish, as he did so often in his writings, turning the awkward moment into a charming and then telling paragraph, even as he dwells on his fears. He was the most charming man I've known, and he got that side of himself into his writing, like everything else, without effort.

Another winter scene is coming—this one a half century later—but first it should be explained that E. B. White was a lifelong hypochondriac, perhaps world class, but not a solemn one. Munching a canapé on my porch in Maine one evening, he clapped one hand to his face in horror. We paused, drinks in midair. "Got anything for cheese in the *eye?*" he cried indignantly. The crisis passed and the moment was affectionately filed away, joining the deadly ant bite at the beach picnic, the bone in his upper spine that was almost surely pushing its way through his windpipe, the passing ulcer or descending thrombus, and the thousand-odd spoonfuls of soup or compote, or forkfuls of salad or soufflé that were suddenly halted and inspected midway to his mouth, with the same "Any *clams* in this?" A clam had poisoned him once—though I don't think I ever heard the meal or the mollusk named—and the cooks and hostesses of the world, including my mother, were out to lay him low again by the same means. No discussion followed a fresh alert. "Nope, no clams, Andy," someone would murmur, and the meal resumed. If your eye fell on him later, you might notice that he was chewing, as always, with his mouth a quarter or an eighth open, ready to discharge any skulking bivalve that had slipped through the lines. Another quirk of his, almost as familiar as his gray mustache or his easeful walk, was a persistent leftward twist of his head, a little adjustment of neck and spine repeated every minute or so, retesting a structure on the verge of collapse.

I never had the feeling that Andy worked on his worries. He wasn't exactly after attention, though that's what he got at the spectacular upper levels of his discomposure. In the winter of 1980, word came to my wife, Carol, and me in New York that a cherished Maine neighbor of ours, Catherine McCoy, had died. There would be a memorial in Blue Hill, early in January, and after discussion we agreed that Carol would fly up to Bangor while I stayed home with our ten-year-old son, John Henry. My mother had died three years earlier, and Andy was delighted by the unexpected visitor, though it was understood that he would not attend the ceremony. Public gatherings—and most private ones, as well—made him jumpy. For years he had passed up family weddings and graduations, town meetings, dedications and book awards, cocktail bashes and boat gams and garden parties. As his literary reputation widened when he was in his forties and fifties, he did make it to a few select universities to receive honorary degrees, but despite prearranged infusions of sherry or Scotch he found the ceremonials excruciating. "So the old emptiness and dizziness and vapors seized hold of me," he writes to my mother after his *honoris causa* Ph.D. appearance at Dartmouth in 1948. "Nobody who has never had my peculiar kind of disability can understand the sheer hell of such moments, but there they are." And when the time came for the encomiums and the enrobing, there in the sunshine at Hanover, he went on, his hood—"white, quite big, and shaped like a loose-fitting horse collar"—became entangled with the honoree in the next seat, Ben Ames Williams: Andy's worst dreams come true. "When I got seated the thing was up over my face, as in falconry," he continues. "A fully masked Doctor of Letters, a headless poet." After that, he stayed home, even passing up an invitation in 1963 to go to Washington and receive the Presidential Medal of Freedom from Lyndon Johnson; the deed was consummated instead by a stand-in, Maine's Senator Edmund Muskie, in the office of the president of Colby College. Andy also skipped his wife's private burial in the Brooklin Cemetery, in July, 1977. None of us in the family expected otherwise or held this against him. And when his own memorial came, eight years later, I took the chance to remark, "If Andy White could be with us today he would not be with us today."

There would be no question of his accompanying Carol to Catherine McCoy's farewell at the Blue Hill Congregational Church—except that a considerable snowstorm blew in overnight, converting the two-lane Route 175 to a slithery corridor the next morning. Carol said she'd drive herself over, but he wouldn't hear of it; he'd drive her—he knew these winter roads. And so she found herself and the writhing public E.B.W. seated side by side near the front of the long church—the "Congo," in local parlance—while preliminary organ music fell about them and the rows filled up with stomping, de-muffling mourners. When the music subsided and the footfalls of the minister were heard, Andy leaned toward Carol and whispered, "I'm having a heart attack."

"I'm not leaving," she whispered back, and kept her gaze straight ahead while he rose, excusing himself, and, half-bending but not unobserved, made his way out of the row and back up the aisle and, at last, through a door into the vestibule. The service and the tributes went on lengthily, at least for Carol. Had she done the right thing? She had no idea what she would find after the benediction and the recessional were over—certainly not the sight of Andy stretched on his back on one of the vestibule benches, a Saxon king atop his sarcophagus, as he responded to the anxious questions of each departing neighbor. "A heart attack," he explained. "I had a heart attack." In time, he arose, bundled up, and drove her safely back to North Brooklin for drinks and a nice dinner.

My mother and Andy White got married in 1929, immediately after my parents' divorce, and though my sister and I were only weekend and summertime visitors with them after that, I soon felt as much at home at their place—on East Eighth Street and then East Forty-eighth Street, in New York, and then in Maine—as I was with my father the rest of the time. A fresh household sharpens attention, and one of the things I picked up was that sense of ease and play that Andy brought to his undertakings. Though subject to nerves, he possessed something like that invisible extra beat of time that great athletes show on the field. Dogs and children were easy for him because he approached them as a participant instead of a winner. In a family photograph, he is sitting astride a bench outside the garage door, in Maine, while he stirs up a dish of mash for his bantam hens. Blond John Henry, then about two years old, is standing close by, and they are looking into the dish with equal interest while Andy mixes and talks. When Andy, without his trying and almost without my noticing it, taught me how to sail or how to row or how to lure a flounder with a bit of periwinkle as bait and—in some part—how to write, ease seemed to be the whole trick. He let things emerge, like the time he unexpectedly put his nearly empty bottle of Pabst or Schlitz down on the carpet in front of his big dachshund, Fred, who sniffed about and soon found that by laying one paw on the neck he could tip the last of the beer toward the top of the bottle and lap it out. Then he ate the label.

When the Whites moved to a year-round residency in
Maine, in 1938, we kept in touch by letters, as everyone did
in those days, but also, I began to realize, through his writings. He'd given up the Comment page he wrote each week
for *The New Yorker,* and the eased deadlines and greater
length of his monthly "One Man's Meat" column in
Harper's suited the hours and bottomless concerns of a salt-
water farmer with a hundred and fifty pullets, a dozen
geese, twenty or thirty sheep, an editor wife (my mother
had continued her work as a fiction and poetry editor with
The New Yorker by long distance, with daily envelopes of
manuscripts and proofs mailed back and forth between New
York and Brooklin), a schoolboy son, Joel, and a full-time
hired man. What he wrote about, along with the weather
and the way to build a double-ended cedar scow for Joe
and the way to keep a city rubber plant healthy with doses
of "sheep-shit tea" (as it was known in the family, if not in
print) and how to hook up a mooring with a chain so the
tide will lift it free later in the morning, was himself. The
arrangement left room for his thoughts about the movies,
automobile design, the railroads, taxation, domesticity, poetry, Florida trailer parks, and freedom. In 1937, a year before he began writing *One Man's Meat,* Andy formally took
a year off ("My Year" as he called it) to try—well, to try
to become a serious writer. Nothing came of it, of course,
but then the *Harper's* assignment came along and saved his
life. He was self-conscious at first as a countryman—he is
abashed as he catches himself crossing the barnyard with a
paper napkin in his hand—but the demands of the work
and his affinity for it soon dismissed such concerns and

somehow put him in place as a writer. The Whites, with their well-staffed household and sophisticated occupations, would always be "from away," in Down East parlance, but no one in Brooklin who knew Andy ever took him for a gentleman farmer. When the war came, he even took on a cow—the first time he leads her out to the pasture, he writes, he feels "the way I did the first time I ever took a girl to the theatre"—and his production goals for 1942 were four thousand dozen eggs, ten pigs, and nine thousand pounds of milk.

I was away much of the time at boarding school and then at Harvard, and then elsewhere as a soldier, but the sense of home and informal but intimate attachment I got from Andy's writings was even more powerful than it was for his other readers. Reading him brought him to me almost in person, as it still does in a 1955 passage about driving on U.S. 1, in Maine:

> *Like highways everywhere it is a mixed dish: Gulf and Shell, bay and gull, neon and sunset, cold comfort and warm, the fussy façade of a motor court right next door to the pure geometry of an early-nineteenth-century clapboard house with barn attached. You can certainly learn to spell "moccasin" while driving into Maine, and there is often little else to do except steer and avoid death. Woods and fields occur everywhere, creeping to within a few feet of the neon and the court, and the experienced traveler into this land is always conscious that just behind the garish roadside stand, in its thicket of birch and spruce, stands the*

well-proportioned deer; just beyond the overnight cabin, in the pasture of granite and juniper, trots the perfectly designed fox.... The Maine man does not have to penetrate in depth to be excited by his coastal run; its flavor steals into his consciousness with the first ragged glimpse of properly textured woodland, the first whiff of punctually drained cove.

The moccasin joke survives—I think of it every year on the same stretch of highway, where the juniper and the foxes are scarcer now and the deer and the neon more prevalent. Reading the passage as a writer, I am struck by its simplicity and complexity, by that "punctually" and "barn attached" and the quick, sentence-closing "fox" and "cove." What I feel for its author comes not just from my knowledge of him at the table or twitchy behind the wheel but from a sense of trust. He has looked at the roadside grunge and granite with the same eyes I do, and he does not labor for reference or add a chunk of scholarship to give them meaning; he waits for the connection—that extra moment—and delivers it with grace. I am included: this must be my thought, too, elegant as it has become. His editor William Shawn, writing after Andy's death, called him the most companionable of writers, but added that "renowned as his writing was for its simplicity and its clarity, his mind constantly took surprising turns, and his peculiar mixture of seriousness and humor could not have failed to astonish even him."

The other sentence-closer in the passage is "death," and Andy must have ceased in time to be astonished at how often the theme and thought recurred in his writing. It runs all through his sweetly comical piece "Death of a Pig," in which he tries ineffectually to deal with the crisis of a young pig of his who has stopped eating. Castor oil doesn't help, nor does his own sense of "personal deterioration," or the ministrations of Fred, who accompanies him on trips down the woodpath through the orchard to the pigyard, and also makes "many professional calls on his own." The pig dies, nothing can be done about it, and it is the profusion of detail—his feeling the ears of the ailing pig "as you might put your hand on the forehead of a child," and the "beautiful hole, five feet long, three feet wide, three feet deep" that is dug for the pig among alders and young hackmatacks, at the foot of an apple tree—that makes its death unsentimental and hard to bear.

The "D-word" also ends two famous essays of his, "Once More to the Lake" and "Here Is New York," arriving without warning in the first one—a piece about taking his young son to a family summer camp where he himself often used to go as a kid. Everything there is the same, or almost—the middle lane, where the horse used to walk, has vanished from the road through the meadow—with the customarily spectacular afternoon thunderstorm thrown in. When it's over and his boy is putting on his wet bathing suit for another dip, "I watched him, his hard little body, skinny and bare, saw him wince slightly as he pulled up around his vitals the small, soggy, icy garment. As he buckled the swollen belt suddenly my groin felt the chill of death."

I was a young man when I first read this, and remember finding the thought self-indulgent and exaggerated, almost a mistake, but this was before I'd begun to feel the brevity and sense of poignant loss that, from the first day, attend our meticulously renewed American vacations.

"Here Is New York," written in 1948, was widely rediscovered in the weeks just after September 11th, because of its piercing vision. Reading the piece now—a revisiting of the pulsing and romantic city he knew and worked in during his late twenties and early thirties—you look for death at the end, since he has just mentioned that a small flight of planes could now bring down the great shining structure in a moment, but he almost appears to have given up on the idea. Has he forgotten the point? It arrives at the tail end of the last sentence, in the famously reversed final phrase: "this city, this mischievous and marvelous monument which not to look upon would be like death." Losing New York is possible, but not holding on to the thought of it—which is all we may have in the end—much worse.

Andy White and my mother wove daily illness and incipient pain into their routines and conversations and their letters as they grew older. Her health was worse than his— she suffered from an exfoliating skin disease, went through a spinal-fusion operation and another dangerous procedure to clear a carotid artery, and endured painful bone deterioration in her old age, as a result of steroid treatments for the dermatosis—but if in the end she won their amazing sick-off, she took no pleasure in it and talked of his symptoms with the same concern and detail as her own. Their conversation became studded with lovingly enunciated medical reference: tachycardia, ileitis, the ethmoid sinuses.

My older daughter, Callie, believes that what was most surprising about the Whites' joint hypochondria was its energy; they were falling apart, they felt terrible, but they weren't depressed. The narcissism and intimacy of their exchanged symptoms could be infuriating, since it excluded everyone else, but it was so dopey that you laughed at it and forgave them. When you turned up at their house after an absence, they'd ask you about your kids and your job and your recent doings, and almost in the same breath bring up a lingering migraine or this morning's fresh back spasm. Someone in the family—someone who'd been reading about astronomy lately and remembered the "red shift" phenomenon as a measure of radiation and distance— named this the "White shift," and it stuck.

All this, as I've said, showed itself late in their marriage, but a moment's effort can bring back for me the way things were at home in better days, a couple of decades back—say on a late morning just after the mail has arrived. Their studies face each other across the narrow front hall, with the doors always open. My mother, in soft tweeds and a pale sweater, sits at her cherrywood desk, one leg tucked under her, with a lighted Benson & Hedges in one hand and a brown soft pencil in the other as she works her way down a page of Caslon-type galleys, with her tortoiseshell glasses down on her nose. Her desk is littered with papers and ashes and eraser rubbings. Across the hall, Andy sits up at his pine desk, facing her; a paste pot and a jar of pencils and some newspaper clips are arrayed before him, next to an old "In" basket, and a struggling winter sunlight touches the white organdy curtains by the north window. There are

messages to himself taped up on the bookcase behind, near
the worn stacks of the Encyclopedia, some bound volumes
of *The New Yorker,* and a trusty Roget's. The wallpaper
here, curling a bit in the corners now, is made of connected
blue-and-tan Coast and Geodetic Survey maps of Penobscot Bay, from the hills of Rockland in one corner, narrow-
ing to a strip above the fireplace mantel, and all the way
around to the waters near Mt. Desert Rock, in the other.
Andy reads a passage aloud from today's letter from Frank
Sullivan or his brother Stanley or a grain merchant in
Ellsworth, and my mother laughs, scarcely lifting her eyes
from the page. Soon the noises of her typing out another
letter to Harold Ross or Gus Lobrano are joined by the
slower clatter of his Underwood: a New England light industry is again in full gear, pouring out its high-market daily
product, and the labor force, for the moment, seems con-
tent. Soon it will be lunchtime.

To me, the Whites' later concern with their health was
a substitute joint effort, more loving than angry, and constituted a fresh form of intimacy as the two grew older. Andy
missed the joy and youth that he had known in my mother
and the passion that she had brought to her work as an editor, an obsessive gardener, and a non-stop letter-writer;
once he told me how he mourned the day when she decided
that she'd have to give up her evening martini or Old-
Fashioned. We in the family often speculated that Andy's
hypochondria wasn't a way to stay close to her as much as
fear of death in another form: if he could intercept each
twinge and malaise as it arrived and bring it squirming to
the light, then the ultimate event might yet be forestalled.

But this is too easy. Rather, I've come to believe that his anxieties were a neurotic remnant of childhood. He was the last child of affectionate but older parents—his father, Samuel White, a piano-company executive, was forty-five when he was born and his mother, Jessie, forty-one. There were two prior brothers and three sisters; the oldest sibling, a sister named Marion, was eighteen years older than he was, and the youngest, Lillian, already a five-year-old. There seems to be no dark family event to seize upon, but one can imagine that a cough or a skinned knee or a passing stomach ache would have brought a rush of attention to young En (as he was called then) amid the daily news and doings of so many vibrant elders.

What is certain is the way that writing about death became a strength for him, and brought a lasting power in his best work. No one who feared death could have written the end of *Stuart Little,* in which the hero-mouse goes off in search of the heroine, a bird named Margalo, who has flown away "without saying anything to anybody." But Stuart is also a romantic, like his creator, and interrupts his search for Margalo to invite a young girl he has met, Harriet Ames—she is just his size—to a picnic. He plans it carefully, but nothing goes right. The day is cloudy, Stuart has a headache, and some idle boys smash the souvenir birchbark canoe in which he means to take her for a paddle. He is disconsolate, and, when Harriet can't cheer him up, she leaves.

The first sentence of *Stuart Little,* to be sure, is just as surprising as its shadowed endings—the fact that the Littles' second child, on arrival, is a mouse, not a boy. White never explains the anomaly, and simply gets on with the story, but some critics and teacher-parent groups—and Anne Carroll Moore, the retired but still formidable children's librarian at the New York Public Library—were collectively aghast. Harold Ross, who read everything, stuck his head into Andy's office one afternoon and said, "God damn it, White, at least you could have had him adopted." The author and his readers—kids and their read-aloud elders—stayed calm, however, and *Stuart Little* sold a hundred thousand copies in the first fifteen months after publication.

Andy was not mouselike, but in these pages he is ready for love, though rueful about the results. In life, he was intensely, almost manically, domestic but always ready to fall a little in love, without the plans or bother of a full affair. Pretty girls, with brains and laughter, entranced him. One of them, a *New Yorker* assistant named Maryan Fox, by a later coincidence became a sister-in-law of mine. He also admired Susy Waterman, the wife of a Maine neighbor, Stan Waterman, and felt that she would be the perfect narrator for the Pathways of Sound recording of "Charlotte's Web"—an assignment he took on himself in the end. For a long time, there was a Steinway baby-grand piano tucked in a corner of Andy's study in Maine, and I can still hear him playing and singing the verse of a lilting old song of his own composition:

> *How often in the greening spring,*
> *'Neath bough and bank reclining,*
> *For love I shall be sorrowing*
> *And gay young girls declining.*

Years later—waste not, want not—he worked a variation of this into *The Trumpet of the Swan.*

On another day, he contrived an epochal whine, murmuring to Carol that he always came in third in my mother's heart: first there was *The New Yorker,* then me (me, Roger), and then, way down the line somewhere, himself. "Are you crazy!" she cried. "How can you say such a thing? You're always first with her—there's nobody else. Then the magazine and then all the rest of us. Everybody knows this."

Death was a more reliable companion. There is not even a concealing metaphor by the time *Charlotte's Web* comes along, in 1952, seven years after *Stuart*: a great short novel that begins with "Where's Papa going with that ax?" and ends, or just about, when Charlotte, the spider, describes her coming death to the disbelieving young pig Wilbur, whom she has saved from that ax. Then comes the line—experienced teachers or reading-aloud parents check to make sure that the Kleenex is handy—"No one was with her when she died."

Andy showed class, that pause again, in waiting to write *Charlotte's Web* until he had the country stuff in it down by heart. He knew how geese sounded when they were upset, and on what day in the fall the squashes and pumpkins needed to be brought in and put on the barn floor—which is to say that he'd still be himself in writing about it, and would not put in a word that might patronize his audience. He must have known as the chapters emerged that this would be his masterpiece, but it would not occur to him to feel uneasy that his best book was for children. Money and celebrity were not much on his mind.

When his old friend James Thurber died, he wrote that he'd known him "before blindness hit him, before fame hit him." Andy also turned down a Book-of-the-Month Club offer for a later book, *The Second Tree from the Corner,* because he did not want to delay its publication until it suited the promotional plans of the B.O.M. He wrote an apology to his publisher, Cass Canfield, for the loss of the promised extra revenue, in which he said, "There are other things in life besides twenty thousand dollars—although not many."

It's my belief—I can't prove it—that there are still readers and writers who feel a debt to E. B. White because of the sparkle and directness they found in a few lines or passages he wrote decades ago. Some of them, to be sure, were third graders who were encouraged by their teachers to write him in North Brooklin, asking whether Stuart ever found Margalo, or what became of Wilbur in the fullness of age: these letters came in by the bagful, and in time Andy had to turn over the task of replying to others. Readers also remember the power of his pieces on freedom and the Constitution—his 1947 "Party of One" letters to the New York *Herald Tribune,* for instance, which took the paper briskly to task when it supported the blacklisting of the Hollywood Ten and others who refused to answer questions about their loyalty or past political affiliations. The *Trib* didn't back down, and wrote that members of "the party of one" were "nearly always as destructive as they have been valuable." White's reply, which pointed out that "a difference of opinion became suddenly a mark of infamy," won a fan letter back from Supreme Court Justice Felix Frankfurter.

White's gift to writers is clarity, which he demonstrates so easily in setting down the daily details of his farm chores: the need to pack the sides of his woodshed with spruce-brush against winter; counterweighting the cold-frame windows, for easier operation; the way the wind is ruffling the surface of the hens' water fountain. Clarity is the message of *The Elements of Style,* the handbook he based on an early model written by Will Strunk, a professor of his at Cornell, which has helped more than ten million writers—the senior honors candidate, the rewriting lover, the overburdened historian—through the whichy thicket. "Write in a way that comes naturally," it pleads. "Do not explain too much." Write like White, in short, and his readers, finding him again and perhaps absorbing in the process something of that steely modesty, may sense as well the uses of patience in waiting to discover what kind of writer will turn up on their page, and finding contentment with that writer's life.

He was a demanding worker. He rewrote the first page of *Charlotte's Web* eight times, and put the early manuscript away for several months, "to let the body heat out of it." Then he wrote the book again, enlarging the role of the eight-year-old girl, Fern, at the center of its proceedings. He was the first writer I observed at work, back in my early teens. Each Tuesday morning, he disappeared into his study after breakfast to write his weekly Comment page for *The New Yorker*—a slow process, with many pauses between the brief thrashings of his Underwood. He was silent at lunch and quickly went back to his room to finish the piece before it went off to New York in the afternoon mailbag, left out in the box by the road. "It's no good," he often said morosely afterward. But when the new issue turned up the next week the piece was good—unstrained and joyful, a snap to read. Writing almost killed you, and the hard part was making it look easy.

What gets left out of an account like this, of course, is most of a life: Andy and my mother's son, Joel, and Joel's wife, Allene, three grandchildren—all grown now, with kids and life stories of their own—and the Brooklin Boat Yard, where Joe built a career and earned a reputation as a master boat designer and builder that matched or continued his father's as a writer. The Whites' pasture isn't here, sloping past the woodlot toward the shore, with the shapes of Harriman Point and then Mt. Desert coming clear beyond as the morning fog thins, nor is Fiddler Bayou, on Siesta Key, Florida, where the Whites passed so many winters. My mind, still in Maine, takes in the rubbly shore of Allen Cove, and the redolent boathouse, its surfaces softened with age, where we changed our clothes before swimming, and where Andy took himself, some days, to write or to work on his Newsbreaks selections for the magazine. Andy, getting ready to swim on a morning when the icy incoming tide has been warmed a fraction by its journey over mudflats, wades out until the water reaches his knees, then unfurls his old Abercrombie & Fitch thermometer and flings it out to the end of its twine tether. If the temperature is bearable—I think the red line stands at sixty-four degrees—he shakes his head and commits himself to the shallow deep.

Many in the family, including my children, have their own lasting and complex attachments to Andy and the Whites' place. My daughter Alice, at about ten—an age when she'd read and been read *Charlotte's Web* over and over again—was shocked to learn that a young pig in residence in an enclosure to the southwest of the garage would be converted to ham and bacon shortly after her departure in September. She worked late that evening, crayoning a large replica of Garth Williams's "SOME PIG!" drawing in the book—the miracle web that saves Wilbur—and had me drive her back to the Whites' that night, so she could secretly thumbtack it to the side of the pen. The agrarian Andy was startled but unmoved, and the pig went to his smoked reward on schedule.

Others in or around the Whites' house are missing as well—Henry Allen, Edith Candage, Shirley Cousins, Tink Hutchinson, Howard Pervear. Andy's lobsterman neighbor Charlie Henderson. Harold Ross—yes, Harold Ross, the magazine's founder and editor—who probably never made it to the Whites' place but who, right up until his death in 1951, was so much a part of their daily thoughts and mealtime conversation that I sometimes almost saw him sitting at the table across from me, with his hunched shoulders and that gap in his teeth. Henry Lawson, Joe and Tooey Wearn, Russell Wiggins, Dottie Hayes. Fifty years of Brooklin friends and neighbors, who all knew or almost knew Andy, and respected his emphatic privacy. (When he was old, Brooklin townspeople would turn away pilgrim tourists who'd come all this distance to visit the shrine. "The E. B. White place? Well, it's hard to say how you'd get there from here. Anyway, I don't think he's around right now.") Sometimes, away for months on end, I felt in danger of falling out of touch, but then another letter from Andy would arrive, like this one from June 24, 1964: "I'm the father of two robins and this has kept me on the go lately. They were in a nest in a vine on the garage and had been deserted by their parents, and without really thinking what I was doing I casually dropped a couple of marinated worms into their throats as I walked by a week ago Monday. This did it. They took me on with open hearts and open mouths, and my schedule became extremely tight. I equipped myself with a 12" yellow bamboo stick, split at one end like a robin's bill, and invented a formula: hamburg, chicken mash, kibbled worm, and orange juice. Worms are hard to come by because of the drought, but I dig early and late and pay my grandchildren a penny a worm. The birds are now fledged and are under the impression that they know how to fly. When I come out of the house at 6 a.m. they come streaming at me from bush and tree, trying for a landing on shoulder or cap, usually overshooting me in the fog and bringing up against a wall. This exhausts them and me." (The stimulating "Letters of E. B. White," out of print for some time, will reappear shortly, in a new and updated printing, edited by his granddaughter Martha White.)

My mother died in 1977, and Andy stayed on alone in the house for the rest of his life. Well, not entirely alone. As he grew older, he began to spoil himself a little, and why not. Sometimes when he was having a bad spell with his head he would check himself into the Blue Hill Hospital for two or three days, until he felt better. He liked a meal out now and then, at the Blue Hill Inn, sometimes with company and just as often alone. He took drives in the afternoon with Ethel Howard, the wife of a Sedgwick garage man, whose conversation he enjoyed; and had occasional visits from Corona Machemer, a Harper & Row editor who had worked with him on late collections of his works. He gave up sailing the sturdy twenty-foot sloop *Martha*, named for the same granddaughter, which Joel had built and rigged for use by a cautious single-hander; he was a morning sailor by now, anyway. Andy worried what might befall him when he was alone, and paid a succession of nurse-companions to be in the next room if he woke up in the night and needed a morsel of talk or a glass of milk. Older women, quite a few of them, set their caps for him, of course, and were disappointed. He told Carol once that he didn't plan to marry again. "I'm afraid I might get a lemon this time," he said.

He was the same, still lithe and only a bit slower, and one evening in August, 1984, when he came for dinner he complained that he'd knocked his head the day before while unloading a canoe from the roof rack of his car, over at Walker Pond; now he was having trouble knowing exactly where he was or what was happening around him. Carol and I smiled at him. "Yes, that happens sometimes, doesn't it?" we assured him.

But he knew better. A couple of months later, after we'd left, he took to his bed and never again knew exactly where he was. It looked like a rapid onset of Alzheimer's, but more likely, the doctors thought, was a senile dementia brought on by the blow to his head that day. He was eighty-five now. Nurses and practical nurses and other local ladies were hired, round the clock, who took extraordinary care of him. My brother managed it all, and somehow managed his own life as well. When I came up for a visit, early in the winter, Joe said that Andy would know me but that our conversation would be interesting. "How do you mean?" I said. "You'll see," he said.

I walked in and found him restless in his bed and amazingly frail. His eyes lit up and he said my name in the old way: "Rog!" He wanted to know how I'd come from New York and I said that Henry Allen had picked me up at the Bangor airport. "Did you fly over Seattle on the way?" he asked. He didn't seem troubled when I said no, and after a moment murmured, "Lost in the clouds."

He died the next October, still at home and able to recognize the people around him. Joe told me that in that long year he'd read aloud to his father often, and discovered that he enjoyed listening to his own writings, though he wasn't always clear about who the author was. Sometimes he'd raise a hand and impatiently wave a passage away: not good enough. Other evenings, he'd listen to the end, almost at rest, and then ask again who'd written these words.

"You did, Dad," Joe said.

There was a pause, and Andy said, "Well, not bad."

Getting There

LATE one night in the summer of 1937 or 1938, a young man at a party—a cheerful fellow named Charlie, the older brother of a girl I'd once been seeing—came into the room where I was, looking for the girl he had brought and was now ready to take home. This was in a house on Parker Point, in Blue Hill, Maine, and the smoky, pretty room was full of young people I knew or almost knew—most of them part of the Blue Hill crowd, but with enough of my sixteen- or seventeen-year-old summer friends from nearby Brooklin in among them to make me feel at ease there, along about midnight. Charlie was from East Blue Hill, not my bunch, but I knew who he was looking for. "Anne? Light of my life?" he said, looking amiably and perhaps a little drunkenly around at us. "Figuratively speaking, light of my life, where are you?" There was some laughter at this, and in time Charlie found Anne—Anne Nevin—and the two said good night and went off together, as they always did. I've forgotten the rest of the evening, but I can still hear the tone of Charlie's question, which came back to me later that night, after I'd got home. Its ease and style—what I would think of in time as cool—dazzled me; I couldn't get over it. Charlie was older, perhaps twenty. I didn't envy him or want to be him, but the moment became one of those flashes which light up the long hallway stretching down the later teens to the door that opens out into adulthood. It promised that what lay ahead for me and others my age was a new life in which we would talk to each other, we young people, in these confident and amusing tones, within an intimacy shared by men and women who were ready for each other now, and eager to find the easy sensual laughter and affectionate idioms and grasped shoulders and wrists and playful glances that would come with our main preoccupation over the next few years. Romance and sex and love itself were almost at hand, and with them the discovery of what sort of men and women we would become, to ourselves and our friends, and, up beyond that, within our marriages and new families.

"Light of my life?"—would I ever be as easy and joyful as that? The delectable question turns to a wisp as we look at it across this stretch of years. It would not occur to young sophisticates today, who are given little time for yearnings before being knocked flat by the rush and crash of experience.

Another passing question that has stuck with me came five or six years later on a narrow staircase connecting some upper stories of the imposing red roofed stone headquarters building at Lowry Field, in Colorado. College has come and gone, it is the fall of 1943, wartime, and I am an Air Force corporal, most recently an instructor in machine guns and power turrets at the Aircraft Armament School but now converted to an official historian, of all things. Somebody at the Pentagon has decided that decent records should be kept about these suddenly overcrowded tech schools that are mass-producing trained personnel to maintain the floods of new bombers and fighter planes headed for the European and Pacific theatres, and has tapped its service records for young noncoms who were college English majors and perhaps can write. On this afternoon, I am going upstairs in search of some files stored in a dusty space under the roof. Ahead of me is a civilian employee in our office, a woman named Bettye, in her middle or upper twenties, and, just behind her, my boss, Tech Sergeant Maury Caples, a cheerful, informal thirty-odd-year-old type, not long ago in the advertising business in Cincinnati. Tromp, tromp we go, we three, when Maury, a step or two below the girl, says, "Have you had your Christmas goose yet, Bettye?"

"No," says Bettye, "but I think it might be coming soon."

"Nothing like a little goose for Christmas," says Caples, as we arrive, laughing together and a little out of breath. I am a married man—I've been married for a whole year now—but the bright-eyed look, a loaded glance, these two have just exchanged is outside my experience. Are they sleeping together? Isn't Maury married, like me? Is something happening between them, or is this just the way grownup men and women can talk sometimes when they trust each other? The last possibility is almost the best. I've grown up a little, myself, right on these stairs. Wow.

Getting there, becoming my adult self, was not a steady goal in my scattered youth, and changes in me, when they came, took me by surprise. Who would expect such a thing to happen on a golf course? Let's reverse directions and go back a few summers again, back before the war to a morning in late August, 1940, when I'd joined my hacker friends Freddy Parson and Bus Willis for another round, there in Brooklin. Where we played was an unfenced but privately maintained little nine holes, right in the middle of town, with bumpy, pasturelike fairways and sunburned greens, where each hole supported an old-style iron flagstick, twisted with years of use and cool to the touch. The shallow, undemanding traps had long since gone to gravel, but lichen-crusted granite ledges, here and there intruding upon a fairway or rising more boldly, like silent onlookers, to one side of a green, offered a greater threat to your score. There was one par five, a fall-away meadow that terminated in a natural bowl, where the strip of rough beyond the green was bordered by knee-high clumps of ball-swallowing ferns. Pinewoods threw their morning shadows almost to the middle of the narrower fairways, and by five-thirty or six on August afternoons began to repeat the process from the other direction. The course started at roadside, just beside the narrow two-lane macadam of Route 175, and at its farther end skirted the inner shore of our harbor. Sometimes, bent almost double under the limb of a hackmatack while I tried to extemporize an irritable slash at my

Kro-Flite, nestled dangerously close to a root, I would peer out toward the green and catch a flash of rippled sunlight from the Reach beyond. Other days, again in the rough, I would straighten up to brush a twig or a bug out of my collar, and find myself monitored by a motionless gull twenty feet away, with a bit of mussel shell at its feet. It was a great seven-iron course, perfect for old gents and free-swinging teen-agers perpetually and hilariously in trouble.

Here, on a clear morning sixty-five years gone, a green Ford pulled up beside the grass shelf that constituted the first tee, and we friends were inspected by a young woman with short reddish hair and a grave stare. "Hi," she said. "Any way a person could pick up a game around here?" Without waiting for an answer, she backed up her car and slid it deftly between my ancient Plymouth roadster and the Parsons' station wagon. As she got out and pulled her clubs from the back seat, we eyed each other uneasily. We were young men in mid-college, just sprung from summer jobs in the city, and thought ourselves a suave bunch. While our casual, pickup rounds often included girls or girlfriends, or even sisters, this was our game, made exclusive by a shared age and ineptitude.

"Hi," she said again, dropping her bag next to ours. She told us her name, and the family she was staying with, out on Naskeag Point, who'd said it would be O.K. for her to just come over like this and horn in. She paused, watching us. "Now I'm not so sure," she said.

We collected ourselves and told her our names. Of course she could come along, Freddy said, but we were only duffers. Bus shook her hand and said he'd just figured out who she must be—and mentioned the name of her fiancé. Didn't he play golf?

Not this week, she told us—he was away and she'd been invited up to get to know the family. She said it lightly.

"I'd be here if I was him," Bus said.

I didn't know the family or their place, but Bus did and even knew how to talk to a self-possessed young woman in her middle twenties—an age that made her as strange to me as any movie star. She wasn't quite beautiful, as I recall; there was something too firm about the line of her jaw, but the way she stood now, looking down the first fairway with her weight cocked easily on one hip and a red tee protruding from between her teeth, was both comforting and exotic.

Perhaps a bit abashed by her own boldness, she said she didn't want to spoil our game. It would be better if she chose one of us to be victim, and to have the two others go first, go on ahead. She didn't want three of us standing around while she fought her way out of the woods. Would that be O.K.?

We agreed, and stood together, suddenly shy before her gaze. "I'll take you," she said, amazingly pointing at me. She asked me to tell her my name again.

I told her, and we two vacated the tee, leaning back against my car together while Bus and Fred teed off— Freddy for once avoiding one of his monster mishits, which had been known to bonk off a farmhouse roof adjacent to our right—and headed down the innocuous par-four first. Glancing sidewise, I noted her stylishly flapped old golf spikes and heavy leather bag, with its three woods and matching irons. The scored, expensive-looking clubfaces were flecked with blackened grass. I was way over my head.

She'd been pulling on a white golf glove, then stopped. "Oh, no," she said. "I keep forgetting." She held up her left hand, which displayed a striking ring on the third finger: a thick little blue-green chunk gleaming within a gold setting. She was wearing a short-sleeved white shirt and a short skirt, with a couple of tees stuck into loops in the top, which she patted momentarily now, looking for a pocket.

"Roger, do you have a handkerchief, maybe?" she said, tugging off the ring. I reached into the hip pocket of my khaki pants and took out a faded, almost decent blue bandanna.

She took it from me, folded it into a long triangle, folded it again, and ran it through the ring. She brought the ends back over each other, making a snug packet, and handed it back. "I'm trusting you—O.K.?" she said. She retrieved the glove she'd tucked under her arm and put it on again, pulling it tight.

I was startled at the assurance and intimacy of the gesture. I took a match folder or whatever it was from inside my left-hand side pocket and stuffed the bandanna in its place, thrilling at the little lump at its center as I tucked it away next to my thigh.

When our turn came, she plucked up an iron and teed off swiftly, finishing her swing with an eloquent slide of the hips at the last moment, so that her lean body seemed to watch the safe flight of the ball. There'd been a click at contact: barely a sound at all. My own three-iron—I'd passed up my driver, which was prone to a low, diving slice—was banged off to the right, as usual, but this time missed the granite shelf out there, which could produce spectacular ricochets. "Shot," she said, picking up her bag. We diverged, and I could hear the rich, clockety sound her clubs made as she walked briskly away, her left hand swinging free.

I sank a lucky putt on the first—eight or ten feet, with the ball bumping and wobbling as it rolled, which happened on these greens—for a five on the hole: five to her four. Possibly we each managed fives on the comeback second, which brought us to the road again, next to where we'd started. Maybe I'd be O.K. We lit cigarettes while we waited for Fred to find his ball, up ahead of us in the marshy right rough of the dogleg third, and I filled her in a little, in response to questions. We were more tennis players, really. We'd grown up here in the summers and had taken up golf early in our teens, because of this handy little course. The proprietor, a shy man named Donald Parson— Freddy's uncle—had leased these acres and converted them to his own use. He allowed his friends and his friends' kids to play here without charge, while he himself turned up only now and then, mostly alone. Sometimes the course stood empty for days on end. None of us had had lessons. We were terrible golfers but not as bad as Fred's older brother Kornie. Kornie was a sketch out here, but a demon sailor who won most of our races. Suddenly sensing the need to account for my pathetic array, I explained that two of my clubs had belonged to my grandfather and the rest—well,

I couldn't remember where I'd picked them up. Weirdly, I had only odd-numbered irons—a three, a five, and a seven—along with a thick, garden-tool sort of sand club, plus my putter and stiffish driver. "I should really get organized someday," I said lamely.

She was too good for me, of course, much as she tried to hide it. I lost a ball in the same boggy stretch where Freddy had gone on that third, and took a seven. I half-shanked my drive on the downhill fourth, and when I'd at last rejoined her on the green it seemed to me that she intentionally misdirected her putt, sliding it well clear of the hole. When I wrote down our scores, I trailed her by four or five strokes. "Let's just play, shall we?" I said, stalking ahead.

She didn't apologize, but went on with her effortless round, gazing with evident pleasure as we topped the hill again, and the green with its circling birches and low bayberry thickets came into view. I stopped sulking. Never mind the painful difference in our scores, I'd take on a different role here: I'd be her host. A couple of holes later, emerging onto the shelf of a west-facing tee, I named three or four of the cruising sloops and yawls at anchor amid the more numerous lobster boats before us in Center Harbor, and pointed out our modest yacht-club fleet, off beyond the spindle. A handful of broad catboats were beginning to stir at their moorings, to the first breaths of the afternoon's reliable southerly. "Ours is the blue one with the tan deck," I said, pointing. "See?" I sounded like a six-year-old.

Something encouraged me to go on. I was an O.K. sailor, I said, better than my sister. These Brutal Beasts could capsize in races sometimes, but mostly you could sail them home again after a squall, with the main reefed way down, even if they were half swamped. One time, I'd rigged a beer jacket between a stay and the mast and run home under that. I couldn't shut up.

She gestured apologetically at the boats and the long sweep of Eggemoggin Reach and the dark line of Deer Isle at its farther rim. "I don't know the first thing about sailing," she said.

Our game finished too quickly—I loved it by now. I can't remember our scores, but she was better by eight or nine strokes. After our last putts had rattled home, I asked if we couldn't play on for another few holes. No—too bad, but she couldn't, she said, making it sound friendly. Something was on with the family that afternoon. She had become a woman again, a stranger.

She pulled off her golf glove, and when I reached in my pocket for the bandanna the lightness of it gave me a shock. When I took it out—my mouth was open—it was partly unfolded, with no weight to it: nothing at its center. "Jesus," I said. I scrabbled in the empty pocket, then pulled it inside out. Nothing.

Her hand was up to her face. "Roger—you'd never?" she said. She'd gone pale.

"It's just got to be—" I cried, pulling out my other pockets, madly frisking myself. "I never touched it—not once."

She seized the pocket where the handkerchief had been, shaking it now and rubbing it frantically through her fingers, and in the same instant we saw that there was a fraying along the seam—a place where you could push the tip of a little finger through. She'd folded the ring away but hadn't tied it, and the repeated motion of the packet against my leg while I walked and swung and walked again had worked the weighted thing free and allowed it to drop. It was gone.

She'd begun to make quick little circles around this last green, staring about intently, as if the ring had only now slipped out of my pocket. She made an anguished sound and stared back down the narrow meadowy stretch toward its tee—the way we'd just come—and then off to the left, her gaze sweeping over the rising grassy spaces and the brushy and sloping wood edges we'd walked, now whiter in the midday sun.

"I'm so sorry," I said over and over as we walked back slowly toward our cars. Fred and Bus had finished and gone home. "How could I have—" She held up her hand and I stopped.

"I can't begin to tell you how bad this is," she said. "This is very, very serious. You have no idea. I can't believe I was so stupid."

She shook away the cigarette I was offering. She couldn't do anything about this now, not today, she went on. But we had to meet again, she said—come back here and walk over the course again, foot by foot, where we'd gone just now, and find the ring. Every shot, every place we were. Agreed?

I nodded—yes, agreed. For a moment, I thought I might be the one to cry.

She kept shaking her head. "Can't God-damned be-*lieve* it," she whispered. "Jesus H. *Christ!*" She looked at me miserably, staring at my face. "It's all my fault, not yours," she said. "Don't even think such a thing—O.K.? And one more thing: don't tell anybody. Don't tell a single soul. Not your family or your friends. Nobody."

I promised, nodding my head again. She could count on me. We'd meet here at the first tee again, first thing in the morning. Eight-fifteen—no, eight. No one would notice—they'd think we were out there for a fast early round. I'd see her again.

Nobody asked. I'd said "Golf" at lunch with my mother and stepfather and kid brother, but they rarely pressed me for details about my days. Before evening, I went back and walked the first couple of holes again on my own, swinging an iron through the tufts and furrows and sedges where I thought I'd been. If anyone stopped to ask I'd say I'd lost a couple of balls. It came to me that a ring was going to be hundreds of times harder to spot than a golf ball; only a gleam, a moment's flicker from the sun, might give it away. I swivelled my gaze to and fro as I tramped, peering intently at grass roots and pebbly shadows and bits of twig. What a triumph if I could produce the ring for her tomorrow morning, holding it up between my fingers like a jeweller: "Voilà!"

It rained in the night, and there was a thick, wet fog everywhere the next morning. I was there first and watched the soft globes of her headlights grow more distinct as she wheeled up quietly, the tires whispering on the wet road. She was wearing red duck pants and an oilskin top, its hood back behind her neck, and when she got out we looked at each other like conspirators. She needs a name here, though I've searched my memory in vain for it. "You sleep?" she said.

We left our clubs locked in the trunk of my car and set off, each swinging an iron back and forth through the sopping grass in front of us as we walked. Within ten strides the road had vanished. "Over here, I think," I said, angling off toward the right. I led the way to the flat ledge and the junipered rough beyond, where we could look in wider circles. Nothing. By the time we'd jumped the trickly stream below the first hole and walked up the patch of rough, our pants were soaked to the knees, and our hair and shoes speckled with weeds and grassheads. She peered down into the first hole, actually lifting the flagstick—you never know—and we turned away and went on, leaving our trails across the whiter sheen of the wet green.

At the third, we had to visit the bog where I'd lost a ball, then cross the fairway to the edge of the opposite woods, where my next shot had landed. Each bush and branch we touched showered us icily, and when we got back to the edge of the fairway my shoes were making squashy noises. She stopped to pull up one sock, then shook her head like a dog and pulled her hair free of her neck. We scarcely spoke, muted by the hopelessness of our work. Every twenty or thirty strides we had to stop to straighten our backs and waggle our wrists, aching from our ceaseless swashings. Anger thickened inside me—this was insane—but I said nothing. Neither of us could be the first to stop. She'd moved out ahead now; perhaps she didn't want me to see her face. I didn't say it, but the fog made it hard to be sure

where I was, once I'd stepped off the fairway in search of a
reconstructed slice or clunker. The course had gone two-
dimensional, a gray page with only the odd birch limb or
moldering stump to let me venture a guess.

On the short seventh, we had to climb the steep side of
the granite cliff just to the right of the green, where another
errant shot of mine had landed amid thick trees. I gave her
my hand at the top, pulling her up behind me. There was
a touch of breeze off the cove, closer to us now but still invisible in the all-surrounding fog, and you could hear the
balsams and the smaller spruce branches beginning to stir
overhead. The fog would lift soon. Then we heard another
sound, steps and rustlings behind us, and with one instinct
dropped to our hands and knees on the crumbly granite together, out of sight. There was the startling plock! of a golf
shot, back on the tee, then a pause and the softer sound of
a ball invisibly striking the green to our right. A man appeared below us, foreshortened, striding out of the mists
with a putter and a single midiron in his hand. For a crazy
moment, I thought it was her fiancé, what's-his-name,
come to find us, but this was a tanned white-haired man,
perhaps in his sixties. He had a canvas sailing hat pulled
down almost to his ears and wore waterproof golfer's pants.
I'd never seen him before: some demented rich friend
of Don Parson's who thought he knew this course well
enough to play it blind. Perhaps he'd even rowed across the
cove from the stone Parson house on the point, and clam-
bered up to the holes here at the back of the shore.

His ball must have rolled off the green after it hit. We
could hear him sighing and muttering under his breath as

he cast about beyond the green, looking for it, and then a private expletive—*grasht!* or *brasht!* it sounded like—when he gave up and walked away, not bothering to drop a fresh ball for his putt. Perhaps he'd been too intent on his game to mark our path before him through the wet or to wonder why it had stopped.

I was laughing, my hand over my mouth. "God, wasn't that something?" I whispered. "He never knew. Did you hear him!"

She turned toward me, rising from her knees. "It's no use!" she said fiercely. "It's gone forever. This is crazy—we'll never find it. I'm leaving tomorrow and it will never turn up. Now I've got to think of something to tell them. This is all so like me—you have no idea."

I couldn't go on watching her, up so close. I dropped my gaze and saw the minute reddish-blond hairs on her wrist and the backs of her hands. Perhaps the wet on her cheeks was from her dank and darkened hair or from the fog. I must have looked as strange and small to her as she did to me. We were helpless, children on a bad outing. She bent to pick up her iron, and, my heart thumping, I walked away.

We didn't leave the fairway for the rest of our round, but when we came downhill on the eighth I took out a ball I'd been carrying, dropped it on the green, and putted it, with my iron turned upside down to make a blade. The ball threw up a little wheel of water as it rolled across the green and past the cup. I held out my club, inviting her to play, but she shook her head.

Back at her car, I told her I'd call her fiancé's family if the ring ever turned up: Bus Willis would know how to reach them. She may have given me a slip of paper with her name and address on it. We shook hands once again, then she took hold of my arm, next to my chest, with one hand. "You've been—" she began but stopped. "Everything's going to be fine, Roger," she said. "You know what I mean."

We raced the next day and I did well. Not a win but maybe another one of the little red cotton burgees they handed out in those days—red for second—or a third-place yellow. I used to smoke fifteen-cent cigars during the races then: Blackstones. When my regular girlfriend, Evelyn, came back—she'd been in New Hampshire, visiting her grandmother—I told her that I'd played golf with this woman who'd showed up and asked in, and next day went back with her to look for some lost keys. Fred and Bus asked me how we'd come out that weird day and I said she'd been too tough for me. I didn't tell anyone that I'd driven out to Naskeag the last morning and parked my car near where I thought her new family's driveway might be. She didn't come by. The next year, I had a full-summer job in New York and only got to Maine for a few days, and the year after that the war came and everything was changed. At some point after Evelyn and I were married, I told her about the ring. After the war, the Donald Parson course was abandoned—now there's a patch of alders down where the first hole was, a driveway in place of the third fairway, and a cottage on the granite ledge above the shore. Nobody remembers a visiting young woman who might have lost something valuable on the forgotten old golf course once.

For a time, I wished I'd paid more attention to things she had told me the first day we played golf. She lived in New Jersey, I think, and she'd met her fiancé...well, perhaps on Cape Cod. She'd gone to some college in Ohio. But none of that mattered. Our two walks together stayed with me, and felt stranger and more intimate as time went by. I kept losing the image of her, but when I thought of her golf swing she'd reappear. I've grown suspicious of some of the colors and details that have worked their way into this account, which may be overpaintings intended to hold a fading work. I was about to start my junior year at Harvard that fall, but in my version of the story I am younger than that, more boyish; she is the expert and I the apprentice. In time, our morning in the fog became more abstract and significant, almost leaving memory for some other place in my mind. She and I, a strange couple, had had a few hours in common and a secret—something no one else could guess. A woman and a younger man, myself at nineteen, had become intimate by association. I'd done my part, held up. Was this what she'd meant with those strange parting words—that I would grow up and be trusted?

Like everyone else, I traveled a lot during the war, and sometimes I caught myself looking for her in a crowded San Francisco restaurant or among the people pushing onto a downtown Denver streetcar. I was a soldier now, no longer a boy, and if our paths should cross we would meet as equals. In wartime, surprise encounters happened all the time. Early one morning when I was heading home on furlough before going off to the Pacific, my train stopped in a place called Ottumwa, Iowa. I lifted the window shade next to the seat where I'd slept all night, and there was Kornie Parson, in uniform, standing on the platform, six inches away outside the glass. He was a flight instructor at a naval air station there, heading to Chicago for a day at the track.

Dry Martini

THE martini is in, the martini is back—or so young friends assure me. At Angelo and Maxie's, on Park Avenue South, a thirtyish man with backswept Gordon Gekko hair lowers his cell as the bartender comes by and says, "Eddie, gimme a Bombay Sapphire, up." At Patroon, a possibly married couple want two dirty Tanquerays—gin martinis straight up, with the bits and leavings of a bottle of olives stirred in. At Nobu, a date begins with a saketini—a sake martini with (avert your eyes) a sliver of cucumber on top. At Lotus, at the Merc Bar, and all over town, extremely thin young women hold their stemmed cocktail glasses at a little distance from their chests and avidly watch the shining oil twisted out of a strip of lemon peel spread across the pale surface of their gin or vodka martini like a gas stain from an idling outboard. They are thinking Myrna Loy, they are thinking Nora Charles and Ava Gardner, and they are keeping their secret, which is that it was the chic shape of the glass—the slim narcissus stalk rising to a 1939 World's Fair triangle above—that drew them to this drink. Before their first martini ever, they saw themselves sitting on a bar-stool, with an icy mart in one hand, one leg crossed over the other, in a bar where a cigarette can be legally held aloft, and a curl of smoke rising above the murmurous conversation and the laughter. Heaven. The drink itself was a bit of a problem—that stark medicinal bite—but mercifully you can get a little help for that now with a splash of scarlet cranberry juice thrown in, or with a pink-grapefruit-cassis martini, or a green-apple martini, or a flat-out chocolate martini, which makes you feel like a grownup twelve-year-old. All they are worried about—the tiniest dash of anxiety—is that this prettily tinted drink might allow someone to look at them and see Martha Stewart. Or that they're drinking a variation on the Cosmopolitan, that Sarah Jessica Parker–"Sex and the City" craze that is so not in anymore.

Not to worry. In time, I think, these young topers will find their way back to the martini, to the delectable real thing, and become more fashionable than they ever imagined. In the summer of 1939, King George VI and Queen Elizabeth visited President Franklin Delano Roosevelt at Hyde Park—it was a few weeks before the Second World War began—and as twilight fell F.D.R. said, "My mother does not approve of cocktails and thinks you should have a cup of tea." The King said, "Neither does my mother." Then they had a couple of rounds of martinis.

I myself might have had a martini that same evening, at my mother and stepfather's house in Maine, though at eighteen—almost nineteen—I was still young enough to prefer something sweeter, like the yummy, Cointreau-laced Sidecar. The martini meant more, I knew that much, and soon thereafter, at college, I could order one or mix one with aplomb. As Ogden Nash put it, in "A Drink with Something in It":

> There is something about a martini,
> A tingle remarkably pleasant;
> A yellow, a mellow martini;
> I wish I had one at present.
> There is something about a martini
> Ere the dining and dancing begin,
> And to tell you the truth,
> It is not the vermouth—
> I think that perhaps it's the gin.

In John O'Hara's 1934 novel, *Appointment in Samarra,* the doomed hero, Julian English, and his wife, Caroline, observe Christmas with his parents, as usual. They live in the Pennsylvania coal town of Gibbsville, but the Englishes are quality, and before their festive dinner Julian's father, Dr. William English, mixes and serves up midday martinis; then they have seconds.

In the 1940 classic movie comedy *The Philadelphia Story,* the reliable character actor John Halliday plays Katharine Hepburn's reprobate father, who has returned home unexpectedly on the eve of her wedding. Standing on a terrace in the early evening, he mixes and pours a dry martini for himself and his deceived but accepting wife (Mary Nash) while at the same time he quietly demolishes his daughter's scorn for him and some of her abiding hauteur. It's the central scene of the ravishing flick, since it begins Tracy Lord's turnabout from chilly prig Main Line heiress to passably human Main Line heiress, and the martini is the telling ritual: the presentation of sophistication's Host. Hepburn had played the same part in the Broadway version of the Philip Barry play, a year before, which also required that martini to be mixed and poured before our eyes. Sitting in the dark at both versions, I was entranced by the dialogue—only Philip Barry could have a seducer-dad convincingly instruct his daughter in morals—but at the same time made certain that the martini was made right: a slosh of gin, a little vermouth, and a gentle stirring in the pitcher before the pouring and the first sips. Yes, O.K., my martini-unconscious murmured, but next time maybe more ice, Seth.

This is not a joke. Barry's stage business with the bottles and the silver stirring spoon in one moment does away with a tiresome block of explanation about the Lords: he's run off with a nightclub singer and she's been betrayed, but they have shared an evening martini together before this—for all their marriage, in fact—and soon they'll be feeling much better. In the movie, which was directed by George Cukor, the afternoon loses its light as the drink is made and the talk sustained, and the whole tone of the drama shifts. Everyone is dressed for the coming party, and the martini begins the renewing complications. Sitting in the theatre, we're lit up a little, too, and ready for all that comes next—the dance, the scene by the pool—because the playwright has begun things right.

Cocktails at Hyde Park or on Philadelphia's Main Line sound aristocratic, but the Second World War changed our ways. In the Pacific, where I was stationed, a couple of Navy fighter pilots told me a dumb story they'd heard in training, about the tiny survival kit that was handed out to flight-school graduates headed for carrier duty. "Open Only in Extreme Emergency," it said—which seemed to be the case of a pilot north of Midway whose Grumman quit cold a hundred miles away from his flattop. After ditching, he climbed into his inflatable raft, regarded the empty horizon that encircled him, and opened the kit. Inside was a tiny shaker and a glass, a stirring straw, a thimbleful of gin, and an eyedropper's worth of vermouth. He mixed and stirred, and was raising the mini-cocktail to his lips when he became aware that vessels had appeared from every quarter of the Pacific and were making toward him at top speed. The first to arrive, a torpedo boat, roared up, and its commanding officer, shouting through his megaphone, called, "*That's* not the right way to make a dry martini!"

Dryness was all, dryness was the main debate, and through the peacetime nineteen-forties and fifties we new suburbanites tilted the Noilly Prat bottle with increasing parsimony, as the martini recipe went up from three parts gin and one part dry vermouth to four and five to one, halted briefly at six to one, and rose again from there. The late George Plimpton once reminded me about the Montgomery—a fifteen-to-one martini named after the British Field Marshal, who was said never to go into battle with less than these odds in his favor. What was happening, of course, was an improvement in the quality of everyday gin. The Frankenstein's-laboratory taste of Prohibition gin no longer needed a sweetener to hide its awfulness: just a few drops of Tribuno or Martini & Rossi Extra Dry would suffice to soften the ginny juniper bite.

Preciousness almost engulfed us, back then. Tiffany's produced a tiny silver oil can, meant to dispense vermouth. Serious debates were mounted about the cool, urban superiority of the Gibson—a martini with an onion in it—or the classicism of the traditional olive. Travellers came home from London or Paris with funny stories about the ghastly martinis they'd been given in the Garrick Club or at the Hotel Regina bar. And, in a stuffy little volume called "The Hour," the historian and *Harper's* columnist Bernard De Voto wrote, "You can no more keep a martini in the refrigerator than you can keep a kiss there. The proper union of gin and vermouth is a great and sudden glory; it is one of the happiest marriages on earth and one of the shortest."

We appreciated our martinis, and drank them before lunch and before dinner. I recall an inviting midtown restaurant called Cherio's, where the lunchtime martini came in chalice-sized glasses. Then we went back to work. "Those noontime cocktails just astound me," a young woman colleague of mine said recently. "I don't know how you did it." Neither do I, anymore. My stepfather, E. B. White, sometimes took a dry Manhattan at lunch, but his evening martini was a boon forever. Even when he'd gotten into his seventies and early eighties, I can remember his greeting me and my family at the Bangor airport late on a summer afternoon and handing me the keys to the car for the fifty-mile drive back to the coast. Sitting up front beside me, he'd reach for his little picnic basket, which contained a packet of Bremner Wafers, some Brie or Gouda and a knife, and the restorative thermos of martinis.

At home, my vermouth mantra became "a little less than the absolute minimum," but I began to see that coldness, not dryness, was the criterion. I tried the new upscale gins—Beefeater's and the rest—but found them soft around the edges and went back to my everyday Gordon's. In time, my wife and I shifted from gin to vodka, which was less argumentative. At dinners and parties, I knew all my guests' preferences: the sister-in-law who wanted an "upside-down martini"—a cautious four parts vermouth to one of gin— and a delightful neighbor who liked her martinis so much that when I came around to get whiskey or brandy orders after dinner she dared not speak their name. "Well, maybe just a little gin on some ice for me," she whispered. "With a dab of vermouth on top."

We drank a lot, we loved to drink, and some of us did not survive it. Back in college, the mother of a girl I knew would sometimes fix herself a silver shaker of martinis at lunchtime and head back upstairs to bed. "Good night," she'd say. "Lovely to see you." I met entire families, two or three generations, who seemed bent on destroying themselves with booze. John Cheever, the Boccaccio of mid-century America, wrote all this in sad and thrilling detail. What seems strange now about celebrated stories of his like "The Country Husband," "The Sorrows of Gin," and "The Swimmer" is how rarely the martini is mentioned, and how often it's just called gin. Alcohol was central to this landscape, its great descending river.

It's my theory—a guess, rather—that martini drinking skipped a generation after Vietnam and marijuana came along. Many thousands of earlier suburban children, admitted to the dinner table or watching their parents' parties from the next room, saw and heard the downside of the ritual—the raised voices and lowered control—and vowed to abandon the cocktail hour when they grew up. Some of them still blame martinis for their parents' divorces. Not until their children arrived and came of age did the slim glass and the delectable lift of the drink reassert itself, and carry us back to the beginning of this story.

I still have a drink each evening, but more often now it's Scotch. When guests come to dinner, there are always one or two to whom I automatically offer Pellegrino or a Coke: their drinking days are behind them. Others ask for water or wait for a single glass of wine with the meal. But if there's a friend tonight with the old predilection, I'll mix up a martini for the two of us, in the way we like it, filling a small glass pitcher with ice cubes that I've cracked into quarters with my little pincers. Don't smash or shatter the ice: it'll become watery in a moment. Put three or four more cracked cubes into our glasses, to begin the chill. Put the gin or the vodka into the pitcher, then wet the neck of the vermouth bottle with a quickly amputated trickle. Stir the martini vigorously but without sloshing. When the side of the pitcher is misted like a January windowpane pour the drink into the glasses. Don't allow any of the ice in the pitcher to join the awaiting, unmelted ice in the glass. (My friend likes his straight up, so I'll throw away the ice in his glass. But I save it in my own, because a martini on the rocks stays cold longer, and I've avoided the lukewarm fourth or fifth sip from the purer potion.) Now stir the drink inside the iced glass, just once around. Squeeze the lemon peel across the surface—you've already pared it, from a fat, bright new lemon—and then run the peel, skinside down, around the rim of the glass before you drop it in. Serve. Smile.

Permanent Party

In midsummer of 1942, a month after I graduated from Harvard, I got drafted and sent to Atlantic City for basic training. As a private in the Air Force (it was a branch of the Army back then), I roomed with four other similarly traumatized young men in a blacked-out oceanside suite at the Ritz Hotel, which had been co-opted as a barracks. Here, for three hot summer weeks, we memorized the Articles of War and learned how to stand at attention, how to salute, and, through training films, how to recognize the Japanese "Betty" bomber, the German ME-109 fighter, and the impartial, skulking gonococcus, all at a glance. We also learned how to march. At six in the morning, with the sun gleaming off the sea and our moving shadows lying long across the boardwalk, we marched from the Ritz down to a mess hall in another hotel, fell out and ate, fell in and marched back. Later that morning we fell out and formed up again, and, accompanied by the blocky dozens of other platoons, marched three miles up the boardwalk (tromp-tromp, sing out, "Onetwo!") to a dusty parking lot, where we did jumping jacks and other calisthenics. Then we fell in and marched sweatily back three miles for chow at the same mess hall. With the country newly at war, no rifles or sidearms or weapons training had yet come our way, but, boy, could we march.

Late in August, one of many hundreds of rumors came true when we packed up and climbed aboard a troop train and began a journey to someplace—no one told us where. Eventually, we would be dropped off, car by car, at un-marked sidings close to the forts or fields where we would begin our technical training. We didn't know anything, not even which side would win this war. All of Europe still belonged to the Nazis, and the early news from a spot called Guadalcanal was grim.

Days on end, stuffed into ancient, sooty Pullman cars, we rolled and clacked westward, while we dozed, played cards, talked, laughed, got depressed, wrote letters, and read endlessly. Unlike in the G.I. movies made about this time, no one sang. I had brought the Modern Library edition of *The Brothers Karamazov* with me, and had chugged along well into the Grand Inquisitor chapter, when a broken drinking fountain interrupted my studies, inundating a heap of blue barracks bags, including mine, in which I had stashed the gloomy Bros. for the moment. At night, we bunked three to a section, taking turns in the upper berth (a delicious single) or squalidly doubling up, head to foot, in the lower. I still recall waking up in the middle of my first night and slowly comprehending that I was staring at the pale toes of Private Pete Hoffman, a fireman from Jersey City.

On our third day, I drew K.P.—the hated kitchen fatigue, but this time a welcome break in the dull, mysterious journey. In a converted mail car, we served up some kind of stew from big galvanized-metal barrels, ladling it into the mess kits of our fellow G.I.s, who complained unimaginatively but ate it all up, every scrap. We K.P.s worked late that night, scrubbing away at the massive pots and then sweeping and mopping the ridged, swaying floor. It was after eleven when the mess sergeant said we were done, and then someone rolled back the wide, boxcar-style doors, and the warm night air streamed in around us. With a couple of my companions, I sat down and lit a cigarette and watched Indiana slowly roll away under my dangling, booted feet. We talked a little, I think, and soon the rumble and creak of our car, the pleasing slither of wheels, and the sidewise-moving dark silhouettes of trees silenced us, yet no one got up and headed off to bed. We had a low moon for company, and the smell of fields and the coolness of the occasional stream or river we passed over (with accompanying bridge-rumble) and the smoothly presented and taken-away details of each small town—a silent station and an empty platform, a light on in somebody's upstairs bedroom, a Purina Chow billboard next to a street lamp, more trees—were hypnotic and lulling. Dozens of trains, it came to me, were at that moment carrying thousands of men like me to someplace new and strange, and eventually to the war itself, but just then, for the first time, I didn't mind at all. I had become a soldier.

A day or two later, dropped off at our own destination during the night, we alighted from our abandoned lone Pullman car in the early morning sun and found ourselves on a straggly patch of prairie with a rim of tall mountains to the west. No one had a clue about where we were—"I think it's Oregon," somebody said—or what anyone had in mind for us. Birds twittered. Then a stubby locomotive slid into view from around the bend, hooked on, and pulled us into the future. We were armorers, it turned out, or about to be, and this was Lowry Field, outside Denver, where we would suck up thirteen weeks of intensive courses in small arms, electrical controls, chemical warfare, explosives and ammunition, bombs and bomb racks, and the like, and a main course in the Browning .30- and .50-caliber machine guns. As such matters were measured in 1942, the change in us from whatever we'd been before—students, for the most part—to tough, coveralled ground-crew maintenance noncoms ready for attachment to some imminently departing Pacific-bound P-47 fighter outfit or B-24 bombardment squadron in line to join the massively growing Eighth Air Force in England, was trifling. Direct combat would not be our lot, and though we knew enough to count ourselves lucky, we had no clear sense of the dimensions of what we'd missed: how our soldier's chance of experiencing everyday fear, with the risk of death or maiming ever at hand, had gone whispering by. And Denver, we'd already heard, was a country club: one of the few cities where the best bars and restaurants had been set aside for enlisted men, not the brass, and where overnight passes grew like clover. I had it made, it seemed. At the same time, the alteration of life and fortune that I and most of my American generation endured over these few months is not something that young men or women today—or so they keep telling me—can quite take in.

Back among my fellow seniors on Commencement Day in Harvard Yard, with the tides of war almost visibly lapping at our toes, I'd run into a favorite professor of mine, Kenneth J. Conant, as he hurried past in full plumage, and took the chance to shake his hand. Three or four vivid courses with him in contemporary and medieval architecture had almost lured me away from my major in English, and when I'd seen him in May, while delivering a late paper to his office in the Fogg Museum, he'd taken a key and a flashlight out of his desk and invited me down to a large room in the basement, where we spent half an hour circling a great table model of the classic dig he'd been engaged upon at the twelfth century Burgundian Abbey Church at Cluny—a work now suspended because the site was in the hands of the enemy. My last Harvard lecture, it turned out, was a private one, and when it was over, Conant, his eyes alight, said, "One of these days. Soon." He'd go back, he meant, and so he did. There's a Rue Conant in Cluny still, celebrating his grand feat of scholarship.

I forgot about this moment in the shocking, boring surge of events after graduation, but one day in March of 1943, a bare nine months later, I thought of Professor Conant again, and wondered what he'd make of my new line of work. Since I'd seen him, I'd finished tech school, got married, become an instructor in machine guns and power turrets, picked up a couple of stripes, and had made Permanent Party at Lowry. Permanent Party! Connoting riotousness, it meant the opposite. I'd be in place, for a change, no longer subject to sudden orders or departures, a noncom citizen of Lowry at least for now, and allowed to take up a residence off the post. In G.I.-ese, I'd found a home.

What I wanted Conant to come look at with me was the Browning Caliber .50 Machine Gun, M2—a lean, sixty-four-pound, five-foot-eight-inch automatic dispenser of destruction, with an interestingly perforated barrel jacket within which the barrel and complicated inner parts banged back and forth at blurry speed and with terrifying noise and smell. I didn't get to fire this weapon often— mostly in the malfunction sheds, where the guns, from fixed downward-tilting positions, fired (or failed to fire) their bursts into underground trenches, while groups of students, by threes or fours, observed and tried to figure out what was wrong with each cunningly botched gun, and how it could be fixed. Learning the Browning, I'd fallen in love with its dozens of slots and grooves and cams, its springs (some coiled within each other) and switches, its ejectors and extractors. In supporting roles were the accelerator, a beckoning forefinger at the front of the oil buffer body, which quickened the recoil; the breech lock, which froze things at firing, and its partnered, instantly-arriving breech-unlocking pin; and, as main player, the slim, pale steel bolt, which, nipping backward with a fresh round in its teeth, simultaneously knocked free the spent casing of the old round and, reversing, rammed the new projectile snug into the same chamber, ready for fire. All this was accomplished with such dispatch and precise, minute tolerances that it was not, as one supposed, the explosion of gunpowder but the heat of friction during extraction that rendered the ejected, clattering cartridge case piping hot to the touch. Professor Conant relished the inventive new as much as the medieval—he'd introduced me to the Mies van der Rohe–designed Tugendhat House, in Czechoslovakia; Frank Lloyd Wright's Johnson's Wax factory in Racine, Wisconsin; and more—and had we been standing together in this cluttered Lowry hangar, with the weapon before us on a tall table, he'd have run his fingertips across its silky metal surfaces and asked questions. "This?" he'd say, pointing inside the lifted cover. "Oh that's the belt feed lever," I'd say in return. "And see how this knob on the front end runs inside that hollowed-out angle, that path along the top of the bolt, and with recoil becomes a cam to pull over the next round. If you lift out this little round piece in the middle and then drop it back down facing the other way, the belt will feed from the opposite side. And this gizmo on the slide is the belt feed pawl, which sort of snaps over the top of each new round and grabs hold."

"'The Belt Feed Pawl,'" Conant would repeat happily, making it sound like a name in Dickens.

These imagined scenes helped pass the wearying and boring hours of repeated instruction, during which we had to present the exact same material each week to another incoming fresh class of students, but our central preoccupation, the Browning .50-caliber aircraft machine gun, still holds up in history. Amassed forward-facing in the wings and body of the new P-47 and P-51 fighter planes, and heavily distributed about each B-17 or B-24 heavy bomber—ten guns, working in pairs fore and aft and in turrets above and below, and singly on either side of the waist—it was the weapon, it could be claimed, that in cumulative numbers and after long bloody trial destroyed the German Luftwaffe and won that part of our war. Modern automatic guns are quicker and deadlier, but the Browning, which employed no electronics or gas-assisted movements, was a little apex of the late American industrial era: a whole New England factory of usefully moving and reciprocating parts slimmed into a narrow box and delivering its product eight hundred and fifty times per minute, at an effective distance of two miles.

This fresh expertise helped stay any guilt over my favored status just then, away from the dirty and distant events of the war, but did not dispel doubts I felt about my value as a teacher. I'd had a .22 rifle and a 12-gauge shotgun as a boy back home, and knew how to use them, but any affinity in me for this sort of work came as a surprise when it surfaced in a mechanical aptitude test I took in my first week in the service. If the Air Force had shoved me into the right place somehow, it showed genius in keeping me on as an instructor, instead of sending me along to employ this stuff on the line, where I would have been instantly lost. Many of the Idaho high school kids and Arkansas rice farmers and Louisville cab drivers and Brockton plumbers who filled up the stuffy, newly thrown-up classrooms at Lowry seemed to take in the workings of the Browning after a couple of peer-

ing glances inside the lifted cover or with one finger running down beside the exquisitely rendered drawings in the
manual. They knew how Dodge truck engines and Motorola
radios and John Deere reapers and family Electroluxes actually worked and where they could go wrong. I knew how
to listen to a complicated lecture and effectively throw back
the same stuff in an exam. Listening to me gabbing away
in front of a blackboard or pointing up inside a Martin 250
CE electrical turret on a platform, they maintained a lidded ennui, a dislike that matched their sour feelings for
everything they'd encountered in the service so far. I was
chickenshit, but given a chance they'd probably win this
goddam war, if they had to.

It was a near thing at that. When I entered the armament school, about half our section had gone to college,
with a couple of grad students thrown in; everyone else
had finished high school. By the time I began teaching, six
months later, there were no college guys in the incoming
groups, and over the next eight months—before the Army
mysteriously converted me, overnight, into a historian—
the class I.Q. plunged downhill. When fewer and fewer of
the students seemed able to pass the weekly tests, tests were
abandoned. When it was noticed that half the students
were falling asleep in their chairs, the chairs were removed,
and we lectured on, six hours at a stretch, to G.I.'s sitting
cross-legged on the floor or out on their feet, with elbows
propped in a window frame. Some of them didn't know
the difference between the numbers ten and zero. We instructors, smoking together during the ten-minute break at
the end of each hour, talked about this in low tones and

wondered whether the service rosters were going to be good enough to carry us to the end. We'd seen the bottom of the barrel.

Evelyn Baker and I got married at ten-thirty on a Saturday night in October, an hour or so after my last Lowry class let out. Eleanor Emery, a Bryn Mawr classmate of my mother's who lived in a square, porched house on Washington Street, filled in—along with her jovial husband and mostly grown children and neighbors—as family. There was candlelight and cake and champagne, and a new service friend of mine, Dan Rapalje, from New Jersey, stood up for me as best man. Rearrangements of this sort were the common thing in these makeshift times, and were appreciated. My mother was there, having made the two-day trip out on the crowded wartime trains, as did Evelyn's father, Roland (Tweaker) Baker, a Republican cotton broker from Boston. This side of the war, an extemporary and exuberant making do, is largely overlooked in the annals. I missed all the arrangements, being on duty, but a half hour or so before the ceremony Mr. Baker took me aside to say that my wife to be had just hit him up for some money. He'd braced himself while Evelyn consulted a little list she'd made up. "How about five dollars?" she said.

She and I had been together for four years, starting just before my arrival at college. Her parents were freshly divorced, and she and her mother and three younger sisters were staying on in their suburban house in Weston, an easy forty-minute bus trip away from Harvard Yard. Her mother,

Mary, vague and charmingly prone to malapropism, ran things with a frazzled good will, and the three lively and variously gifted girls turned to Evelyn—and then to Evelyn and me—for direction and entertainment. Here, at home inside a Jane Austen novel, I passed my college weekends, carving Sunday roasts and getting the station wagon serviced, explaining the double finesse in bridge, lacing up ice skates, sharing by radio the fall of Paris and the night bombings of London, giving the horselaugh to Wendell Willkie, teaching the racy lyrics from "Pal Joey," and picking up the dogs at the vet after their shots, having fallen not just in love but into a family.

Evelyn, thin and brown-haired, with a strong chin, was tougher than anyone I'd met before. A full-scale diabetic since the age of six, she ran her case without fuss or complaint, shooting each day's doses of insulin into her thigh, and backing away from nothing in life. Once in a while she'd unbalance and begin to slide into the daze of an insulin shock, and her mother or I would have to grab her waving hands and make her take some orange juice or bites of a Hershey bar in response. The early diagnosis of her disease had come only a few months after the discovery of insulin, and her first specialist, the godlike Dr. Eliot Joslin, of Deaconess Hospital, took her as a young child into a ward of recent amputees and said, "Take a look—this will happen to you if you don't take your shots." Enraged more than cowed, she became a model case, cited in the journals, who lived to eighty without losing her limbs or her eyesight. Her father, another bully, saw an absent son in her.

One Saturday in our first autumn together she stationed me next to a high stone wall at the foot of a hill in Framingham, and told me she'd come by here shortly on her horse. Tweaker was a fox hunter, and though the local hunt had run out of foxes they made do with drag races instead, with decoy sacks of meat towed around the woodland course in advance, to lure the hounds. On this day, all played out as advertised—the baying hounds, the tootling horn, the scattered, rushing riders in pink or black habits, the thick sounds of hoofs on green turf. There was Tweaker, on his white hunter Feathers. And here suddenly came Evelyn, yards above me in the air on her enormous, gasping animal, her face white and excited as she cleared death by an inch or two and flew away up the hill. She scorned and hated this, I knew, and soon afterward told her father the hell with it, he'd have to break his neck on his own.

Tweaker, a ferocious Tory, saw no reason that his girls should go to college, and Evelyn, forever ashamed at her lack of a degree, paid him back as a serious and insatiable lifelong reader and full-bore liberal Democrat. In this, she resembled her grandmother Baker, who'd been thrown in jail for picketing the State House during the Sacco-Vanzetti trial. Tweaker was a throwback. Later in the war, when I'd gone off to the Pacific, he began providing a small monthly stipend to Evelyn and her nearest sister, Tudie, whose husband Neil MacKenna, was an infantryman in Europe. But he and Evelyn fell into a dispute about race one day, when she held that it was a disgrace that our armed forces were still segregated during a war that was supposed to be about democracy and equality, and the next month the checks stopped coming.

In Denver that winter, Ev and I—I never called her Evvie, as others did—put up in a couple of hotels or back at the Emerys' house, and then in a modest white-brick apartment house on Sherman Street called the Bahamas. I was still in school but got off on Saturday nights and Sundays, and also, weirdly, twice a week after taking a midnight bedcheck in my barracks. This was legal but exhausting—I had to be back on duty by seven in the morning—and in November I got sick and was toted back to Lowry in an ambulance. Once there, I was told I had the flu—there was a semi-secret epidemic in progress on the post—and that every infirmary bed was taken. I was ordered to go to bed in my barracks and have my buddies bring me food from the mess hall and soft drinks and apples from the PX. Each morning, though, I'd have to get up and get dressed and go on sick call again, so they could check on my case. I protested that I had a wife and a little apartment back in town, where I'd be warmer and better looked after. Couldn't I call a cab each morning and come out for sick call from there? "Oh, no, that would never do," said the medic captain, smiling. "People might say we're not looking after you."

I got better, resumed my classes in time and graduated—and shortly thereafter became aware that the Army Air Force had lost me. I'd fallen back by a week while ill, and when my original group finished up they'd been shipped out to a factory school in Detroit for a last three weeks of training—every man of them and my service record, too. Slowly, over a few days, I realized that I'd become invisible. I appeared on no duty roster; and when I turned up for morning roll call nobody said my name. It was too good to be true. Warily at first and then with the louche air of an outcast dog, I hung around the Rec Room playing pool and then slide into line early for my undeserved chow. I had plenty of passes tucked away, some of them still legal, and spent happy hours in town with my new wife. Sometimes we walked the neighborhood, arm in arm under the trees, or took in an early double feature at the movies before dinner. Reluctantly I'd grab a late cab back to the post, in case someone missed me. Nobody did. It was the other way around, in fact, because soon I noticed that I had company in my loony exile. Before long there were twenty or thirty of us: a league of derelicts. The great rushing apparatus of the war—millions of men going somewhere else in a hurry, with fresh-cut orders in hand— had sprung a leak and cast us loose. Our pool and Ping-Pong and sack-time skills shot upward. Now and then a sergeant or the Officer of the Day would stick his head in the door and look us over, but Lowry had three full shifts of students in place by now, which meant that there were always extra G.I.s idling about at odd hours. Couldn't this sweet deal last for the duration? Surely none of us would be dumb enough to give in to conscience and spill out a confession. The empty paydays were a problem, but perhaps there were civilian jobs to be picked up on the side. Was there anything doing in the private armament sector?

Evelyn, meantime, had found a job as an assistant secretary in a private school, and I began to notice a certain impatience in her when she'd come home and discover me still there, or there again, finishing the Denver *Post* crossword at the end of the day. "Is this my fault?" I'd cry, spreading my arms. "Jeez."

This Peace of God lasted almost three weeks, as I recall, until one of our number sailed off on an unauthorized furlough to visit a girlfriend in Milwaukee and got nailed on the way back. The response was swift. Teams of officers and noncoms went through every squadron at Lowry One and Lowry Two, sweeping us up like suspects in a bank heist—a good fifty of us by now—and threw us into a special barracks while they cast about for our lost papers. Every fatigue duty from around the sprawling base now fell to us—KP and latrine clearing, painting and maintenance, weeding and hangar sweeping, day after day, all administered with an irritable or vengeful zeal. I remember four successive sub-zero February nights when I was in charge of six furnaces and three insatiable coal stoves, the sweat freezing on my wrists and eyebrows as I trudged from barracks to barracks. It was uncalled for—we had violated no rules or orders—and when we rebelled, melting away in hilarious numbers while marching to the next vile job, our C.O., a major, went bonkers and dispatched M.P.s to escort us to work. We were prisoners, or just about, and when this came out—in the time it took for our indignant letters to get home and take effect—the major was fired and disgraced. I'd already got free, having wangled myself a day job in Personnel, in the ancient red-roofed Headquarters

Building, and before long word came down that they'd found my service record at last—sorry about that—and that I'd go to instructors' school for a week, and then take up my first class that following Monday.

In a snapshot of me taken in early spring of 1943, I am wearing minuscule wire-rim eyeglasses—the compulsory back-up pair I'd been required to keep on hand to slip on during gas mask drills; I had fallen back on these when two prior pairs of horn-rims snapped within days of each other that winter when I stepped outdoors into the four-thirty a.m. sub-zero cold, on the way to the dawn shift at Lowry. A reticence of memory surrounds these times, because of their blandness, but perhaps also from the way everyday contentment slips through our grasp. We'd found ourselves a one-story brick house on Garfield Street—an almost new cottage in a modest, treeless development not far from the field. Two flights of narrow concrete steps led up the lawn to the front, where a stepped-forward, Tudorish sector of the little living room made room for a side-entering front door. Inside, there was comfortable furniture, a bedroom and adjoining tiny guest room, a dining nook and kitchen, and, out in back, a garage and a bit of yard with, yes, white picket fencing. The rent, I think, was eighty-two dollars a month, payable to owners now also off at the war somewhere. This overhead closely matched my entire take-home pay as a new corporal, but with Evelyn's small salary and a hundred or so each month in checks from home tacked on we stayed afloat. Though carless, I was invited into an instructors' car pool; one of our older sergeants—Albert, from Little Rock—had money and drove an ornate black LaSalle, with white-wall tires. He had high blood pressure, he kept telling us, and would never live to forty. At home, Ev and I drank Old-Fashioneds before dinner—at whatever odd time it occurred—and listened to my Ellington and Coleman Hawkins and Muggsy Spanier records, played on our portable. Friends and family came out to visit: Evelyn's mother and her sister Tudie; my new stepmother Betty, livelier and funnier here while away from her kids; and a college classmate of mine, Larry Brown, who unexpectedly presented us with an Old English Sheepdog puppy we named Mandy. Larry, an ensign, was taking a crash course in Japanese at the Navy Intelligence School in Boulder, and bowed and sucked in his breath whenever he spoke. Evelyn and I were at home in Denver, knowing the names of the nearer mountains, making free with our no-fare privilege the bus and trolley routes, and exclaiming over the exuberant weather, which dropped deep billows of dry snow overnight and then sucked them away in the high-altitude sunshine by noontime the next day. We saved up for the movies every week—*Casablanca* and *Shadow of a Doubt* and Eric Von Stroheim as General Rommel in *Five Graves to Cairo* turned up, among others. Once, we caught the slick Phillips 66ers basketball team, and another night some great rodeo at the Denver Stock Show. That summer, we grabbed tickets for the Jack Teagarden All Stars' date at Elitch Gardens, and when we swung close to the bandstand, dancing, saw the mournful maestro taking his temperature behind a held-up sheet of music. We had a cat, Henry, to keep Mandy company, and Evelyn acquired her first printed stationery, with "535 Garfield Street" at the top, and perhaps wrote home even more often than before. In another photograph, I am sitting on our tiny Victorian sofa on a Sunday in clean, freshly pressed suntans, with my legs crossed, smoking a pipe.

We ate up domesticity—Ev, I think, because of her scary father, and I, after all this time, still in reaction to my childhood's departed mother. My father, after a decade on the beach as a bitter divorced man, was happy in his new marriage, and had cleared out my bedroom and my sister Nancy's bedroom to make room for Betty's two young sons. Nancy was in Boise, Idaho, with her professor husband, Louis Stableford, now an Air Corps lieutenant, and their young daughter. A bit later they were transferred to Topeka, Kansas, and produced another baby, a boy. Countless young Americans in service were flourishing in this extempore style, with nothing in their lives within their control but—if they were anything like us—finding freedom in each day's release from the grownup business of war. We were also lonely: that was the surprise. What I missed most were the new friends we'd made as a couple together, back home: the beginnings of what we were going to be.

Evelyn and I had gone to a lot of jazz joints in Boston and New York during the years we'd been keeping company, and this part of our lives took a nice upward jag or jump in my senior year when we became friends with George Frazier, an older man who was writing a lively twice-a-week jazz column, "Sweet and Lowdown," for the Boston *Herald*. I'd written him a letter adding something to an item

in one of his columns, or perhaps even correcting something, and he wrote back in friendly fashion and asked me
to give him a call, and soon I was invited up for drinks at
his place, in an apartment house next door to the Harvard
Crimson on Quincy Street.

George was tall and lean, with expensive clothes, gray
crinkly hair, a perpetual Chesterfield in his hand, and a
slight limp: a case of polio in childhood had left him with
a turned-in right foot and, in time, a nice exemption from
the draft. He'd been at Harvard about ten years earlier, and
at graduation had won the Boylston Prize for Rhetoric,
the hallowed award given to the writer of the best senior
class essay. One of the runners-up in George's year was
Harry Levin, the eminent future Joyce scholar and the
Harvard English Department's most relentlessly intellectual professor.

"How did that Boylston thing happen?" I asked George
once.

"Pah," he said, with a dismissive gesture. "Levin froze
at the plate."

George's wife, Mimsi, was pale and great-looking, with
a wide swatch of crimson lipstick, like Billie Holiday's.
She was the first woman I ever heard say "fuck." Together,
George and Mimsi and Evelyn and I stayed late at the better jazz places in Boston, and we were excited about the
trumpet player at the Savoy Café on Massachusetts Avenue:
Frankie Newton, who recorded for Blue Note and had a
great touch with the mute. He was said to be able to hold
converse with Professor Levin about Joyce, though I never
heard them talk (or play) together. Sometimes Evelyn and

I went back to the Fraziers' apartment after one of these outings to listen to more records. One June night, we four stayed up all night there, drinking Tom Collinses and laughing.

When Evelyn came out to Denver for our wedding she gave away her big, staid Old English Sheepdog Topper to the Fraziers. George had just gotten a new job in New York as entertainment editor of *Life* magazine, with an unlimited after-hours expense account, and when we heard from him next he told us that whenever he or Mimsi called up Nick's or Café Society Downtown or the Ruban Bleu for a reservation, they asked for a table for three. Topper got the extra slot.

Looking for music in Denver, Evelyn and I began to hang about a Denver nightspot called the Embassy, and picked up a friendship with the band leader, Clyde Hunt, a slight, cheerful Negro (as we all said then) vibraphone artist in rimless glasses. A couple of times Clyde and his wife and a player from his quartet—the piano player Fletcher or the guitarist Ben Sohier—came by for Sunday lunch, and the Hunts would produce snapshots of their young kids, back home in Chicago.

Moments like this have come flickering back as I've been writing this chapter, and the emotion they carry comes as a surprise. I've kept quiet about my trifling Army career all these years, because I was ashamed of my safe, lowly status. I had volunteered for the Navy and then the Marines shortly after Pearl Harbor, but was told that no service would take me because I was so nearsighted. Still, I knew that some college friends of mine had already grown into command positions here and there, while I was playing house, and others had begun to die in faraway places. A returning, persistent memory of Denver in 1943 is of me and Evelyn downtown at night, where we encounter two or three lieutenants coming along Market Street in our direction: young newly made officers, with no overseas or combat ribbons. Evelyn is wearing a flowered cotton summer dress, with a skirt that just comes to her knees, an open cardigan sweater, and low pumps. Her hair is waved, in the fashion of that time, and she has fresh lipstick. As the little group approaches, she takes her hand away from my right arm, and I shoot them one of my flyboy highballs—back straight, head and shoulders slightly turned in their direction, elbow firmly crooked, and the short salute snapped off and done with in an instant—and what I get back is something embarrassed and half-hearted. Their gaze takes us in, and the yearning there, just for that second, breaks your heart.

This state of things could not last, nor did we entirely want it to. When we got home on furlough, in June and again in January, sitting up the first night on the high-speed, streamlined Burlington Flyer, the war had come closer. We always kept up—the attention everyone gave to the news in that time is astounding—reading two Denver newspapers every day, and regularly getting packages from home containing the *Times* and torn-out sections or columns from the *Herald Tribune* and *PM*. We saw *The Nation* and *The New Republic*, and read Janet Flanner and Molly Panter-Downes and Richard Rovere and the wide-ranging Reporter at Large war stuff in *The New Yorker* each week. At night, of course, we tuned in to Sevareid and Murrow and Bob Trout and William Shirer, from London and North Africa. After the fall of Stalingrad, the map of Russia appeared so often on the front page that it came to resemble a classroom chart, with thick arrows pointing to places like Orel, Kursk, Vitebsk, Pinsk, and Smolensk, where men were dying in enormous numbers as the tide of war rolled westward. In my furlough stopovers in New York, some of the service men and women you saw on the street wore the uniforms of other countries, and officers going by or climbing into staff cars included majors and commanders and colonels. Dinner guests at my father's were just back from Washington or had fresh news from Moscow; things were looking up for our troops in Sicily, they said, and we might even be wrapping up in New Guinea in another few weeks. They asked me for the "G.I. viewpoint," but I demurred. Back in Denver, before my transfer from the Machine Guns and Power Turrets shift into a nine-to-five historian, a tech sergeant on leave from the Eighth Air Force turned up one day before class, in his wings and ribbons. He was a brother or cousin of one of our fellow instructors, out on a pass from the local military hospital, where he was recovering from wounds. His B-17 had been to places like Hanover and Wilhelmshaven, but he did not elaborate. "Don't fly in the low formation," he told us.

Before this, I'd been accepted for armament officer training school and also for the administrative O.C.S. school in Miami, but was told there were lengthy back-ups in the quotas. Unexpectedly, in February 1944, something better came along—a chance to join a group of Public Relations noncoms headed for the Central Pacific to staff a Seventh Air Force G.I. magazine. (I'd just had a story published in *The New Yorker,* which might have helped my chances.) Within days, it seemed, we'd closed up our life in Denver and gone home on a final furlough; Evelyn took up chores at the Whites' farm in Maine, and, away from her now, I became the managing editor of *Brief,* a fifteen-cent, slick-paper weekly, published in Hawaii but covering a westward beat of four million square miles. For a time our stories centered on skimpy B-25 raids to distant small islands in the Gilberts and Marshalls, but after the bloodlettings at Tarawa and Kwajalein, the invasion and capture of the Marianas brought full-scale, hardened runways and a shot at Japan itself. One afternoon at Hickam Field, in Honolulu, an Intelligence major we *Brief* guys knew ran off a private screening of some still-classified film footage of the Eighth Air Force's disastrous B-17 raid on the German ball-bearing works at Schweinfurt, back in the previous August—part of a massive double raid that also included the Messerschmitt works at Regensberg. Bad weather had separated the main groups, and once the escorting P-47 fighters had to turn for home at the end of their fuel limits, the waiting Focke-Wulf 190 and Messerschmitt 92 fighter groups launched attacks over a distance of almost two hundred miles, in relentless waves. When they exhausted their ammunition, other groups appeared, and when they, too, at last departed the flak attacks began. Some of this grainy or sun-flared black-and-white footage still sticks in mind— a progressive, jolting panorama of explosions and flames, with the bombers, under ferocious attack, losing their formation and drifting out of their places in the sky. One of the great dark B-17s is on its back and spewing debris, while another, trailing a thin plume of vapor, pursues a tilted, stately path off and down to the left, with a jammed rudder or dead pilot. In among the chunks of falling, failing planes you can spot the hunched little forms of bailed-out American crewmen from a stricken plane overhead, with their arms clasped around their waists or knees as they rip past in free-fall, waiting for a safer level before they open their chutes. There are plenty of Browning .50s to watch in action, with the masked and muffled waist gunners at their stations dodging and flinching as they swing the pivoted guns back and forth and fire, the thick belts of ammunition feeding snakelike from over their shoulders. They gesture and try to yell whenever another FW flickers into view, spewing gunsmoke, and is instantly past, over their heads. This was not quite the stuff we were teaching at Lowry— nor would the decision have been quckly made to show this film there, I think, if the chance had come. Two hundred and thirty B-17s attacked Schweinfurt that day, while another hundred and forty-six went off to Regensberg (these planes labored on from their targets all the way to bases in North Africa), and sixty of the total, with six hundred crewmen, went down. The attack was called a success, but on October 14, the Eighth's B-17s had to go back to Schweinfurt again, two hundred and ninety strong this time, and again lost sixty planes and crews, with another twenty or thirty planes crashing on landing or being written off from battle damage. Five dead airmen and forty-three wounded were taken off the planes that got home. After this, the Eighth Air Force called off daylight raids over Europe until the arrival of the long-range P-51 fighters, in the spring.

A few months after this, I wrote a piece about a B-24 bomber that had been simultaneously hit by Japanese flak and fighters while on a mission from the Marianas to Iwo Jima, and, although heavily damaged, had made it home again to its base on Tinian in a falling flight that stretched across eight hundred miles. Four of its crew were wounded in the battle—one of them, the co-pilot, severely—and the rest were banged up in the landing, when the plane, with one wheel down and no brakes, slid the full length of the runway and broke in half. All survived and all got Purple Hearts. When I talked to the crew, some in their hospital beds and others recuperating at a rest camp, I realized that some of them still didn't know how close they'd come to disaster. An aerial burst from a Japanese fighter had knocked away the top turret canopy, and the co-pilot lay semi-conscious in his blood in the freezing stream of air. One of the four engines was gone, another was leaking fuel at a perilous rate, and a third kept running away in midflight and had to be controlled by manipulating its feathering button, but most of the crew members only knew their own part of the picture. When I asked the tail gunner what he'd thought about the runaway engine, he turned pale. "What runaway engine?" he said. I wrote all this for *Brief*, and then, in a longer version, for *The New Yorker* (it was my first reporting piece for the magazine), but what the Army and Navy censors wouldn't let me say in the piece was the news that the pilot, although unhurt in the action over Iwo Jima, had gone to pieces on the way home, unable to fly or to speak because of his terror. With the co-pilot wounded, the flying for most of the journey was extemporized by one of the gunners, who had washed out of pilot training school back home. The pilot, a captain, composed himself near the end and pulled off the tough landing, when the brakeless, screeching hulk banging down the runway was slowed a little by parachutes that had been strapped to the waist and tail gun positions. Several of the survivors swore to me they'd never fly with that particular captain again.

I'd become a wily old noncom, in suntans now white with laundering. I'd gotten tougher, and felt an old lag's distaste for the length of our sentence and our foul-mouthed, relentlessly male jokes and beefs. We *Brief* guys had our own jeeps and a weapons-carrier truck, and kept our own hours. We cultivated the right officers; knew our way through the red tape at Pearl Harbor (some days you could see Admiral Nimitz throwing horseshoes just below the balcony outside the censors' office); and hit up the best post bakery for warm, fresh-from-the-oven Danish at five in the morning. Hiding our stripes, we got into drunken officer parties, and picked up word about the Iwo Jima and Okinawa invasions before they happened.

With the war in Europe ending, our style and sector of the fighting had already begun to prosper. Shiny, enormous new B-29 bombers flooded the fields at Guam and Tinian, and after some unexpected difficulties with the weather and Japanese fighters at the prescribed twenty-five-thousand-foot level of operations, went down to five thousand and with mass incendiary raids systematically burned Japan into submission. Our stories in *Brief* covered all this with restrained exuberance, mentioning the targets struck—Kobe, Yokohama, Nagoya, Osaka, and the others—but not the cost: three hundred and fifty-seven thousand civilian dead in sixty-seven cities. Eighty-five thousand died on March 9, 1945, the night of the great fire raid on Tokyo. A returning B-29 bombardier told me later that the updrafting torrents of flame at five thousand feet had blown some of the planes around him upside down. Hiroshima and Nagasaki, when they came, felt like more of the same. One of our writers, Bob Frederick, got into Hiroshima on the second day anyone was allowed there, and we ran his story, in our next-to-last issue, under the headline "Too Great for Tears."

It wasn't until after I got home that I could begin a personal accounting. John Brackett, Walter Ebbitt, and William (Boopa) Sturtevant, school or summer friends all, had died in flight-training accidents. Freddy Alexandre went down in action over the English Channel while piloting an RCAF Mosquito fighter. Harry Blaine fell in the first wave at Saipan, and our college classmate Demi Lloyd, a Navy aviator, was killed there two days earlier. Orson Thomas was lost at Wake Island; Bob Nassau and Paul Carp in the Mediterranean. A childhood friend of Evelyn's, Gordy Curtis, died in the invasion of Sicily when the Army transport he was piloting was shot down by friendly fire. And so on. Three classmates lost their lives in B-17s or B-24s over Europe: Bill Emmett on his fifth mission, Frank Joyce on his eighteenth, and Robert Rand on his forty-third. At Hickam Field, I'd drawn straws one day with Larry Swift, to see which of us would go out to the Marianas for a stretch to write little hometown stories for stateside newspapers. He won the toss, and a week later got into a B-25 bomber and flew a low-level mission over Tinian, to see what that was like. He and I had come overseas together, as part of the *Brief* project. He was ten years older than I, and curious; in New York, in peacetime, he'd been a reporter with *PM,* the serious-minded crusading tabloid. He must have been excited about the B-25 run, with the fixed bow cannon and the frag bombs and the machine-gun bullets smashing men and buildings just below, because when it was over—these harassing raids only took twenty minutes or so, round trip—he got back on another plane, then another, all in the same day; it was never clear how many. In time, one of the B-25s he was in hit a tree or ran into Japanese ground fire, and went in. A little before this—in May, 1944—Evelyn's sister Tudie had married Neil MacKenna at Fort Benning, Georgia, two months before he shipped out to Europe as an infantryman. She got him back at Camp Pickett, Virginia, the following February, seven months after he was severely wounded at Belfort Gap, France. He'd lain semi-conscious for twenty-eight hours on contested ground, and played dead when a Wehrmacht patrol came by, shooting anyone who moved.

I observed Christmas of 1945 on the homeward-bound carrier Saratoga, converted to a transport. I took another troop train, shivering in the winter weather, then checked out at last from Fort Dix and into the Algonquin Hotel, where I found my mother and Evelyn having lunch in the

Rose Room. We'd not seen each other for twenty-two months, and in that space—with Hiroshima and the Holocaust a part of our consciousness now; with Germany and Russia and much of Europe laid waste, Hitler and FDR dead, and an end at last to the killing—our world had changed beyond imagining. I'd not been in the war, exactly, but like others back then I'd got the idea of it.

Ancient Mariner

M R. Hopper, paint me a seascape. Give us an islanded bay—a sunlit reach, with water moving around ledgy, beachless shores and bold rises of spruce and hackmatack. Darker water, please: we're Down East, and a fingertip trailed idly overside here comes up pickled. Next, as centerpiece, a classic little keeled sloop, gaff-rigged, as in your day, just now close-reached and throwing an occasional splatter of white off her starboard bow as she steps along in the first morning breeze. The man at the helm sits at ease, his right hand on the windward coaming and his left on the tiller; his sneakered right leg is comfortably up on the seat, and his gaze, behind shades and a faded Red Sox cap, is contented, for he has been here many times before. The islands here are unchanged except for their thicker recent growths of pine and fir. Without thinking he registers the nearer run of island shapes and shores: Conary and White, with Bear lower between them; the sweet cove next to Devil's Head, on Hog. There's the rim of Smutty Nose, up to port. Soon he'll pick up the "tongg" of George's Bell. With this breeze, why not stand right out into Jericho Bay? Forty years ago, in this selfsame Herreshoff 12½ (that's a waterline length), he might well have passed within a yard or two of this tack on the identical moment in August. The lone sailor is lucky and knows it, so why should he remind himself so perversely—I'll take it from here, Mr. Hopper—how many people, within view and beyond, begrudge him his happiness?

He is an old summer sailor is why; he is me, and I know that the aversion, while mostly unspoken, runs wide and deep. It is not a burden, but it's there all right, a little onus that can never quite be shaken, and it turns an apparently harmless pastime into something only awkwardly shared, except with other sailors. Involuntarily, I am in holy orders. Let me list a few of the disbelievers and disapprovers of my morning sail aboard *Shadow*. The preoccupied lobsterman who waves a gauntleted hand as he skews his vessel toward his next buoy. (He is working; I am playing.) The distant, growly yacht running down toward Swans Island, and the nearer, bouncing, earsplitting runabout. (They are going fast and straight; I am going slow and in zigzags.) The kids coming down the gangplank onto the club float, with their spinnaker bags and their tactics. (I have happily given up racing.) My local friends and neighbors, at the general store and the post office and the boatyard. (They live here; I am forever from away.) But I am thinking even more of city friends—at home or in my office, in New York—who do not sail and know that I do, and can hardly bear the idea. "Going—uh, sailing, will you be?" they offer a day or two before my vacation starts. "Going off in your—uh, boat, I suppose?" I nod, I hope not too cheerfully, and we change the subject.

Some of it must be the language, although the argot of sailing, to my ear, is not much more arcane than that of golf or cooking or opera or flytying. But say "sloop," "close-reached," "starboard," or "tiller" (as I have done here), or murmur "halyard," "jibe," "headsails," "genoa," and the rest with any air of familiarity (it's "heads'ls," I mean), and you are instantly seen as a dilettante, a poseur or a snob, a millionaire, and, almost surely, a Republican.

Is this fair? More to the point, is it true—can mere lingo do such damage? I doubt it. Out on the water, even during one of those eventless, inexorably slow, time-flattening stretches of sailing—nothing doing, nothing to do—I realize once again that my eye and hand are reacting almost on their own to the thousand sights and sounds and movements of sailing. The look of the mainsail along the luff, an infinitesimal tug on the tiller, the lift of the stern on a quartering sea—all lead by reflex to a countering small movement of my own. I am sailing and, like countless thousands of other summer skippers, old and young, I am calling upon knowledge and responses that lie dormant during long months ashore but are there to be drawn upon for a lifetime.

I've sailed here in bigger if not better boats, as well, with summer charters of cruising yawls and sloops and cutters, ranging from thirty to almost fifty feet, which have taken me with friends and family up and down and east and west of this bay and archipelago, on day sails or easy overnighters or more, for over forty years. Boats named *Hanau* and *High Heels, Eastward Ho* and *Pauline.* Bermuda Forties by Choi Lee and Hinckley; sloops by Rhodes and Alden. Also *Aquila,* a stiff-bowed Crocker cutter, and the sweet *Nasket II,* a Crocker ketch redesigned and built by my brother. I've also passed countless undemanding hours and days aboard boats where we've regularly been invited along: *Astrid, Mary Leigh, Hopeful, Jarge's Pride, Sprite,* and *Ellisha.* Anyone with small boat experience and the extra bucks can carry this off, but given these ledge-studded waterways and stiff tides what you should also have at hand is a bit of local knowledge. Awake at night in the winter, I summon up visions of dozens of rock- and ledge-strewn bars and tricky narrows that I know the look of and have mostly managed to shun. There are the Triangles and the Boulders, Rudder Rock and Colby Pup and Spirit Ledge, and two or three Channel Rocks, all set off in italics and asterisks on the charts I first studied and shuddered over as a teenager. There's the notorious submerged knob or spindle just east of Bear Island which I have seen impale bigger and more impulsive vessels than mine, leaving them to teeter there like a compass needle until the tide relents. There was that overlooked small type *"shl rep 1967"* on my much-folded chart, there between Saddleback and its smaller companion Enchanted Island, which I bumped onto and then off of while reaching through this pretty passage with friends of ours aboard; embarrassingly, they were a summer couple new to the region who were thinking about learning how to sail. "It's simply a matter of knowing where you are," I said, with my suave fingertips on the wheel. "Oop."

There's a much-visited flat ledge on the western side of the anchorage at the Barred Islands which I forgot about—we were easing along with sails down, looking for a place to drop anchor—because Carol and John Henry began exclaiming over a nest of young ospreys they'd spotted through their binoculars on a nearby niche: bang. Carol was embarrassed because we were under scrutiny by twenty or thirty landlubber witnesses aboard one of the Camden dude ships, but I insisted that this was one of those no-fault mishaps—we'd only bonked the ledge with our keel—that could befall anyone. A few days later, visiting my brother Joel in his office at the Brooklin Boat Yard, I asked if he'd ever encountered that flat ledge at the Barred Islands. "Two or three times, easy" he said. "We were there last in September"—he'd been aboard his Danish-built, Aage Nielson cutter *Northern Crown,* with his son Steven and daughter-in-law Laurie, among others—"and we smacked it hard. Laurie was in the head and she fell off the pot."

Having Joe's yard so close to hand was a sweet convenience in my cruising years, and I used to turn up there every week or two with a wheezy engine or a jammed winch or stopped-up head. I awaited my turn and paid full rates, but the service was terrific. In time, of course, this imbalance between brothers—I the summer amateur in shorts; he the soft-spoken Down East sage and provider, in wood-smelling denim—began to get to me, and I reminded myself that I, too, had a profession. "Goddam it, Joe," I said one morning. "Couldn't you come around some day and borrow a comma?"

Getting back to sea, there was also an early evening when, off on an overnight with Carol and young John Henry, I dreamily nudged our bow onto the mud bar poking out to the south from White Island, and stuck fast there on a going tide. There we lay, despite kedgings and curses, a couple of miles from our front porch but thankfully hidden from view by the loom of the island. No one came by as the sunlight and the water waned and we lay at last on our beam ends, under the stars drinking Scotch and listening to the trickling sounds of our diesel fuel emptying onto the gravelly mud. We found a Sox game on the radio, and along about the top of the sixth the returning tide gently took us off, and we went home.

The rewards of mild summer sailing outnumber the scares and goofs. With my eyes closed again, I can run the obstacle course of hidden shelves and weed-buried granite outcroppings that delivers you into an overpopular anchorage at the bottom end of Winter Harbor, and I probably still could perform the sequence of short swings that take you into the dozen yards of safe water, too small to fit onto the chart, just inside York Island. There you awakened at first light to the sounds of cropping sheep and, up in the cockpit again, found the loom of Isle au Haut, closer than expected, on the other side. Still in bed in New York, I can bring back the faint squeezing sounds from our anchor rode, up forward, as a night breeze touches our sloop and sets her on a fresh heading. Or the look of our old fox terrier Willy sitting on the stern seat of our green dinghy while I row him back from an early morning pee on the beach, and now pricking up his ears as he looks over my shoulder and spots Carol coming up from the cabin with a towel to wipe the dew-drenched cockpit cushions. Or maybe it's the smell of bacon that's got him.

A million such moments are in my sailing brain. The fog dispersing at Perry Creek to disclose a *New Yorker* colleague of mine and his wife quietly reading aboard their pocket-size schooner *Tyhee,* not twelve yards away. "Thought that was you," he calls over. Another day brought our fabulous twenty-mile dash from Center Harbor all the way to Islesboro in a smothering fresh northwester, closed hauled and rail down on starboard tack the whole way, doing seven-and-a-half or eight knots in our sloop Megaptera; and then, heading back, the same thing all over again, boiling along in the other direction almost faster now, with the sheets eased only by a foot or less: two fabulous slants in a single day. Or the afternoon along about 1939, back in my teens, when the thermometer and the wind went every which way and finally, as we tacked through the Bartlett Island Narrows, delivered a six-minute snow storm, there on the last day of August.

Later—not long ago—here comes one of those fierce fair-weather afternoon squalls which descend so quickly in these parts, this time a bit north of Hat Island Ledge, blackening the distant waters and churning the waves around us to a froth. Aboard a sturdy forty-five foot cutter, we're in no real difficulty but we need to take in sail. I get the engine going and hand over the helm to a visiting friend of ours, a retired two-star admiral who had recently been an intelligence advisor to the Joint Chiefs of Staff. "Just keep her in the wind," I say and go forward with Carol to rein in and drop our big genoa. Only he doesn't. Down on my knees, with the wind grabbing at us and the rain streaming and our arms full of slippery flapping nylon, I feel the boat yaw this way and that while loose sheets and heavy blocks bang about over our heads. "Hans!" I yell back at the Annapolis-trained skipper astern. "What the fuck are you *doing!*"

I've given up big boats now that I'm in my eighties, and one repayment for this loss is that I will no longer find myself sailing grandly past that working lobsterman amid the pot-strewn waters of Western Way or Casco Passage. Boats like his are bigger and more powerful than they were when I first started sailing around here, and they're stuffed with electronics. But he's fishing four hundred traps now, a huge enterprise, and his loans have gone sky-high, even as his overburdened, over-managed fishery slides into decline. No reason remains for him to look upon me as a neighbor; he may even know my ancient waterfront cottage, which has been climbing crazily in value and remains one of the reasons he and his kids can't get access to our common shore. (All this pain and irony is reported on at length in an essential new book, *The Edge of Maine,* by Geoffrey Wolff.) There's still a chance, I tell myself, that he won't mind *Shadow,* since she's been around here even longer than he has. Mostly, though, I stopped chartering forty-footers because I'm afraid of making a dumb mistake. Everybody who has sailed this drowned coast of Maine, with its great depths and steeply shoaling ledges and tall islands, has had the experience of idly watching the dark water below his hull turn a paler blue and then bring up the terrifying white of an unexpected shoal or giant boulder—*Christ, what have I done!*—just below. You swing the wheel and pray.

No, thank you. Here I am, still aboard *Shadow* and thinking about the pleasures at hand. Even at this easy level, I am dealing with shifts and forces and counter-flows—wind and tide and current—that are nearly invisible to the hapless nonsailing friend I have brought along this time, who now (the wind has freshened) looks at me with dislike, because I am in another realm: a medicine man in a baseball cap. It can't be helped, but sailing is exclusive. What the landsman senses and perhaps envies is exactly what grabs me at odd moments in a small boat in August. Here—for the length of this puff, this lift and heel—I am almost in touch with the motions of my planet: not at one with them but riding a little crest and enjoying the view. I smile across at my friend but say nothing. Eat your heart out, pal.

La Vie en Rose

A SATURDAY evening in May, 1949, and I am taking a moonlight leak in the garden at Ditchley. Hedges and statuary cast elegant shadows nearby, but I've had a bit of wine and it probably doesn't occur to me that this is one of the better alfresco loos I have visited—the Italianate garden installed by Sir Geoffrey Jellicoe in 1935, as a culminating grace note to the celebrated Georgian pile of Ditchley Park, in Oxfordshire, designed by James Gibbs and built in 1722. Ditchley, with a deer park and a village within its borders, is headed inexorably for the English Heritage Register but for the moment remains the country home of my old friend Marietta FitzGerald and her delightful, fairly recent second husband, Ronald Tree, who is standing a few feet to my left here, in identical posture, his chin in the air as he breathes in traces of boxwood and early primrose. Beyond him, also aiming, is Major Metcalfe, a neighbor of Ronnie's and another dinner guest of his on this evening. He is the same Major Metcalfe who proved such a staunch friend to King Edward VIII at Fort Belvedere during the difficult abdication days, in 1936, and who stood up as best man the following year, when the King, reborn as the Duke of Windsor, married Wallis Warfield Simpson in Monts, France. Major Edward Dudley Metcalfe, M.V.O., M.C., I mean, who at any moment, surely, will invite me to call him Fruity, the way everybody else does. He and I are in black tie, and the moonlight lies magically on his satin lapels, just as it does on mine. Ronnie is wearing a beige velvet smoking, perfectly O.K. for a country host, I guess, but he looks less dashing or narrow, less *right,* than Fruity and I do. Good old Fruity.

Soon we three will amble back up the terrace steps, toward the tall lighted doors and the sounds of conversation and rattled dice within. My wife, Evelyn, ravishing in her silk top and shimmery gray skirt, will look up from the backgammon table, where she has taken on Ronnie's first son, Michael (he's in his late twenties), and has just realized that she's in over her head. "How much is eleven pounds?" she whispers urgently. It's around forty-five dollars, I figure quickly—big bucks, to us—but of course none of this is for keeps. Only it is, we find.

Memory stops here. Nothing more can be made of that ancient weekend. Evelyn and I were impostors—not members of the bon ton but a visiting, unembarrassed American couple, still in their twenties, on a lucky six-week dive into England and France, mostly paid for by the magazine

Holiday, where I was an editor and writer. I was scouting the Continent for writers and picture ideas, or some such scam. We had married in 1942, were separated by the war, and when it was over swiftly acquired New York jobs and friends, an apartment in the upper reaches of Riverside Drive, a two-tone Ford Tudor, a bulldog, and, sixteen months before this, a baby daughter, now in the hands of an affectionate grandmother. The works. But, given this chance, we grabbed it, booked passage on the slowpoke liner *De Grasse*—the only French Line vessel as yet restored to the Atlantic run after the war—and after six entrancing days and nights debarked and did the tourist thing. Westminster Abbey, the bombed-out City, St. Paul's. Green Park in the spring sunshine. The British Museum. Oxford and the Trees. Paris. The Orangerie and the Cimetière Père-Lachaise. Our rented Citroën Onze—with its chevron-striped grille, crooked-arm gearshift, low power, and sneaky reverse gear—would carry us faithfully along the uncrowded two-lane routes to the south. What was the French word we needed for "windshield wiper," after ours gave out during a thunderstorm outside Le Puy? Why, *essuie-glace,* of course. Who could forget that? There was a funeral going on at the cathedral in Chartres when we arrived, the soaring gray columns enfolded in black at their base. The next noon, on Ascension Day, we walked into Bourges Cathedral to blazing candlelight and mauve sunlit shafts above, just in time for a raft of first Communions. "Be joyful, *mes enfants,*" said the white-hatted bishop to the three-deep rows of pink-cheeked, well-combed nine-year-olds. "You are being accepted into the one true Church, here in the most beautiful structure in the world." Why, yes—where do we go to sign up?

We were lucky, but this was long ago and one wants more than a pee on the grass or the tink of a funeral bell, behind the altar at Chartres, to bring it clear. But only anecdote continues to work. Late at night aboard the *De Grasse,* Evelyn is dancing with our friend Tom Hollyman, a *Holiday* photographer, and Jean Hollyman with a young purser. At our tiny table, with its crowded champagne glasses and triangular white C.G.T. ashtrays, I am in deep converse with a fellow-passenger, Alfonso Bedoya, the Mexican movie actor who was such a hit last year as the bandito chief in *The Treasure of the Sierra Madre.* (Encounters like this happened all the time on the Atlantic run just then. The dearth of shipping—the *De Grasse* herself had recently been raised from the bottom of the Gironde estuary, where the Germans had scuttled her—made for a travelers' bottleneck, where celebrities and the rest of us squashed cheerfully together for a few days at a time.) Here, sometimes in French, sometimes in Spanish, Bedoya is discussing monetary or agricultural issues—I'm not always sure which, though I nod in agreement—in emerging Latin America. Part of me is listening to him and another part following the ship's five-piece dance band as it shifts shamelessly from "La Seine" to "J'Attendrai," but in truth I am only waiting for my new friend to flash his enormous teeth and cry, "Badges, badges—I don't have to show you any steenking badges!"

In London, I know, we caught Laurence Olivier as Chorus and Vivien Leigh as an anguished Antigone at the New Theatre, but not a word or gesture of it comes back now. Instead, I see us sitting down to dinner at the Café Brevaux, in Paris, with *The New Yorker*'s Janet Flanner, where another guest of hers, Tennessee Williams, seizes Evelyn's hand and presses it to his forehead. "What do you think?" he asks, and Evelyn, shaking her head sadly, supplies the right answer. "I think you're really getting sick," she says. Looking for a second opinion, he produces a thermometer from an inner pocket, shakes it down, and furtively takes his temperature behind a menu. "Go home, Tenn," says Flanner, in her field marshal's contralto, but he stays on and does away with a white-asparagus salad, his veal Marengo and *fonds d'artichauts à la crème,* and, a brave though gravely ill playwright, remains as well for a *mousse au chocolat* and the cheese platter and coffee and a tiny Armagnac and then, why not, one more.

Southward in our Citroën, we came out of the mountains at Alès and on from there to Les Baux (no one else turns up for lunch at the fabled Baumanière) and Arles and Nîmes (there's a bloodless Provençal bullfight in the blazing-hot Roman amphitheatre) and Tarascon, and, with the sea now shining off to our right, Saint-Tropez and Antibes. Arrived at our destination, we're at breakfast on the terrace of the modest Hotel Metropole, in Beaulieu-sur-Mer, when we are startled by the unmistakable sounds of a Boeing 377 starting its four propellers—*WHEE-EEE-eee-ouzzzze*—and warming for takeoff—*RhhhOUUMMMM!*—from a room on the second floor. It is the S. J. Perelman family—Sid and Laura and twelve-year-old Abby and ten-year-old Adam— or, more accurately, the pair of caged mynah birds they have brought along from Singapore to this wildly accidental meeting, here by the lapping Mediterranean. The Perelmans had been in the Far East for three months and, with many stops along the way (giving the mynahs a chance to tune up their act), were by degrees heading home.

Perelman, already a Mt. Rushmore eminence on the landscape of American humor, was more a friend of my mother and stepfather's than mine, but, anxious for company as tourists are, we two families palled up, ate and drank and swam and talked together and, jamming all six of us into the Citroën, drove up the corniches and then back down from Menton, mousing around (as Sid put it) among the white villages, with their withered trees, dusty pétanque courts, and alley-like streets, half empty in this off-season. Mornings, Abby serenaded our breakfasts from above, practicing on her well-travelled cello. Sid, natty and with his gagman's jaw always fractionally agape, followed every conversation with terrifying attention. He and the tall, dark-eyed Laura liked it here and arranged to rent a villa in Èze for an extra week or two. When we looked the place over one morning, the kids went rocketing off down a steep path to the shore, while Perelman conferred with the owner and a rental agent. There was a discussion of some sort between the two locals, and Sid, his eyeglasses glittering, offered free translation: "*Hélas,* these hectares themselves find encumbered."

That afternoon, we went to Monte Carlo in two cars, and, while Laura took Abby and Adam off somewhere, ventured into the Société Anonyme des Bains de Mer et du Cercle des Étrangers de Monaco for a spot of gaming. The long rooms were not stuffed with slot machines and customers in shorts, as they are said to be now, but did not exactly come up to expectation. A bare two tables were in business in the curtained, fusty Public Gaming Rooms, with others shrouded in tattered baize. The handful of players, bending over their skimpy stacks of thirty-franc chips, appeared to include some local widows, making a late-afternoon stop-off before the evening rates and lighting came on. But the quiet commands from the formally garbed croupiers were straight out of E. Phillips Oppenheim, and the suave Sid now faltered a moment before a vacant seat. "Do you know how to do this?" he whispered. "Sure," I said and slipped in. I lost two early bets on Rouge and another on Passe, got eleven chips back for my one on a Transversale Pleine, and, encouraged, plunked down four on No. 26—the traditional spot for an opening thirty-seven-to-one long shot. Around went the little ball, to the croupier's *"Mesdames, messieurs, faites vos jeux. Les jeux sont faits—rien ne va plus!,"* then slowed and bounced—rickety-tackety tipitty-tup—and nestled sweetly into my slot. There was a gasp—it came from me—and piles of oblong chips, triangular chips, and variously tinted round chips slid smoothly to my part of the green. "Jesus, what did you do!" Perelman cried, but I was no longer of his party. Seizing a casual stack of counters from the top of the pile, I tossed it toward the man at the middle of the table—I really did this—who raked it into a slot next to the wheel. *"Merci, monsieur,"* came the murmured response (with little bows) from the band of croupiers. *"La maison vous remercie."* I smiled, extracted a Sobranie from my silver case, and accepted a light from the slender, white-gloved countess at my shoulder.

I had won perhaps fifty dollars and, staying on, added a lucky ten or fifteen more before we arose. Perelman, betting his kids' birthdays, then his hotel-room number subtracted by the number of letters in his name, worked like a trooper and wound up seven or eight bucks to the good. "Never again, Étienne," he said as we walked out into the late sunlight. "You must swear to stop me." Not till the next day did I give him a break and confess that my expertise and gambling manners had all come out of the Encyclopædia Britannica, consulted back home before my departure, which had a terrific "Roulette" entry in the "RAY–SAR" volume. I took notes.

Our last stop—Evelyn and I had to start back—came the next afternoon, when we pressed a call on W. Somerset Maugham at his Villa Mauresque, next door on Cap Ferrat. Perelman, a fabled reader, told me he had once written the grand old man of British letters to express admiration for his effortless style, and won a similar mash note in return. Now they had a date. In the Perelman wheels this time, I think, we noticed Maugham's adopted Moorish symbol— for good fortune—here worked into an iron arch at his entranceway. The same sign appeared on the covers of *Of Human Bondage* and *The Moon and Sixpence* and *Cakes and*

Ale and the rest, which the world had snapped up in staggering numbers over the previous decades. A flood of bestsellers and long-running West End plays had earned him this comely retreat, in a part of the world that even then looked lightly on his private life. Here, twisting and turning around corners, up hill and down dale, we followed the raked driveway onward through stunning groves of palm and pine and splashy bougainvillea. "The royalties! The royalties!" cried Sid in pure admiration and purer envy, as we drew up at last at the flowering stone steps and spreading red-tiled roofs of the shrine.

Maugham appeared, a frail gent of seventy-five, slightly bent in his soft shirt, pleated summery trousers, and suede pumps. With his skimpy, slicked-back hair and heavily lidded eyes, he suggested a Galápagos tortoise, wise and of immense age. He shook hands with us each, repeating our names, and told Abby and Adam to make themselves at home. Indoors, tea was produced and Maugham's cheerful partner, Alan Searle, introduced. Two house guests, the tall poet C. Day-Lewis and a slim, long-necked woman in gray, floated in and silently took places in the vast low living room. All went well except the conversation, which soon became a trickle, unhelped by Maugham's famous and extraordinarily demanding stammer and my sudden realization that the woman next to me, Day-Lewis's companion, was the novelist Rosamond Lehmann, whose *Dusty Answer* and *The Weather in the Streets* I had sighed over while in college. Silences fell, broken by thumpings and running feet above, from Abby and Adam. "They're in my st-study, I believe," Maugham said, smiling, as Sid bolted from the room. Dadly noises arose from the stairs. We picked up a bit after a round of Maugham Specials, a grenadine concoction prepared by Searle. Sipping mine, I saw Evelyn gesture with her eyes toward the window over Maugham's shoulder, and, shifting my gaze, caught sight of a paper airplane as it sailed slowly down from above and impaled itself in a jacaranda.

Ever the host, Maugham pulled over his footstool and sat down again, one leg tucked beneath him. "Tell me, Mister Angell," he said, "have you ever worn a s-s-sarong?" I had to ask him to repeat the word and then said no, not yet. "Oh, but you m-must!" he cried, wrinkling his wrinkles with kindness. "V-very *cool*—but they do f-f-fall off!" On the way back, Perelman lit into his progeny. "This was a big, big disappointment," he said. "I don't see how we can take you anywhere." Silence. "Listen," he resumed in a different voice, "what was it like up there?"

These tales and name-droppings grow dim with repeating, and hearing them once again, in the fashion with which we stare into the too small black-and-white snapshots in a family album, we look into their corners and distant porches or mysterious windows in search of something more—times of day, a day of the week, other names and other tones of voice, beyond recall. What in the world did Evelyn and I talk about—beyond our adored but absent baby, I mean— all those weeks and miles? How did we survive the shrivelling boredom of long days on the road, through landscapes relentlessly renewed and snatched away but never entered? Conversation saved us, but I can't bring back a word now.

What books were we reading, which crisis were the French and British papers and the Paris *Tribune* full of each day? What fears or sadness woke us up at night, either or both of us, and made it hard to sleep again? With effort, if I wait not too eagerly, I can sometimes bring back her voice. She was happy on this trip, and could prove it. She was a full-blown diabetic, but here in France, while eating two exceptional meals every day, all over the map, and drinking down the splendid wines, she was able to cut down her daily insulin—a stab in the thigh, mornings and evenings—to her lowest levels in a lifetime. We divorced in the sixties and she died—can it be?—almost ten years ago.

On the *De Grasse* again, homeward bound, we were old hands. We told our new friends the Sidney Simons—he was a painter and sculptor coming back from a spell in France—which deck chairs were out of the wind and which dinner service to sign up for (the *deuxième,* except on cabaret nights, so you could leave earlier and grab a better table by the floor). In our cabin, Evelyn told me that she had wept a bit in the taxi on the way to our train to Cherbourg, but couldn't tell if it was from leaving Paris or missing Callie. I said we could do this again, maybe next year, and make it a shorter trip. We never did. Life and work and a second daughter intervened, and there was the money problem and the kids' summers to think about, and almost before we knew it the *De Grasse* and every other Atlantic passenger vessel were gone, swept clean away by the airliners' seven hours to Orly, and by Eurail Pass and Junior Year Abroad, and by the hundreds of thousands of kids and travelers and shifting populations, from all over the world, who filled the fabled capitals and charming roads and did away with our postwar afternoon, leaving only these moments.

On the *De Grasse* the night of the Captain's Gala, a day and a half before New York, Evelyn and I are in close embrace, dancing to the Jerome Kern chestnut "You're Devastating." Our dancing has picked up, and we know how to let the slow lift of the floor tip us together, and to wait for the sensual tilt and counterflow of the departing wave. The bandleader, Tony Prothes, gives us a little nod as we swing by. He remembers us from the trip over, I've decided, but of course he's good at this. Like our cabin steward and the second sommelier and the barman Charles—Jules? Gérard?— he goes back to the *Normandie,* before the war. Half an hour later—or is this on another crossing, years later?—I am sitting at a cabaret table next to Mme. Hervé Alphand, the wife of the French Ambassador, whom I met at a cocktail party earlier in the evening. Tall and olive-skinned—I think she is Greek by origin—she will become one of the great Washington hostesses. She is wearing an amazing evening gown, and when I say something about it she suddenly spreads the skirt's thick folds so they cover my knees and those of the man on her opposite side. The three of us are under the multicolored skirt, which lies in glistening heaps, holding us together. "Mainbocher," she says, smiling. "It's *élégante,* don't you think? It brings pleasure."

At the Comic Weekly

Working Types

I'VE gone off to work at *The New Yorker* on more than ten
thousand mornings, and can't quite get out of the habit.
My second office there was a slotlike space inherited from
the august, pipe-smoking Geoffrey Hellmann, and next
door to the saintly William Maxwell, who became my
colleague and mentor in the fiction department, and the
editor of my nonbaseball stuff. In time, I edited him, as
well—a happy back-and-forth that was often the custom
in those days. In editorial temper, he was a keeper-inner
and I was a taker-outer, but we so enjoyed each other that
the difference never came up. Later on—this was still in
the magazine's red office building on the north side of West
Forty-third Street—I became august, too, and moved into
a nice corner office down the hall, where one of the windows offered views into other *New Yorker* offices up or
down a flight or directly across from me, all containing fel-
low-writers and editors, who could be observed typing or

telephoning or reading newspapers or snoozing or (a lot of the time) staring morosely at the wall. My new space had been occupied twenty years earlier by my mother, then the fiction editor of the magazine; the first time I opened the closet door I found myself facing a long vanity mirror and, preserved beneath it as if in the Smithsonian, a round box of her Coty face powder. When I mentioned the coincidence of occupancy to the psychiatrist I was visiting back then, his jaw fell open. "The greatest single act of sublimation in my experience," he proclaimed.

I remember running into Maxwell in the hall one day after lunch, when I was carrying a present I'd just bought for my five-year-old daughter, Alice, at the Music Masters store in the lobby—a 45-RPM Little Golden Record of Tom Glazer singing "The Little Red Hen" and other kiddy folk songs. I winced when Bill asked what it was, because I knew that his daughters Brookie and Kate had been brought up since the nursery on a diet of Debussy and Schubert, with Chopin for breakfast. "Oh, Roger!" Bill exclaimed, when he peeked into my package. "You're so worldly."

Maxwell had a great feeling for my work, and was patient with me when the process was reversed. I learned more from trying to edit him than the other way around. I still recall a recalcitrant sentence of his, near the bottom of a galley, that we stared at and scribbled over together for a good ten minutes. "It's still not clear," I said at last and when Bill, leaning his head on one hand, murmured, "I don't want to be *too* clear," I saw, as if in parable, the artist's heart that ruled his editor brain. Other contributors who had already sensed this preference and sensibly entrusted their work to his care included Eudora Welty and John Cheever and Frank O'Connor.

And here, within a page or so, has emerged a problem for anyone in trying to bring back a trove as rich and fraught and jumbled in private recollection as *The New Yorker*. Reaching into a mountain of meaning and back issues, I have produced a ghostly whiff of my mother and Bill Maxwell shrivelled to an anecdote. More is always required. If I were to go on at decent length about Maxwell, I'd bring up the loss of his mother in the flu epidemic of 1919, when he was ten, and point out how often he returned to this appalling event in his fiction—she died six or eight times in the pages of *The New Yorker*, I think. His last and best novel, *So Long, See You Tomorrow*—we ran it in the magazine, in two successive issues in 1976—begins with his mother dead again and his father almost undone by her death, endlessly walking the floor of their house after supper, with the son (the future author) walking beside him, with one arm around his waist: "He would walk from the library into the front hall, then, turning, past the grandfather's clock and on into the library, and from the library into the living room.... Because he didn't say anything, I didn't either." In the book and in his later stories Maxwell reconstructed a household and a family and his home town, Lincoln, Illinois, as it was then, putting in furniture and seasons and times of day, along with relatives and neighbors and children and servants and dogs and conversations, to the point where readers came to know these streets and living rooms and kitchens almost as if they had emerged from their own recollections and family letters: a work of art. Alice Munro, a modern master, likes to take vacation trips to authors' locales, like Faulkner's Oxford, Mississippi, and she told me once that Maxwell's Lincoln, Illinois, was just about her favorite.

Still in my Maxwell piece, I'd mention his brilliant conjectures in the same book about the elusive and (as he insists) unreliable powers of memory that surface so powerfully when we go back to our hoarded scraps of scenes and tones of voice. "Too many conflicting emotional interests are involved for life ever to be wholly acceptable," he writes, "and possibly it is the work of the storyteller to rearrange things so that they conform to this end." And surely I'd have to look for some tie between Maxwell's scholarship and literary classicism and his wide-eyed, sometimes infuriating purity of gaze, that preserved innocence that began in him—or so I believe—when he understood that he'd have to keep his mother and her absence clearly in sight for the rest of his life.

That portrait belongs in another book that I no longer expect to write. Other New Yorker pals and paladins would be there, too—William Shawn, Frank Sullivan, James Thurber, John O'Hara, Ogden Nash, Donald Barthelme, V. S. Pritchett, Saul Steinberg, Brendan Gill, Edith Oliver, Jim Geraghty, Garrison Keillor, William Steig, Veronica Geng, Charles McGrath, Charles Addams—whom I knew and served with or under, and observed and edited (some of them) and had drinks and lunch and laughs with but can't get around to here. I feel an obligation, a lost chance, with but a few. It's too bad, for instance, about Victor Pritchett, perhaps my favorite editee ever, going back to my days as an editor with *Holiday* magazine, for which he was writing pieces about Spain and London's inner City. Early in the sixties, Carol and I became closer friends with the Pritchetts, Victor and Dorothy, during a sweltering August when by accident they sublet the apartment directly upstairs from us while Victor did research for a forthcoming travel book of his about New York. When we asked them at last, gently enough, about some pounding noises we'd been hearing overhead it came out that it was only the sound of bare heels: the two were going around naked up there, to keep cool. I was still Victor's editor a quarter century later when, in his eighties, he produced a late rush of fresh and vigorous new stories. In one of them, "On the Edge of the Cliff," a story about an old man in love with a young woman, there came a passage that brought Victor himself, unmistakable, into the room with me. "From low cliff to high cliff, over the cropped turf, which was like a carpet, where the millions of sea pinks and daisies were scattered, mile after mile in their colonies, the old man led the way, digging his knees into the air, gesticulating, talking, pointing to a kestrel above or a cormorant black as soot on a rock, while she followed lazily yards behind him. He stopped impatiently to show her some small cushioned plant or stood on the cliff's edge, like a prophet, pointing down to the falls of rock, the canyons, caverns, and tunnels into which the green water poured black and was sucked out into green again and spilled in waterfalls down the outer rocks. The old man was a strong walker, bending to it, but when he stopped he straightened, and Rowena smiled at his air of detachment as he gazed on distant things as if he knew them."

This passage is cited (and no wonder) in a vivid new biography, *V. S. Pritchett*, by Jeremy Treglown, which relieves me of any remaining promises I'd made to myself to keep Victor whole and someday try to get him down on paper. Enough will stay on in my mind, including a last luncheon in London that Carol and I had with him and the rueful and vivid Dorothy, when the sunlight fell across the table and glanced off our empty cups as we lingered late with our talk and laughter. Victor, well along in his eighties by now, told Carol that he'd been startled to find himself dreaming lately about the Queen Mother, who was over ninety and still going strong.

"Well, that's not surprising, is it?" Carol said. "She's so lively—doesn't everyone here still dream about her?"

"Erotic dreams?" Pritchett said.

I'd need to talk about Shawn, the quickest reader and most perceptive editor I've known, but also, in his later years, the most contradictory and self-destructive. His extreme shyness, his privacy and courtesy, and his killingly long work weeks have already been set forth and extolled in memorials, as have his lavish compliments and commitment to writers whose work he admired. For all that, the stubbornly clinging portrait of him is of a small, nervous fellow, terrified of elevators and prudishly on guard against the arrival of a four-letter word in his magazine. This misses him by a mile. At his daily best, he was outsized in intellect and imagination, and if thought-burdened, anxious first of all that the magazine might stop being funny. He knew all the bad words but believed that once he'd given

way about the ban to some star fiction contributor or department writer—Pauline Kael kept snapping at his heels
about this—he'd have to do the same for others, and the
magazine would soon be awash in street talk.

He and I became at ease in time, and shared some private jokes. One of these concerned my old jazz writer
friend, George Frazier, who in later years had begun writing a popular weekly column, "The Lit'ry Life," in the
Boston *Globe,* in which he would comment in the fashion
of Pepys or a latter-day H. L. Mencken about journalism,
music, Harvard, clothes, sports—anything. Here, every
few months, he would drop in a little boosting item on my
behalf, which I can now offer only in paraphrase: "When
is William Shawn going to take his faltering hand from the
wheel of *The New Yorker* and turn it over to the oh, so qual-
ified Roger Angell?" The suggestion embarrassed me, of
course, but if Shawn was irritated he must have been aware
that I'd had no part in the matter. We also both knew that
the proposal was beyond unlikely: it was loony. After that,
whenever another version of Frazier's grand plan for me appeared, Shawn, blushing but enjoying the moment, would
say, "So, we've had another little message from your friend
up in Boston," and watch me writhe. "'Friend'!" I would
cry. "Bill, the guy is killing me!"

What I'd like to add, since it's barely been noticed, is
that Shawn was a genius editor of fiction—a reader apparently attuned to the many dozens of conflicting voices and
weird takes that were surfacing in our mail every day back
then. He was just as quick about humor: quicker. The ongoing Perelmans; the young Keillor casuals; the first Woody

Allens; the crazy Trows and wild young Fraziers; the pearl-
like Brickmans and convoluted Gengs—all excited him and
made his day. "I don't know what this is," he sometimes
said, pink with pleasure, "but it's wonderful."

He loved the bafflng, mysteriously moving first Donald
Barthelme stuff, and in 1965 saw at once that we would absolutely have to take his short novel, *Snow White,* in its entirety:
Snow White dreaming of a prince while she lives in a close
domestic arrangement with Bill, Hubert, Henry, Kevin, Edward, Clem, and Dan, and at one point complaining, "I am
tired of just being a horsewife."

"I suppose we'll have a lot of complaints about this,"
Shawn said to me, "but who cares when it's the real thing?"

The New Yorker fiction department took a jolt in 1975
when an unexpected compulsory retirement policy took
away Maxwell and the long-tenured regular Robert Henderson. It was to Shawn's credit that he allowed the department to reform itself around a much younger nucleus of
editors—Chip MacGrath, Daniel Menaker, Fran Kiernan,
Veronica Geng, Linda Asher, and, in time, Pat Strachan.
Suddenly transformed from the youngest to the oldest fiction man, I was the titular chief, but fiction buying and editing now became a looser and more entertaining process,
particularly after we took on the emotional and fervently
intelligent Geng. "Jesus *Christ,* how can you all be so goddam stupid and pigheaded not to see that this story is absolutely the one best [worst] thing we've seen around here
in months or maybe goddam ever?" she'd cry, after a difference in opinion had surfaced. Tears and slammed doors

generally followed. Door slamming, a retort that had declined to invisibility under the gentle Shawn, was back, accompanying a general playfulness and decline of formality. Chip and Dan and I became world-class pushpin flingers. (A heavyweight, sharp-pointed leaden pushpin, delivered underhand with a last-minute spin imparted by a reverse snap of the thumb and forefinger of the flinger, will fly arrowlike toward its target, fifteen feet away, and stick fast in a plaster wall or a posted old Nixon photograph or outlandish manuscript page.) We also joined a larger group at the magazine who'd become adept at forging Shawn's signature on a faked memorandum or a pink buck-slip, or imitating his mothlike voice on the telephone. Sandy Frazier was unmatched here and could engage you for several minutes of polite, wildly uncomprehending conversation with the great man before reality or a suppressed giggle allowed you to expel a breath. Chip was athletic and boyish, and after we'd moved to new quarters across Forty-third Street, in 1989—Shawn had departed by then, succeeded by Robert Gottlieb—he sometimes set sail up and down the long new corridors on his inline skates.

From time to time back then Shawn would be approached by one or another of the staff's intellectuals and asked why the magazine didn't run more world-class fiction. How come Mailer's stuff didn't make the grade here? Where was Gore Vidal or Italo Calvino or Gunter Grass? Why didn't we stop our old dependence on agents and submissions and cut down our number of fiction readers and editors and simply commission stories from the known élite? Shawn, in his customary mode of polite agreement, would appear sympathetic to the suggestion, and sigh miserably over the state of things, but of course he knew better. Commissioned fiction is one way to do it but perhaps not the best, since it eliminates surprises and does not leave room for the essential guarantee of quality, which is the rejection. Almost every *New Yorker* fiction writer, no matter how well established or beloved by readers, faced the possibility that a clunker of his or hers would get the heave. Shawn, to be sure, granted protection to S. J. Perelman and Jerome Salinger, whose pieces, never seen in manuscript by the rest of us, would magically appear in galleys a day or two before the issue they were to run in was ready to close; if they were ever turned down we never heard about it. But other top-rank contributors were not so fortunate; John Cheever and John Updike, when interviewed together on an early Dick Cavett show, admitted to the occasional *New Yorker* rejection with something like wry pride. E. B. White suffered a rejection now and then, too, although the decision would nearly demolish Shawn. He found it painful to disappoint anyone about anything, and the semi-independent status of the fiction department allowed him relief when he'd been given a bad story written by a staff member or an exalted author. "They didn't like it," he'd say miserably. He had no such option with his fact writers, and many a windy or arid or bottomless piece of reportage inexorably appeared in the magazine as a result.

Knowledge of our sternness undoubtedly cost us some prime submissions by writers too certain of their own importance to face disappointment, but we held firm. This in turn, led to the curious and hilarious occasional phenomenon of the *sub rosa* submission—a story or novel selection from a great sensibility first introduced by a quiet telephone call from the sensibility's agent to a particular editor friend at the magazine, sometimes Shawn himself. If we liked this great story or section of a novel and wished to run it, fine, the idea went, but if somehow we didn't then it never had been submitted at all and could scarcely be said ever to have existed, so word of its presence in our office could not be permitted. Some fiction actually did make it into our pages by this means, including stories by Saul Bellow and Bernard Malamud. Shawn played along with the rigmarole, though reluctantly, and I recall a morning when he appeared at my door with a manuscript chunk of Norman Mailer's outsized Egyptian novel, *Ancient Evenings,* in his hand. "This isn't exactly a submission," he began, "but *if it were,* do you think you could perhaps take a look..." I did read it and thought highly of one section of its many pages, but Mailer would not consider a cut and the whole sneaky project went up in smoke.

In Shawn's latter days, in the early eighties, he began training McGrath as his possible successor at the top—a better candidate, I believed, than the previously tapped Jonathan Schell or Bill McKibben, whom Shawn had been forced to abandon, to his great distress, when faced with strong opposition from much of the staff. Shawn, though well along in his ninth decade by now, did not want to go at all, of course, and the McGrath apprenticeship, like the others, languished on the vine. One afternoon, piqued and frustrated by the whole thing, Chip determined to force the issue after his eye had fallen upon a dilapidated life-size, cotton-stuffed dummy that had lately been kicking around the fiction department in various low poses and positions. Chip called me into his office on our twentieth floor, which by chance lay directly above Shawn's, on the nineteenth. "Listen," he said, his eyes wildly alight. "It's time for action. I'm dressing the dummy up in my shirt and tie and this old Press jacket. Then I get Shawn on the phone and say, 'Mr. Shawn, this is McGrath and I can't stand it *one more minute*! Look out your window'—and then, ZAM, here I come, straight down past him, with maybe a whole bunch of galleys tied to my hand. That should settle things, wouldn't you think?"

"Do it," I said.

Only he didn't.

In time, all the young fiction department people of that era took their leave, one by one, and moved up to distinguished careers elsewhere: Chip (who had become the fiction editor and, under Tina Brown, the magazine's deputy editor) at the *Times;* Dan Menaker as a top editor and then the top editor at Random House; and, a later arrival, Deborah Gottlieb Garrison, who is a poet in addition to her other talents, to a double post in publishing as an editor with Pantheon and the poetry editor of Knopf. She'd begun at the magazine as a summer intern. I think back on them at times as my protégés or children but in reality they were Shawn's. There in the late seventies and early eighties, we were regularly publishing stories by Raymond Carver, Donald Barthelme, Peter Handke, Alice Munro, Ian Frazier,

William Trevor, Mary Robison, Stanislav Lem, John Updike, Garrison Keillor, Muriel Spark, Veronica Geng, Edith Templeton, Max Frisch, George Trow, V. S. Pritchett, and Ann Beattie, which felt enough like a renaissance or a great party to make us feel that we'd all had a Medici hand in it, though there's an equal chance that it was just the luck of the draw: a lot of very good writers getting hot at the same time. Either way, we loved it.

These fragments of Shawn will not be amplified into a portrait or position paper, even though there may be some fresh things still to be said about his great gifts and his diffident, relentless eminence. It saddens me to realize that I have joined those who have no wish to linger within the great William Shawn National Forest after its recent strip minings. He was amazingly generous and friendly with me, and, I believe, almost relieved that he did not need to count me among his acolytes. Here comes one last Shawn story, to lighten us up: a family tale. It's opening night of his son Wallace Shawn's new play "The Hotel Story," in the summer of 1981, at the La MaMa Theater, on East Fourth Street. The theater was a tiny one, with no room backstage, which meant that the large cast—there are seventy-six characters—had to stand about in costume on the street until it was their turn to go on. Ann Beattie, a friend of Wally's, had volunteered to play the walk-on bit of a hooker, and during the intermission that first evening saw the playwright's parents standing uneasily together under the marquee, with Shawn in his customary dark suit, black shoes, and funereal necktie. "Mr. Shawn!" she said enthusiastically, hurrying toward the startled editor, who blushed

and bowed, and, staring at the creature before him in platform shoes, pink stockings, clingy skirt, purple eye shadow,
and thick crimson lipstick, at last recognized a valued contributor. "Miss *Beattie?*" he whispered, his cheeks scarlet.
"What are you doing here?"

Barthelme I want back, as well. Nobody reads him
much these days, not even "The Indian Uprising" or
"Views of My Father Weeping"; not "Critique de la Vie
Quotidienne" nor "Paraguay" nor "Kierkegaard Unfair to
Schlegel"—the titles jump out at you, just like his writing. Not *Paradise,* a novel, nor the limpid "Overnight to
Many Distant Cities." Categories seemed to accumulate
around him of their own accord, but a brief rundown of
some common ingredients in his fiction brings back his
unique swirl of colors and contexts: museums, headlines,
orchestras, bishops and other clerics, babies, savants and philosophers, animals (gerbils, bears, porcupines, falling dogs),
anomie, whiskey, fathers and grandfathers, explorers, passionate love, ghosts (zombies and others), painters, princes,
balloons, nothingness, places (Paraguay, Korea, Copenhagen, Barcelona, Thailand), young women, angels, and a
panoply of names (Goethe, Edward Lear, Klee, Bluebeard,
Cortés and Montezuma, Sindbad, President Eisenhower,
Eugénie Grandet, Snow White, Captain Blood, the Holy
Ghost, Daumier, the Phantom of the Opera, St. Augustine,
and Hokie Mokie the King of Jazz). This explosion of reference, this bottomless etcetera, probably accounted for
his brevity—short stories and short novels—and for the
beauty of his prose. His names and nouns were set down

in a manner that magically carried memories and over-tones, bringing them intact to the page, where they let loose (in the reader) a responding flood of recognition, irony, and sadness. The Barthelme sentences, which seemed to employ references or omissions in the place of adjectives or metaphors, were sky blue—clear and fresh, and free of all previous weathers of writing. It was this instrument that allowed him to be offhand and complex and lighthearted and poignant all at the same time. In an early story, "Philadelphia," a man named Mr. Flax describes an imaginary tribe and culture in this fashion:

> *The Wapituil are like us to an extraordinary degree. . . . They have a Fifth Avenue. . . . They have a Chock Full o' Nuts and a Chevrolet, one of each. . . . They have everything that we have, but only one of each thing. . . . The sex life of a Wapituil consists of a single experience, which he thinks about for a long time.*

Many readers had difficulty at first cottoning to writing like this. They were put off by Barthelme's crosscutting and his terrifying absence of explanation, and those who resisted him to the end may have been people who were by nature unable to put full trust in humor. Donald was erudite and culturally rigorous, but he was always terrifically funny as well, and when his despairing characters and ragged scenes and sudden stops and starts had you tumbling wildly, freefalling through a story, it was laughter that kept you afloat and made you feel there would probably be a safe landing.

He was also an inspiring teacher of young writers, eventually becoming the centerpiece of a celebrated program at the University of Houston, in his old home town, to which he returned in 1981. I once told Donald that I'd been talking with an old pupil of his, a young man who'd also taken writing courses under John Barth, at Johns Hopkins. It was clear to this fellow that Barthelme was the better writer, but he'd decided that Barth, in a very close contest, might have been the better teacher.

"God *damn!*" said Don.

"Why, which did you want?" I said, startled.

"Both!" Don cried. "Both, of *course.*"

He died at fifty-eight, in 1989, and his not knowing that he's out of contention for the moment is the only comfort I can find in that. Reviewers of his day called him a postmodernist or a minimalist or both, but his effect on readers—or on readers like me, at least—had nothing to do with groups or attitudes. The attitude I see him in is sitting and smoking in my regular armchair at my place—he always did this—with an expiring expression of sociability on his face as the warring forces of intelligence and kindness and alcohol and privacy and preoccupation inexorably begin to distance him from the gathering even as he wishes to stay on and keep the evening's sadness at bay. We counted on each other—a great many people felt this way about him—he perhaps seeing in me on older, semi-establishment New York guy who appeared to laugh or cower at the same things he did, and who also, as an editor, could reliably comb the hay out of his writing (this was his phrase). Dazzled, I stuck close to him because he knew so much—art and jazz and philosophers and gumbo—and because he had quickly and surprisingly taken me and Carol and John Henry in with his wife Birgit and their daughter Anna and, later on, his wife Marion and their daughter Kate, at their place on West Eleventh Street. We were family, and on evenings and weekends got to share his strange, smart friends and his dashing, knifelike thoughts, as we hung together (in both senses) through the scary seventies and on into the eroding eighties. "Equanimity," he said, "begins with breakfast." As long as he's here in the same city with me we'll be all right, I used to think—or was that something Veronica Geng said?

One day in the late sixties, Donald needed to get somewhere upstate and dropped into his neighborhood Hertz office for a rental. All went well until it was revealed that the applicant did not possess a credit card. "We'll need some identification, then," the Hertz man said unhappily. "What is your occupation, Mr. Barthumb?"

Don—already sensing the onrushing scene from "Mondo Donaldo"—confessed that he was a writer. He wrote books.

"What are some of your books?" said the Hertz guy, slightly retrieving the application form that lay between them.

"Well, *Snow White*."

"*You* wrote Snow White? Any others?"

"I have a new one just coming out, *Unspeakable Practices, Unnatural Acts*. It's a collection."

"Well, there's a lot of that going on these days, isn't there?" said Hertz. "That'll be seven hundred dollars down, cash."

Three more *New Yorker* friends, as seen in short pieces I wrote about them in the magazine, will wrap up our office visit, although Harold Ross, the first subject, would be startled at such familiarity. He knew me as a contributor and, uneasily, as a grownup version of the kid he'd sometimes run into at the Whites' place. He died five years before I went to work at the family store, but I seemed to find him—or *hear* him, almost—in a new collection of his letters that I reviewed early in 2000.

Oh, Christ

Harold Ross, the founder of this magazine, in 1925, and its uniquely attentive shaper and editor until his death twenty-six years later, has achieved a niche of fame and obscurity that would appear to keep him mercifully safe from the attentions of a fresh biographer. Exempt from the yappings and shin-bitings that have greeted recent memoirs centering on his successor, William Shawn, Ross stands upon a farther hill like a Martin Van Buren of American journalism: a good man of whom one knows just about enough. In truth, Ross himself was patronized and misrepresented in posthumous books about him and his magazine written by celebrated colleagues. James Thurber's *The Years with Ross* (1959) managed to suggest that Thurber himself, not Ross, had been mainly responsible for the magazine's reputation, while Brendan Gill's *Here at The New Yorker,* published in 1975, savaged him for his boorishness and limited education, and diminished him by anecdote. These lingering hurts were put away in 1995 by Thomas Kunkel's *Genius in Disguise,* a foursquare, fully researched biography that cleared up some paradoxes about the man (Ross the gap-toothed Aspen rube as one of the founding sophisticate members of the Algonquin Round Table; Ross the habitual "God-damn"er and "Oh Christ"er who wished to protect young women on his staff from the sight or sound of the shorter expletives; Ross, the publisher of Nabokov and Edmund Wilson, asking "Is Moby Dick the whale or the man?" and so on). Ross is also a central figure in the balanced and useful *About Town: The New Yorker and the World It Made* (2000) by Ben Yagoda, which draws upon six decades of archives while assessing the magazine's fortunes during its accumulating editorships and extremely various eras.

No serious reason remains, then, for anyone but scholars or obsessives to take up still another book about Ross and his "fifteen-cent comic paper," which suggests that the most recent entry, *Letters from the Editor: The New Yorker's Harold Ross* (Modern Library), should be read simply for pleasure, in which it abounds. The collection comes from Kunkel, the grateful biographer, who notes in his introduction that Ross, who never wrote a word for the magazine, "was, with the possible exception of the protean Edmund Wilson, the most prolific writer in its history," if one counts the letters. Prolific in this case doesn't necessarily mean lengthy. "I hope your God-damned stomach is better since you've quit writing," Ross writes to E. B. White (whose furlough was temporary). To the poet William Rose Benét, he is encouraging and corrective, in thirteen words: "We like your stuff, God knows, but this verse, damn it, is obscure." To James Thurber, he notes, "While bathing this morning, it came into my mind that what that dog is doing on your New Year's cover is winking, dog winking. I'm not exactly clear on how a dog winks but it's probably as you've drawn it." In 1930, the unknown young John O'Hara receives "I don't know of any job and I'm not likely to hear of one, but if I do, I will let you know. Maybe the only thing for you to do is to keep on writing and become a writer." O'Hara complies, and then some, and hears a different tone fourteen years later: "Dear John: I regret to report that there is nothing doing as to the proposed $3,200 advance. I formally put it up to the big-scale fiscal man and the result was a laugh, in which, in the end, I joined."

These are excerpts, but almost every letter in the book's four hundred and eighteen pages contains similarly brusque and entertaining clarities—the Rossian nub—which makes this a read-aloud, or read-across-the-room, sort of book. One-sentence mailings turn up as well, even in the daunting condolence form: "White: Was very sorry to hear about your father, and send my sympathy, which is about all I have to say, except that after you get to be thirty people you know keep dropping off all the time and it's a hell of a note."

Ross wrote letters all the time, frequently logging several hours at it in a single day. Some were handed over to secretaries for correction and retyping, but surviving *New Yorker* editors and writers who recall the steady thrash of Ross's old Underwood upright emanating from his nineteenth-floor, West Forty-third Street office have told me that they looked forward to perhaps receiving something from the daily outpouring of inquiries and encouragements or afterthoughts. The messages, pristine in type in the book, actually arrived in an imperfect rush of grimy black lines on yellow copy paper, with hurried X-ings out and penciled-in corrections; sometimes Ross would produce an opening three or four lines of gibberish—it looked like code—before noticing that in his hurry he had placed his fingers on the wrong deck of keys. Ross often stalked the halls, hunched and scowling with the burden of his latest idea or question, but these in-house letters, conveying the same urgent and disheveled impression, also appeared to bring him into your office, so to speak, and nearly in person. When Brendan Gill took exception to the sense of intimidation his boss sometimes conveyed, Ross wrote back, "I don't try to scare anyone, although occasionally I don't give a damn if I do probably."

The notes, in any case, got passed around, and, as Kunkel has observed, were often tucked away for posterity, in spite of their dashed-off informality. Salutations are curt and pauses for throat-clearing or attitude-seizing absent. The man was too busy for bonhomie or style. He hid very little and knew what was on his mind—an ever-increasing burden that he groaned and complained about even in the act of dealing with it—and amazingly shortened the distance between his thoughts and their departure. He always sounded like himself, which is the whole trick.

Ross had a full-scale life away from the magazine as well, and one finds him making a backgammon date with

Bennett Cerf, firing off a reminder to Noël Coward that he has tickets to take him to the circus, offering to sell Jimmy Cagney a used tractor for four hundred and ninety-nine dollars and twenty-five cents, and imploring Ambassador (and former bootlegger) Joseph P. Kennedy to help with a wartime shipment of Haig & Haig to Chasen's restaurant, in Hollywood, of which he was a backer. His divorce from his first wife, Jane Grant, and the arrangements for her support become a clenched-teeth obbligato running through the book, once producing a letter to her lawyers which he famously signed, "Very truly yours, Ross, Ross, Ross, Ross & Ross, sgd/H. W. Ross, By H. W. Ross." But there is no levity within the position papers, ultimatums, and near-resignations that follow the trail of his lurid struggles with Raoul Fleischmann, the publisher and co-founder of the magazine, whom he mistrusted (with some reason) and in the end despised.

Kunkel calls Ross an "organic complainer," which is another way of saying that he was victimized by his insistence on quality and clarity in his magazine, and by the natural scarcity of editors and writers who could produce it. When the irreplaceable Whites moved to Maine, Ross somehow suppresses outrage. "If you will do a very little bit of timely Comment it will help out," he says to White (who had begun writing his longer "One Man's Meat" columns in *Harper's*). To Mrs. White (as he invariably addressed her), who continued editing from long distance, he writes, "As to your sharp-shooting of the issues, and your recent memo about this, I say do it your way. I deplore your way, but since you can't do it another way, I'll settle on it."

The loudest outcries went to writers of humor, on whom he was almost pathetically dependent. "I have come to expect little from writers, including writings," he grumbles to Frank Sullivan, a friend and funny man, whom he often addressed more directly. "I cannot refrain from urging you to write a piece. If you don't do one, you are a little bastard" comes at the conclusion of a 1941 note that began, "Dear Frank, old fellow." He is still at it in 1946: "GOD DAMN IT, WRITE SOMETHING! As ever, Ross." He would not have used the capitals to a writer of less ability.

His health and his teeth weren't good ("Honest to Christ, I am more dilapidated at the moment than Yugoslavia," he writes to White), and office troubles had begun to compound themselves in wartime, when so many editors and artists and staff writers went off to the service that he found himself at his desk seven days a week, and seriously considered scaling down to two issues per month. But Ross loved the work, there's no getting away from it, and a tinge of enjoyment sifts into a summary whine of his, to Alexander Woollcott: "I am up to my nipples in hot water, what with half of the staff going off to war, a limitation of fifty-seven gallons of gasoline for six weeks, the Holy Name [Society] demanding that we stop printing 'son of a bitch,' and so on. This war is much harder on me than the last one."

Ross was never sunny, but his powers of attention lighted him up, particularly when he was dealing with writers and their copy. One of his notorious query sheets turns up here in a 1948 letter to Thurber about a casual of his, "Six for the Road"—a routine (for the magazine) sort of notation in which Ross lists fourteen items worthy of the author's immediate attention. No. 11 is typical—"Very unexpected to learn at this late date that there's a bar in this place. Not mentioned before, and the definite pronoun has no antecedent"—but No. 3 brings Ross to near-frenzy: "This mixing up of a dinner party and an evening party that begins in the afternoon baffled me for quite a while, and I have come up with the suggestion that the party be made a cocktail party with buffet dinner. I think this is a brilliant suggestion. You never later have the people sitting down to dinner, nor do you take any notice whatever of dinner," etc. etc. One can almost hear Thurber's cries of irritation, even from this distance, but he has been poked or maddened into a tiny but perhaps useful fix, which was the main idea.

Ross's query list for the Thurber casual brings up his celebrated question to Vladimir Nabokov, on the galleys of the eighth chapter of his "Speak, Memory" series, which was electrifying the magazine in the late 1940s. Nabokov, describing a garden party at Vyra, a family country estate at the time of his boyhood in pre-revolutionary Russia, is at full tilt with "A torrent of sounds comes to life: voices speaking all together, a walnut cracked, the click of the nutcracker carelessly passed, thirty human hearts drowning mine with their regular beats—" when Ross steps in marginally to ask, "Weren't the Nabokovs a more-than-one-nutcracker family?" Well, uh, yes—and, taking the infinitesimal point, the grand master Nabokov, surely the most abundantly gifted artist ever to appear in the pages of the comic weekly, steps back into the flow, bends over, and turns *the* nutcracker into *a* nutcracker.

It's surprising that Ross never saw himself as a writer, or succumbed to the notion that he was growing into one. I think he sensed instead that he was a genius appreciator of clear writing and strong reporting, and understood that the care and comfort of those who were good at it required full-time attention. When the first-rate Profiles reporter Geoffrey Hellmann decided to go to work for the better-paying *Life* (it was a temporary aberration), Ross goaded him with "What is the temperature over there? Do you need any pencils?"

He is almost fatherly in a mini-crisis with the touchy Whites that blew up when a one-letter typo slipped into an E. B. W. proof—"hen" had become "her"—and he could always sound unfeigned appreciation for a writer's best, even in a rival magazine. In 1940, after White had published a piece in *Harper's* on the meaning of freedom, Ross wrote to him, "I think it is a beautiful and elegant thing, probably the most moving item I've read in years and worthy of Lincoln and some of the other fellows that really went to town." And he concludes, "Knock me down anytime you want."

Ross's *New Yorker* got better and deeper near the end of his tenure (he died in 1951), and the editor who had once expected so little of his contributors must have been startled by what was happening. Writing to John Hersey, whose account of the atomic-bomb destruction of Hiroshima had been given an entire issue, in 1946, he says, "Those fellows who said 'Hiroshima' was the story of the year, etc., underestimated it. It is unquestionably the best journalistic story of my time, if not of all time. Nor have I

heard of anything like it." And when Rebecca West, who
had written some notable pieces for the magazine, dedi-
cated her book "The Meaning of Treason" to him, he was
astounded—"just overflowing with gratitude and goodwill
to you.... I consider that I have now crashed American letters, which gives me much amusement."

Ross knew his own value, but his tenure at the magazine, to hear him tell it, was all about process. He didn't
give a damn what people thought about him or how he
would be weighed; he just wanted to get the stuff right on
the page. "It's all right for people to say that we are too
fussy, that ten or twenty slightly ungrammatical sentences
don't matter," he writes, "but if (from where I sit) I break
down on that the magazine would break down all along the
line." Similarly comes the confession "I still find journalism glamorous," in a long and uncharacteristically personal
letter to the editor of *Current Biography,* in which he re-
counts, among other things, his departure from high school
after two years, in favor of full-time newspaper work on the
Salt Lake City *Tribune.* And, writing to the artist Gluyas
Williams in 1934, Ross says, "I'm employed by *The New
Yorker*...largely as an idea man. That's what I regard myself as, at any rate, and what I think my chief value to the
magazine is." This city-room angle on the world elates the
old sourpuss again and again in this refreshing and uncyn-
ical anthology. Who gets the royalties to "Happy Birthday
to You"? he suddenly asks a Talk editor. To the actor Fredric
March, he declares, "The belief that 'none' is a singular pronoun is an old American legend which grew out of an error
made in a common-school grammar many years ago." To

E. B. White, an accomplished countryman by now, he takes up a dictionary exploration of "compost," both verb and noun, which must have required three or four pages out of his Underwood. And in a memo to Shawn, his most valuable discovery, he wants additions to a coming June Talk piece that will explore more fully the story behind the home-plate umpire's little hand brush, and the ball capacity of his pockets. "Are these brand-new balls, or are they balls that have been played with some, and been knocked foul?"

For Ross, the invention of his magazine was just another good story. "*The New Yorker* is pure accident from start to finish," he wrote to George Jean Nathan. "I was the luckiest son of a bitch alive when I started it. Within a year White, Thurber, Arno and Hokinson had shown up out of nowhere....And Gibbs came along very soon, and Clarence Day, and a number of other pathfinders I could name if I spent a little time in review....And Benchley was alive, for instance." They were lucky, too.

Ms. Ulysses

"Nobody said not to go," begins Emily Hahn's 1937 Reporter at Large piece "Round Trip to Nanking," and so, at the outset of the singularly bloody and dangerous Sino-Japanese War, she gets on a train in Shanghai and goes, carrying an evening dress tucked inside a hatbox. "There were young men, dinner parties, and dancing in Nanking," she offers by way of explanation. In 1932, after spending a year in the Belgian Congo, she determined, "with my usual sublime self-confidence," to walk out, via elephant trail, to Lake

Kivu and thence all the way to the East African coast, accompanied by a baby baboon named Angélique and a pygmy guide. "Like all pygmies," she wrote, "he was incapable of getting lost." Her surprising first-person piece "The Big Smoke," about opium (her own opium smoking, I mean), begins, "Though I'd always wanted to be an opium addict, I can't claim that as the reason I went to China." Actually, she went for the weekend, to drop in on an old friend, and stayed for nine years—a reasonable turn of events, to hear her tell it.

Hahn, who died in 1997 at the age of ninety-two, was the magazine's roving heroine, our Belle Geste: a reporter inveterately at large, whose work, arriving from all continents, encompassed a hundred and eighty-one pieces and eight decades. Her datelines, taken together with her smashing good looks—enormous, green-flecked dark eyes; an oval face; a plungingly intelligent gaze; and a generous mouth always on the edge of an arriving smile or giggle are misleading, suggesting another trenchcoated, news-hungry gal reporter among the guys, a Jean Arthur, or perhaps a beautiful, thrill-seeking flibbertigibbet, a Carole Lombard. She was something more rare: a woman deeply, almost domestically, at home in the world. Driven by curiosity and energy, she went there and did that, and then wrote about it without fuss. Her pieces from the thirties and forties switch effortlessly between the Reporter at Large configuration and the offhand, first-person casual—a form famous for its lack of exclamation points. "She spoke of extraordinary things as if they were everyday," a former colleague of hers said; and I remembered that once, when she and I were talking idly in the hall, she murmured that she used to dream in Chinese.

What is disconcerting about her now that she has gone is how few of us, even among the old-timers, can claim a close friendship with her, much as we admired her. "She was a sweet-tempered feminist, who didn't dislike men," William Maxwell said. "She didn't see why she shouldn't do whatever they did, including sexually." Philip Hamburger recalled first meeting her in the Oak Room of the Plaza, where Harold Ross introduced them. "A beautiful woman," he said, "and smoking the biggest cigar you ever saw. I always liked her but I can't say I really knew her."

Hahn had no end of friends, but she didn't hang out, she was always busy writing, or moving on—to Brasilia or Nairobi or the British Museum, to a zoo conference somewhere, or perhaps back to her home at Little Gaddesden, in Hertfordshire, where she had a house, Ringshall End, and a happy long-term marriage to a University of London historian, Charles Boxer, whom she saw there for ninety days a year, thanks to the tax laws and to their shared preference for an intimacy built around absence. For years, she didn't have an office at the magazine, and we all counted ourselves lucky to catch a glimpse of such a staff celebrity, on the run between her books and her pieces, her departures and her children.

I was luckier than most, for I had first encountered Hahn under unforgettable circumstances. One day when I was twelve years old, she stepped out of a cab in front of our house on East Ninety-third Street, carrying a monkey in her arms—a monkey for me. Because my mother was her editor, she had heard about my boy-naturalist inclinations and had determined, all on her own, to find me the most ravishing (and most inconvenient) pet imaginable. "Don't let her bite you," she said, handing over a small, solemn-faced, greenish-brown macaque, with a belt around its waist. "If she does, bite her right back—bite her on the ear—and she'll never do it again." She was right about that, it turned out, but by then I was convinced that she always knew exactly the right thing to do.

Another Hahn moment has stayed bright in my mind. One morning in 1962 I was alone in a Down elevator at the office, when the door slid open at a lower *New Yorker* floor to admit Hahn. "Why, Roger—how are you?" she said.

"Not so hot, Emily," I said. "In fact, right now I'm headed for Idlewild, to fly to Juarez for a divorce."

"Well, good for you!" she cried instantly. "Trying to make yourself happy is the only thing anybody can do. That's what I've always said, anyway. Try not to worry about it."

The Mickey Hahn story (her mother gave her the nickname) remains fresh and vivid, even in the broad scale. Born in St. Louis, she grew up in a powerful and iconoclastic family sisterhood, and took a degree in mining engineering at the University of Wisconsin, mostly, it seems now, because no one there expected a woman ever to do such a thing. She took a cross-country trip in a Model T (E. B. White had already made the same pre-writer hegira), and arrived at an early age in the pages of *The New Yorker,* thanks to her per-

fect pitch in the little arias of the casual. Her trip to the
Congo lasted longer than she expected (she'd gone broke),
but changes of scene and fortune came easily to her. In
China next (where she became an official *New Yorker* correspondent), she had an extended affair with a married Chinese artist and poet, Zau Sinmay.

The main event of her life, one can say, began with a
scandalous adventure: she fell in love with a British officer,
Charles Boxer, and bore a daughter, Carola, out of wed-
lock. He was imprisoned by the Japanese after the fall of
Hong Kong, and their reunion and marriage had to await
the end of the war. She had remained free by claiming to
be Eurasian (she looked the part), and contrived ways to
visit him under the eyes of his captors. When it came time
for her to accept repatriation she brought their child to her
father's prison in a rickshaw, past the barbed wire, for a
movielike farewell. She writes about the moment with her
usual economy: "Charles was waiting. He must have guessed
I would take some such risk this last time. He turned and
started walking step for step with the coolie, and I broke
yet another rule and turned my head and looked straight at
him. So did Carola."

Given this flamboyant early résumé, and Hahn's ceaseless postwar journeys and writings (ultimately, there were
fifty-two books), it should not come as a surprise if we sometimes overlooked both how lighthearted and how complicated she was, and what it was that she cared about in the
end. What she tells about her two years in the Congo (in
her early published diary, *Congo Solo,* and in a novel, *With*

Naked Foot) isn't just the romance of being a lone young American in such a place but the cruelties that white men inflict on African women. Hahn's move to China and her affair with Zau Sinmay placed her in a cosmopolitan and historically turbulent milieu, which she wrote about in her best-selling biography of the Soong sisters; but her long-running series of placid *New Yorker* casuals, in which Zau becomes Pan Heh-ven, lingers on the ironies of colonial life, and of a traditional Chinese wife who is not permitted to cross the street alone. The best thing that Hahn wrote about her straitened years in Hong Kong during the Japanese occupation was a story, "The Baby-Amah," about Carola's nurse, who had to be left behind in 1943, when her employer had a chance to go home. A two-part Reporter at Large piece about that long trip home with her child, via India and Cape Town and Rio, with a shipload of missionaries and exchanged prisoners of war, barely touches on the risks and fears of a wartime journey but turns instead to the alcoholic misdeeds of some returning merchant seamen, whom she liked better than anyone else aboard.

Hahn gravitated toward the unexpected and the informal. She was an even more spectacular reader than world traveler. Her daughters remember mealtimes at home in Hertfordshire, with everyone at the table behind a book: their father invoked a rule of silence at meals, and their mother always broke it, with giggles and whispers. Hahn resolutely refused to learn the first thing about cooking, her younger daughter, Amanda, who was born in England after the war, cheerfully recalled the other day. "She kept offering to make us rice, but who wants rice?"

Hahn turned out major works of reporting—on the Philippines, and on diamonds and their history, for instance—as well as biographies of D. H. Lawrence and Raffles of Singapore, but an almost greater concurrent flow was made up of low-key memoirs and books and novels for children. In a multipart 1958 Reporter at Large piece, "Last Days of the Maharajahs," she makes small talk with a maharajah's wife as they sip a Coca-Cola at Phoolsagar Palace, and then finds out that Her Highness of Bundi has never visited the nearby city of Agra. She has never been anywhere, in fact. "You see," the Maharanee says apologetically, "I'm in purdah."

The central preoccupation of Hahn's later writing years was zoos and monkeys and wildlife preservation, and particularly primate intelligence and animal communication. She became a distinguished scholar of the subject, and was elected to the American Academy of Arts and Letters. "Either you have gibbons in your blood or you haven't," she once wrote disarmingly, but of course it was a chance to dwell among the voiceless—how eagerly she seized it!— that drew her into the company of celebrity chimps and gorillas, like Washoe and Booee, Colo and Toto, and their painstaking keepers and researchers. When I went into her empty office (she'd given in and accepted one, after she reached her nineties) a couple of days after she died, I spied a bulletin board that was overflowing with yellowed newspaper stories and photographs of gibbons and tamarins and chimpanzees and gorillas. "OPEN-HEART SURGERY PERFORMED ON ORANGUTAN," one headline read. The photographs made me smile, the way monkey pictures do, and I thought of how Mickey Hahn had looked—that gleam of everyday transcendence—at the moment when she cut them out and pinned them up on her wall.

G.B.

i. The Music of the Spines

Shawn's office and Gardner Botsford's office were close to each other at the magazine, down at the east end of the nineteenth-floor corridor, but galactically separated in tone and context. An appointment or shy summons to see Shawn took you past an outer minion and through his rarely opened door; inside (he rose as you entered) he'd be at the middle of his long, altarlike desk, with ancient columns of manuscripts and galleys rising on either side. Many staff members, sharing notes later, found that any meeting with him, even a two-minute session, felt significant and uneasily exciting. If there was something deadly about these encounters, it was probably your fault: you'd half-wanted to be taken in on a major decision or to become the recipient of another of Shawn's astounding compliments. Leaving, you let out a breath and hung a right into Botsford's place, a low-pressure chamber, where persiflage and laughter were encouraged, and high-level work was conducted in a low-key manner. Botsford's invariable reference to the magazine as "the comic weekly"—it was an early Ross description of his brainchild—was not intended to disparage Shawn or the complex and very different magazine that grew during his reign, but only to laugh a little at the immense seriousness that hung about the place in its upper middle age. Shawn actually appeared to believe that his *New Yorker* had come to represent something much larger than its individual issues, its Comment page, its range of talented contributors, and its loyal readers; perhaps it stood for, or even was, Western civilization itself. Botsford, his first lieutenant and most important and reliable editor of non-fiction, thought this was bushwa. He allowed himself pleasure over a pretty good issue, or a surprising Profile, or a telling Rovere column, but went home at the end of the day for an angst-free martini with his friends, and sometimes got through an entire evening without ever mentioning *The New Yorker*. Here's a passing bit of news about him I wrote in a Talk of the Town piece in 1999, after he'd retired:

A departing dinner guest at the Gardner Botsfords' apartment on Gramercy Park can find himself at a sudden loss for words, right in the middle of the thanks and farewells. The process is always the same. Somewhere between the promise to meet again soon and a parting hug, the visitor's gaze falls on a narrow, six-shelf wooden bookcase, there beside the elevator, where, willy-nilly, wandering attention picks up the book titles "Beginning Polo," "Music in Geriatric Care," and "Adultery and Divorce in Calvin's Geneva," all on the same row. What? Just down the line comes "Pray Your Weight Away" and "Selected Lithuanian Short Stories." The elevator arrives and the thanks are distractedly resumed, but a helpless backward glance discovers "Toilet Training in Less

Than a Day," on the shelf below, not far from "Modern Volleyball" and "The Sexual Christian." The door clanks shut, and up (in the little round window) go the host and hostess, who are smiling. They understand.

The Botsford apartment occupies the upper floors of a handsome brownstone, which means that the elevator hall and the bookcase are part of the place, too. And what better spot to stash "Gardner's Library," as old friends think of it—a unique selection of volumes never to be taken down and opened, never to be discussed, reviewed, collated, or arranged? You can't tell a book by its cover, but in this case you can. Their owner and curator, the narrow and amiable Botsford, who is eighty-four, was once an editor at this magazine, with an office just inside the anteroom where inbound, not-yet-published books, destined to be sent along to reviewers or cast aside, accrued in teetery stacks. Running his eye week by week down the nonfiction titles, he became impressed by a sweep of unexpected subject matter and the acute seriousness of certain obscure authors—which, when combined, promised extremely low sales. He began to pluck out some of the unlikeliest volumes— "The Law and Your Dog," "Septic Tank Practices," "Successful Fund Raising Sermons"—and stashed them in a bookcase in his office, where, slowly gaining company during the sixties and seventies, they became a solace for him and his colleagues. When he retired, in 1982, writers and editors and artists found themselves mourning "The

Handbook of Wrestling Drills," "Creative Insomnia," "What Can I Do with My Juicer?", and the rest, but not to worry: Gardner's Library went with him, carefully boxed up, and can still be visited by its exegetes.

"I don't believe there's as much of this kind of publishing anymore," Botsford said to a visitor. "The special special book, the book with an audience of three—I don't know where it's gone." He went on to explain that two broad principles had governed selection of the treasure, which now numbers a hundred and six volumes. There were to be no joke titles—you had to be rigorous about this—and no work that didn't bear its title on the spine. "That's because no one will ever open any of the books," he said. "They are not for reading. Some people don't understand this."

The visitor pointed out that certain themes appeared to recur. Here was "The Personality of the Horse," not far from "Breaking Your Horse's Bad Habits." And would a geographer be drawn first to "The Passaic River" or to "Hamtramck Then and Now?" Might not a scholar wearying of "Refrigeration in America" be tempted to skip over to "Father of Air Conditioning"?

"Pure coincidence," Botsford said sternly. "And please don't move a book closer to any other book. These are arranged on the John Cage principle. Chance makes the music. Look here"—and he gestured toward "All About Guppies" and its neighbor "The Best of Stanley G. Weinbaum."

The visitor, freed at last into art, made a random cast across "Haikus for Jews," "An Essay on Calcareous Manures," "Meet Calvin Coolidge," and, yes, "Who's Who in Saudi Arabia: 1978–79," nestled together on the right-hand side of the second shelf, and felt a twangling chord of happiness descend.

"It would be nice to find a few more," Botsford said, "but I have to rely mostly on friends. Tom Nagel, a professor of philosophy at N.Y.U., brought me this one not long ago." He pointed to a paperback by Kendall Crolius and Anne Montgomery, with its title prettily printed in red: "Knitting with Dog Hair."

Knitting what—mittens? And with whose hair? Could time and love produce a Pekinese tea cozy? Saluki socks? A Lab lap robe? A guilty but familiar impulse crept over the visitor, and when his host departed briefly, summoned by the telephone, he sneaked down the book and began to read.

ii. Never Better

Every meeting with Botsford—down the hall; on a street corner, unexpectedly; at your doorway before dinner—began the same way, with your own "How are you, Gardner?" and his firm, upbeat "Never better!" You came to count on this and to laugh at it with other friends and colleagues of his—some of us even began to call him "Old Never Better"—and only with time did you sense how well the riposte served him, diverting attention from sadness or symptoms, encouraging the social or conversational pleasures just ahead, and also stepping off an elegant little distance away from intimacy. Botsford, who died in 2004 at the age of eighty-seven, was an editor with the magazine for almost forty years and a continuing presence around the place in the two decades after he stepped down. His long and famously happy marriage to the *New Yorker* writer Janet Malcolm—it was the second for both—had its roots in their editor-writer attachment, begun when she was a young contributor of shopping columns, and maintained (through her nine books and ninety-odd reportorial and critical pieces) until the end. He relished her success and his own anonymity. Once at a splashy New York party, she introduced him to a well-known gossip columnist who had been seated at her table. "And what do you do?" the lady asked without much interest. "I'm a bowling instructor," Botsford said.

The instructor, in fact, had edited A. J. Liebling, Joseph Mitchell, Janet Flanner, Mollie Panter-Downes, Richard Rovere, Geoffrey Hellman, and dozens more of the vivid figures of the magazine's postwar journalistic flowering. Hired a couple of times as a young Talk of the Town reporter (the first time didn't take) by the magazine's founding editor, Harold Ross, and lured into editing by its second, William Shawn, he rose to an easy, semi-anonymous eminence: a number two man, had there been a masthead. He was also connected to the magazine through his stepfather, Raoul Fleischmann, *The New Yorker's* first publisher, and, one could say, through New York itself, where he grew up in the twenties and thirties as a rich East Side, private-school kid, then a fabled charmer (he was a terrific dancer) and early devotée of the city's parties and pleasures.

There was an Astaire-like deftness and sense of style that went into the Botsford editings, which were applied swiftly with a fine-point mechanical pencil. His pleased expression and the fresh light that had entered your leaner and smarter paragraphs lifted you both, and you walked unhurriedly down the narrow avenue together and turned the corner to the next page. Often a writer—this writer, for one—couldn't quite remember what had disappeared from his text, or find where the scalpel had been slipped in. "Well, yes," Gardner would say, happy with the compliment. "A nice piece and let's enjoy it." Another long-term contributor, Mark Singer, recalls an early Talk piece of his that had grown miraculously stronger after a trip across Botsford's desk but had lost its significant, irreplaceable ending: "I went in ready to do battle, but he just gave me that smile and said, 'Too much is too much.' I try to keep that in mind."

Tall and bald, with a straight back, Botsford wore his beautiful tweeds inconspicuously. Modesty and courtesy came naturally to him, but he was stuffed with surprises. He graduated from Yale but didn't return for reunions or honors; he mistrusted Old Elis and smiled happily whenever the Yale football team took a licking in a big game. Bores and self-important types were "sashweights" in his lexicon. A lifelong liberal and Democrat, he gave Ronald Reagan's name its original "Reegan" pronunciation if it had to be spoken. Women he liked were called "dearie" and trusted male friends "Old Cock." He beamed at the approach of an icy martini or a lowdown joke—he was an appreciator above all—and conversations at the Botsfords'

apartment or their deeply porched hilltop house in the
Berkshires wound their way trustingly into the night. His
laughter was world-class, a collapse into wheezings and gasp-
ings and table poundings: nothing held back.

He was cool in both senses of the word. "He crackled,"
in the phrase of Alastair Reid. Another old pal, Charles Mc-
Grath, recalls a summer when he and his wife, young and
short of cash, and with a new baby, were presented with the
Botsford cabin, on a lake in Putnam County, for a couple
of weeks at no charge. Maybe Gardner and Janet were rent-
ing my summer cottage in Maine just then—the time I returned to find a sheet of paper in my old Underwood
upright, with the nicely spaced message "The Instrument of
the Immortals. Write, Anatole, write—all France is waiting." Botsford or maybe Voltaire—there was no difference.

We thought we knew him, but then two years ago, well
into his eighties, he produced a trim, unweepy memoir, *A
Life of Privilege, Mostly,* which told us how much he had
been keeping to himself. Who could have guessed that he
was such a graceful and agile writer, for starters? He had
been a rich kid, yes, but who knew about the five live-in
servants there at 151 East Seventy-fourth Street, or the runaway trip around the world that he and another playboy
college friend had managed, just before the war put an end
to such jaunts? He became an infantry officer in Europe
after that, but who else would have kept quiet about his intelligence mission (he spoke perfect French) to make contact with a key member of the Resistance a day or two after
his own landing at Omaha Beach, or his capture of a valuable collaborator spy? None of this inconspicuous gallantry

is dwelt upon, any more than his two serious wounds, his Bronze Star and Croix de Guerre and five campaign stars, or the moment he found himself face down in the snow at the time of the deadly Battle of the Bulge, with an enormous tank of unknown provenance pausing above him in the darkness. The fun of it gets more space—an AWOL sojourn in Paris in the wild first week of Liberation, and later the appreciations of peacetime and his early days as the Sunday-night man at the magazine, closing the late Cinema and Theatre columns and the Letters from London and Paris. He grows up in the book, without regret, and it finishes with a meticulous sad accounting of the late tenure of William Shawn. What I go back to in my own copy of Gardner's book is a little gallery of photographs in the middle pages, where so many old friends of mine and his— Shawn, Joe Liebling, Maeve Brennan, Janet Flanner, Mollie Panter-Downes, and the eloquently calm Janet Malcolm, each a different kind of genius—regard me from the page but are now joined, and in my mind almost more clearly— by our man Gardner.

Here Below

On a spring Sunday a couple of years ago Carol and I drove out to the Palisades Cemetery, which I hadn't visited in forty years. The place was harder to find than I'd expected, and we had to ask for help at the back door of one of a row of wooden houses that ends with an antique store on the corner of Route 9W. Redirected, we poked our way up a little private driveway and then through some tall shrubs to find the graveyard. It was a quiet, foggy morning, and once there I felt as if we'd walked into a green and gray room furnished with leaning stones. Many had surfaces thickened with lichen and decay, where inscriptions had become indistinct, with some words missing. It was like a half-heard conversation. There were rusty iron chains lying on the long grass here and there, and fenced-off small enclosures that you could reach only by opening a stiff little gate. Early lilacs were in bloom and there was intense spring birdsong all around us. (When you visit a cemetery the stage effects arrive without effort.) Some of the hundred-odd stones dated back to the eighteenth century, but in among them I found some bygone friends of mine, including Bentz and Kitty Plagemann. There were long-ago Snedenses as well. Palisades is a village on top of the steep west bank of the Hudson, about twenty miles above New York City, and Snedens Landing lies off a narrow, twisting road that leads down to the river.

Now, near the western fringe of bushes in the cemetery, Carol found one of the markers we were looking for: a tipping-forward silvery granite oblong, with the letters fading into invisibility. With effort—and a few impromptu rubbings done with a pencil and a scrap of notebook paper—we made out

ISAAC D. TALLMAN

ENGINEER
Was killed on the N.Y. & E. RR
While running the night express
ENGINE NO. 97
Caused by a rock laying on the track
April 11, 1855
Aged 30 years, 3 months
and 26 days

There were a couple of vanished lines, and then, near the bottom, in small italics:

No more to make the engine rattle
No more to sound the shrill whistle

Another eloquent marker nearby was a tall and faded pinkish-brown slab—perhaps it's brownstone—with a scalloped top and the pleasing old willow-tree-and-stone-urn drawing, barely visible here, that you find in this part of the country. Care and money had gone into its making, and pain, as well:

DANIEL POST

Who died July 22ᵈ, 1814
aged 52 years.
A pale conſumption gave the fatal blow!
The ſtroke was certain, but the effect was ſlow,
With wafting pain death found me long opreſs'd
Pityed my ſighs, & kindly brought me reſt.

We looked about for another favorite of mine, but decades of acid rain had smudged away its name, leaving the decedent anonymous. The stone, as I recall, once presented the name and dates of a departed lady—perhaps another one of the local Posts—who had succumbed around the turn of the old century, with a closing *"Who died of epilepsy* in her sixty-first year."* At first glance the asterisk looked decorative or accidental, but at the bottom of the stone it was repeated, in footnote fashion, and the medical slur corrected: ** apoplexy.*

A few weeks later Carol and I headed up to the Berkshires to visit friends and on the way decided to make a further swing to the north and pay a call at the Stockbridge, Massachusetts, cemetery. It's an impressive place, still almost the main event in town. We'd walked around here before, when one of my daughters was attending a nearby boarding school, and had come to know some family graves, including that of John Sergeant, a multi-great-grandfather of mine, on my mother's side, who had come to this area as a missionary to the Mahican Indians in 1728. He was the first settler of Stockbridge. I own a tall Queen Anne secretary of his, part of a striking four-piece set in gleaming cherry—he married money—now scattered among my closer relatives. He is said to have sat at the secretary while he wrote his weekly sermons in the language of the Stockbridge tribe.

It was the Fourth of July, a blazing-hot summer's day, and Carol and I and our fox terrier, Harry, were the only visitors. We kept losing our bearings among the rows and neighborhoods of graves and surrounding tall firs. The young dog, white against the green grass, cast eagerly about, keeping a steady pull on his leash and panting in the heat. There was a small house almost within the confines, with a back fence adjoining some of the oldest graves. A woman sitting in the yard asked us if Harry wouldn't like some water, and brought out a big metal cooking vessel, filled almost to the brim, which he lapped up noisily, with his forelegs in the pot. When she and Carol began talking she said, "When people asked why we lived right here, so close to the cemetery this way, my father always said, 'It's not who's outside who matters, it's who's in.'"

The John Sergeant gravestone—it's pronounced "Surgeant" in the family but "Sargent" locally—had once been elevated, lying flat on four legs like a pool table, but thanks to our informant we knew to look for it now at ground level. The raised stone had been tottering, she'd said, and had lately been repositioned:

HERE LYES
the body of the
Rev^d Mr.
John Sergeant who dy'd
the 27th Day of July AD 1749
In the 40th year of his Age

The monument has a long extolling verse below this, with a joke—a joke back then, at least—at the end:

Here's not a Sergeant's body or a Sergeant's MIND
I'll ſeek him hence for all's alike
Deception here
I'll go to Heav'n, & I ſhall find my Sergeant there

There was a scattering of later Sergeants nearby— Sewall and Erastus and George—dating on into the nineteenth century, all of them recently cleaned to a startling and elegant white.

What we had come this distance to see once again, however, was not a family marker, and though I thought I knew its shape and location, not far from the roadside stone wall, it kept eluding me. Hot and out of patience, I said, "I give up—it's got to be around here somewhere," when my gaze went down again and there it was, bang at my feet, and almost exactly as remembered:

Erected to the Memory
of Solomon Glezen jr
who, made Prsoner by the
Insurgents, fell at the Battle in Sheffield Feb 27th
1786, in the 26th year of
his age

Oh for a lodge in some vaft wilderness
Some boundless contiguity of Shade,
Where rumor of oppression & deceit,
Of unsuccessful or successful War,
Might never reach us more.

All this was carved in a modest lowercase. I had written down the poem when I first found it, years ago, and its
elegance and startlingly modern and apposite thought
quickly imposed itself in my memory. The verse—this
took a while to find—is from a much longer poem, "The
Task," by William Cowper, a British poet long out of fashion. Somehow I'd convinced myself that Glezen was a
British officer who'd died in captivity during the Revolu-
tion, but the date of his death didn't match up. That same
night, I mentioned this puzzle to Gardner Botsford, the
friend (along with his wife, Janet) we'd come to visit in
South Egremont, and he instantly said, "It was Shays Re-
bellion that got him. There was a firefight in Sheffield, and
a lot of local men and boys got killed." Daniel Shays led
a brief and doomed uprising of local farmers, swiftly put

down by the militia. The armed dissidents had been enraged by economic conditions imposed by the lawyers and
merchants of coastal Massachusetts: an argument perhaps
not quite sufficient to die for, as Glezen's little editorial reminds us.

I am not a churchgoer or a stone-rubber, but over the
years I've logged a surprising number of hours at Père-
Lachaise, in Paris; at Hollywood, rising sweetly beside the
James River in Richmond, Virginia, where the old soldiers'
graves, once tended by the Daughters of the Confederacy,
were badly in need of mowing; or at Woodlawn Cemetery,
a No. 4 Lexington Avenue express subway ride away from
me in the Bronx, which offers hilltop stands of enormous
trees and a nice range of urban housing, from Jay Gould's
massive Grecian temple to Fiorello LaGuardia's wayside
nook, which befits his stature better than his grand contri-
butions to our city. I have also called at Hope Cemetery, in
Barre, Vermont, where generations of stonecutters from the
local granite works have left memorials celebrating their
worldly preoccupations—a soccer ball, a racing car, a tilt-
ing biplane, and an armchair. Here also is that much-
photographed life-sized double bed, wherein a couple sits
stiffly up hand in hand above the granite percales, he in his
breakfast wrapper and she in a chaste negligee: a celebra-
tion of eternal fidelity barely marred by the fact that the
widower (who'd ordered the monument) later married
somebody else. Nor can I forget the churchyard gravestone
I was guided to in East Haddam, Connecticut—an ancient
news extra saying goodbye to a parishioner who walked out

into the sunshine after Sunday services a century or two before and was struck dead by the falling clapper of the steeple bell. There's an inexorable secular echo here in the diner who strolled out of Le Pavillon, on East Fifty-seventh Street, after lunch (this was in the sixties), and was terminally conked by a dumbbell accidentally nudged off a high windowsill by a maid of the television celebrity Arlene Francis. No last words were taken from the victim, but Le Pavillon was a five-star eatery, and it's always been my guess that his last nanosecond of consciousness may have produced the thought You should have passed up the profiteroles.

Two or three times each summer I pay a call on my own future retirement home, in the Brooklin, Maine, Cemetery. Brooklin, with a population of eight hundred, has ten graveyards, the most beautiful of which, the Naskeag Cemetery, sits across the road from the gemlike Beth Eden Chapel. Most of the others are half-forgotten family plots, containing Babsons and Freetheys who go back to Revolutionary days. The Brooklin Cemetery has a more purposeful, everyday air, and lies in the middle of town, which is to say across Route 175 from the First Baptist Church, and a hundred yards or so north of the Brooklin General Store and the Friend Memorial Library. The front sector, close to the road, holds the older stones, going back to the late eighteenth century: skinny marble or granite markers now weathered to seagull white. Later graves illustrate current options in the memorial line: pink or oatmeal granites, and thick, low slabs offering smooth façades with roughened tops, like weathered roofing. There are floral and religious motifs, and, just lately, darker blocks faced with what look like color engravings, running to seascapes and lighthouses, beside the names of the departed. Fifteen years ago, Carol and I met here with the friendly cemetery representative (a sign on his pickup truck advertised his other line of work, taxidermy) and for two hundred and twenty dollars signed on for a nice double, close to an oak tree in the northeast corner.

"That's—uh, per year?" I asked.

"No, that's the whole of it," he said.

What we visit here, to be sure, is not just our own plot, now marked off with green metal tabs, but my mother and stepfather's graves, a couple of yards to the east, and also, close at hand, that of my brother Joe, who died in 1997. The oak tree was planted by Andy White when my mother died, in 1977, and it has thrived. Mother, a passionate gardener, would appreciate its flecked shade and those festive three- or four-leaf sprigs that oaks let drop during a windstorm. I think she would also put up with the little memorial piles of stones and mussel shells, faded bunches of wildflowers, or plastic pigs that visiting-pilgrim readers of *Charlotte's Web* or *The Elements of Style* keep putting down in front of Andy's grave, though she'd want them cleared away the next morning. Similar symbols of respect get dropped off at Joe's grave by people who loved his boat designs. What would drive her batty, though, and (if it were possible) would result in a three- or four-page typed letter to me or someone else in the family, laying out this fresh problem—"appalling problem," in her words—and its possible solutions, with afterthoughts scribbled at the end and up the sides of the page in pencil, is the slovenly state of the two stones: hers and Andy's. Sad and bereft after she died, he'd picked a mournful charcoal-gray slate for her marker, which was matched eight years later by his own glum replica next door. The gravestones are mid-sized, with a classic curve along the top and elegant shoulders, but the years have demonstrated that slate—or this slate, at least—ages poorly. A corrective metal sheath or splint now covers the top of both slabs, to check the fine cracks that have appeared along the sides and front. The fading slate, now silvered to a happier tone, has almost smoothed away the names and dates. Soon the Whites' wish for privacy, well known to everyone in town, will be complete.

Mother's gravestone was the first decision of any magnitude Andy had to take on without her. With the help of an art-director friend of mine, Hank Brennan, he settled on a subtle English style called Centaur for her stone's elegant, slightly flared type face—KATHARINE SERGEANT WHITE in three separate lines; then a single small design, more a plus sign than a cross; and then her dates, 1892–1977, below. If, as seems likely, Andy wondered about her reaction, he might almost have heard her response here: "Well, perhaps, but are we sure about the capitals? Do you think of me as a capitals sort of person?"

Design and arrangement had always fallen to her in their forty-nine-year marriage, and her Olympic-scale worrying would have briskly taken on the darkness of the slate had she still been around. She would have set her mind to finding out everything about the durability and legibility of slate, as against granite and marble and limestone and porphyry: her letter to me would instruct me to consult somebody in *The New Yorker*'s checking department about all this, with a backup verifying conversation with Joe Mitchell, who'd written about graveyards so well. There was also the question of site. The spot Andy had picked out was way in the back of the Brooklin Cemetery, close to the woods and so many yards removed from the nearest existing graves that Mother's lone stone, when first put up, reminded me of the mystery slab in "2001: A Space Odyssey." Andy's adjacent 1985 grave and the subsequent natural proliferation of Brooklin deads have done away with this distracting idea. The only provision about her burial that Mother left was that there were to be no prayers or Bible readings of any sort. But if, as seems possible, Mother and Andy did actually talk about the standoffish gravesite at some point, I can unhesitatingly provide her train of thought: *We don't want anyone in town to think that we're snobbish or distant, or that, good heavens, we want to* hide. *We've lived here a long time and we have friends who are buried here, but this is their cemetery, not ours, and we wouldn't want people thinking that we're taking up space in the middle of things because we want to be accepted in ways that we're not—that now we're one of them and not From Away—just because I'm gone. This way we're showing respect. But will they understand?*

William Maxwell once told me that one of the great mercies we are provided with is that within a few months after someone close to us has died the vision of him in sickness or great age is replaced with a much younger memory of that same parent or husband or friend, now seen at his youthful best. I thanked Maxwell for this wisdom and later passed it on unhesitatingly to others, in letters of condolence, but now I'm not so sure. Most memories of my mother are affectionate and cheerful, but still center on the bottomless worries and overthoughts that descended on her late in her life. And not always so late, come to think of it. Last summer, my nephew Jonathan Stableford, who is now close to sixty, unexpectedly told me about the time he'd competed in a Fourth of July footrace in Brooklin at the age of ten or eleven. Brooklin always puts on a parade up Route 175 on the morning of the Fourth, and later celebrations at the nearby town green, but back then the road that branches off from the Williams General Store toward Naskeag Point would be closed off for athletic events. Jon entered the Boys Twelve-and-Under 100-Yard Dash and won it, collecting a prize of thirty-five cents. He was headed for the candy counter inside Williams' when his grandmother appeared, gave him a congratulatory hug (well, sort of), and put her foot down when she heard the plans for his loot. "This is town money," she explained. "It's not exactly ours. You'll understand this some day." And in no time she'd persuaded him to donate the thirty-five cents to the Library, across the street.

I groaned and laughed when I heard this tale, which so perfectly summed up Mother's noble sense of duty and her terrible—no, appalling—judgment about kids. For her a fistful of candy never had a chance against the complicated right thing. She loved us all, anxiously and bemusedly, but forgot to hand out kisses because we were great runners or really good-looking or the smartest kid on the block. Stuff like that went without saying, only she never said it.

Nancy Franklin, in a remarkable piece about my mother in *The New Yorker* in 1995 (she'd never met her), wrote, "It's funny; as an editor she was maternal but as a mother she was editorial." This made me laugh, not cry, and it has come to me over time that my own way of loving her was often simply to try to cheer her up. Despite Maxwell, I don't envision her much at a younger best—slim and stylish at lunch with me in Schrafft's, around the corner from her office, in 1928, say—but instead find her sitting at the head of the dining-room table in North Brooklin, in her seventies, with her elbow on the table and her head wearily resting in one hand while she eats. Andy is at the other end, and Carol and John Henry and I—or maybe this is earlier, with my two daughters there, instead—in our usual places. Callie and Alice, burnished with their sailing suntans, are wearing skirts instead of shorts, for Grandma. It's our customary last dinner together before we Angells head back to New York at the end of another vacation. Andy's martinis have brushed aside the sad import of the occasion for the moment, and he is regaling us with the latest neurotic doings of his Norfolk terrier Jones. Late-August sunlight falls into the room, competing with the table candles, and the usual homemade mint sauce and homemade piccalilli are in their usual silver dishes. Mother smiles and sighs and picks at her roast potato, and, watching her, I try to imagine which of her immediate deep concerns is topmost at the moment: whether the blue Chinese willow-pattern vegetable dish on the mantel behind her should be left to Alice, as written on her current and endlessly rewritten twelve-page adjunct-to-her-will list, or, for some complex reason, to Callie or perhaps to another granddaughter altogether, Kitty Stableford; how many of her nine grandchildren attended or ever will attend a school or college where they would get to learn their way around not just *Middlemarch* but *Cranford*, too; why the cosmos, some blossoms of which are in the arrangement she's put together this afternoon in the copper vase in the far-left corner of the living room, has been looking so leggy of late and whether the northwest bed, where the cosmos are, doesn't need a wholesale cleanout and replanting this fall; whether Jean Stafford, the widow of Joe Liebling, was drunk again when she called last night or in the grip of something more dire; whether Edith Candage, in the kitchen, has remembered to get the dessert Floating Island egg white whipped to a proper firmness; whether poor Catherine Allen's failing eyesight will keep her from laundering and ironing these organdy curtains, come spring, and, if not, who in the world can be found to replace her; whether Joe, away at the moment on a cruise east to the Bras d'Or in his cutter *Northern Crown*, may encounter the tropical depression in the Caribbean mentioned on the radio tonight, on his way home; whether Roger, never as lean as his father Ernest, hasn't picked up a bit of weight over this vacation with too much beer and too many lobsters and may be overloading his heart; why Ernest made me carry that enormous frying pan around my neck on our 1915 honeymoon camping trip, and so perhaps beginning the back troubles that have been killing me ever since; whether Vladimir Nabokov doesn't still have a couple of pieces of short fiction in him for the magazine, and whether the current fiction department is still regularly in touch with him and Vera, and how long has it been since I've had a letter, one of those "V.N." specials, from him; who that new person in checking is who last week crazily circled a phrase of Andy's on a galley and wrote "zeugma?" in the margin; whether Milton Greenstein will call us back tomorrow about the estimated September tax figures we've mailed him, and about Shawn's concerns about the paperback of the appalling Gill book; and isn't it time for seconds? She puts down her fork and lights up a filtered Benson & Hedges.

What can I say? Looking at Mother, I suddenly remember the line "In the absence of faith, indecision is the mind's great stay against death," which I've happened upon again just lately in some book. It's by a French writer, Benjamin Constant, and now I suddenly want to relay it to her, here at the dinner table, because it so perfectly applies to her. But then I think better of it. Mother doesn't talk about death or really think about it, ever, and it won't exactly make her laugh in the first place. So I turn and say, "Did you hear about Carol's idea for a name for our house here, out on the point? The kind of thing we'd put on the side of our station wagon, if we had a station wagon?"

"You're putting a name on your station wagon?" Mother says in alarm.

"No, no," I say. "Try to pay attention. This is a joke. She wants to call it 'Beside the Point.'"

Andy doubles over, laughing into his napkin, and my mother, smiling and radiantly herself, shakes her head and begins to laugh, too.

Jake

THE only piece of advice I ever got from William Shawn
was something he said to me in 1956, in my very first week
as an editor at the magazine. "It's no great trick," he said,
"to edit a piece of fiction and turn it into the greatest story
ever written. Anyone can do that. It's much harder to take
a story and help that writer turn it into the best thing he
is capable of this week or this month." I've tried to keep
that in mind. What you hope for is that the writer will sense
how this process works, and will learn to trust it. Sometimes, though rarely, this can happen almost at once, with
a writer you've never met before, and when it does you remember it. One such meeting came early in 1976, after I
read a manuscript called *O'Phelan's Daemonium,* by a writer
I didn't know named John F. Murray. In the first sentence
of the story we learn that the narrator, a man called
O'Phelan, has tried to blow his brains out with a .16-gauge
shotgun but has succeeded only in messily grazing his fore-

head. O'Phelan is middle-aged, and in his words, "an epi-
sodic paranoiac schizophrenic. Also manic depressive, also
alcoholic." His brother, Martin, a well-to-do broker and
apparently his self-appointed minder or keeper, meets him
at the Islip Airport, on Long Island, and puts him on a
plane to Boston, where he is to enter "St. Hogarth's Clinic,"
for treatment. In real life, this is McLean's. O'Phelan gets
himself there, though unwillingly, since he has been through
this many times. "No need to show me around," he says,
"I've been here before."

The story unfolds quickly. In the clinic, we meet patients of every description—lawyers, children, shoplifters,
securities analysts—all of them traumatized or drugged or
despondent or crazily cheerful. Many have forgotten who
they are. There are staff doctors and mental health special-
ists, of course, but no one knows quite what to do with
O'Phelan this time around. On the way to keep an appointment at Mass General, he slips away from his atten-
dant and goes to the Ritz Bar, where he begins to drink
vodka. He calls a cab driver he has encountered, a man who
also has a pilot's license, and arranges to have himself flown
back to New York. In the city again, he goes to the apartment of a woman friend of his, called Lady Jane, and soon
after he arrives there's a pounding on the door, and he
knows that it's Martin, Martin his brother, there to take
him back and start the whole thing over again.

There's much more—events unfold at breakneck
speed—but what holds a reader is the story's unique style and
spirit. It's depressing but also funny and surprising. You learn
hopeless and frightening things about the narrator and his

plight, and you sense that he is both desperate and exhilarated. There is something stylish about him, almost jaunty. It's a hell of a story—one that stays with you.

We decided to buy this, of course, and to work with the writer on some necessary editing—it needed cuts and clarifications all the way along—but when I called the agent with the news, she seemed startled. "You're taking something by *Jake Murray?*" she said. I made a date for Murray to come in to the office and see me. When the moment arrived, I went out to the twentieth-floor reception room and found a tall, thin, shabby man with some missing teeth and a huge bandage over one side of his forehead. He was wearing an ancient orange parka, with rust-colored bloodstains all over it. "I'm Jake," he said, watching my expression. "It's all true."

What was also true was that Jake was an ideal writer to work with. We talked over the manuscript in some detail, and he agreed to take it back and work on some sections and passages, and bring it back in a week or two. When it came back, very quickly, he not only had fixed the rough places but had taken a few suggestions of mine and turned them into something much better. The story had taken on fresh life. He was excited and pleased, and so was I. The process had worked. The story went into galleys, and he took these back, after we'd met again, and made the same kind of sharpenings and smoothing he'd done before. The man was a pro.

I had learned a little more about him. John F. Murray belonged to a large and distinguished Catholic family from the South Shore of Long Island. They were society people, and there was plenty of money there. Sometimes the Murrays had been compared with the Kennedys. Jake Murray was one of seven children. He had gone to Yale and served overseas in the Second World War. He had written a novel, *The Devil Walks on Water*, I now remembered—it's about the monster New England hurricane of 1938—which received enthusiastic reviews. He had also been a successful copywriter and executive with some top-level advertising companies, and he'd been married three times. He had three children.

When I got to meet him Murray was down on his luck, and almost down and out. I'm not sure I ever passed an hour with him when he wasn't drunk or getting over being drunk. Early on, he asked for an advance on our payment for the story, and I was able to get him a check for two hundred dollars. When he came back the next morning, it was gone—he told me he had been robbed. But I'd been warned that this would happen. I'd had a call from a brother of his, Tom Murray, a stockbroker, who asked if we would please not give Jake any more cash; just send the rest of the money to the agent. In the story, O'Phelan's broker brother is called "the hateful Martin," but Tom Murray, I found, was the opposite. He was a sweet man. He seemed to know where Jake was every day, and he had set up a network of friends and cops and bartenders who kept an eye out for him. There was a powerful strain of attachment among the Murrays, I began to realize after a conversation about Jake I had with his sister Jeanne (an old acquaintance of mine), who told me that late one Christmas Eve she'd had to call the Southampton Police Department to come over and get her brother, who was carrying on noisily under her windows. The next morning, Christmas, she turned up early at the jail and bailed him out. She told this with laughter, and Jake laughed, too, when I mentioned it to him. "Just like her," he said. But no one was happier about the story the magazine had bought than Tom, or more proud of what his troubled brother had managed to do.

The story ran that spring, and was much admired and talked about. There was a flurry of mail from readers, and inquiries from publishers. Everyone at the magazine was delighted, Shawn above all. I'd brought Jake in to meet him, and they talked about more stories up ahead. We'd found a new writer, and there was no telling what would happen next.

Nothing happened until the following January, when another manuscript came in from Jake. It was called *O'Phelan Drinking*, and turned out to be a direct continuation of the first one. I was disheartened—how could he expect to do this all over again—but when I'd reread it I saw that it was written with more confidence than the first one and that there was more to it. Picking up the first story, it takes our man to "St. Justin's Hospital" in the Village, for alcoholic rehab—to St. Vincent's, that is—where once again O'Phelan knows the ropes and remembers the doctors. The patients and their dilemmas are done with greater skill this time—it's riveting but appalling to meet them. Again, the tone is strong and certain, but there is much more feeling. There's a sustained flashback in which O'Phelan picks up his young children at their mother's house in Connecticut—the family has busted up—and takes them on a vacation to Nantucket. He holds things together, just barely, and delivers them home again. Every moment for him has become risky and terrifying. O'Phelan wakes up in the hospital again, and later that day, when he slips out of an A.A. meeting in the Village and buys a pint of 100 proof Smirnoff, you want to cry out "Stop—my God, don't do that!" But you also understand the calm that O'Phelan finds in the booze, and the sense of order it restores.

When Jake Murray came into the office this time, he looked worse than before, and there were fewer traces of his old élan. He was looking forward to our sitting down again and going through the editing process, so he was disappointed when I told him that this would have to be put off for a couple of weeks. We were in a busy time of year, and I was swamped with other stories and writers. I'd call him in a couple of weeks, the first chance I got. But Jake didn't want this pause. Some days when I came to work or back from lunch, he'd be sitting there in the reception room, waiting for me. Other times he turned up late in the afternoon. One morning when I came in early, around seven-thirty, I found him there, asleep, with his old work boots sitting side by side on the next chair. Wait a couple of weeks, I begged him when he woke up. But he was back that same afternoon, and in bad shape. Shawn and I conferred, and agreed to do nothing. It was January, full winter, and we didn't know if Jake had anyplace to go. Tom Murray said that he'd take him off our hands, but he was back again in a day or two, and noisy. Shawn called me in and said he was sorry, but this had to stop. The receptionists were getting upset, and there were other visitors to think about.

When I went out and gave Jake this news, he grew stubborn. "I'm a staff member and I demand to see Mr. Shawn," he said.

"You're not a staff member, Jake," I said. "You're a trusted contributor, and you can't see him right now. Come back when I'm done with my other stuff, and we'll do the story together."

"I just want a place to hunker down," he said,

"You can't hunker here," I said.

He stood up and looked at me. "This is it?" he said.

"This is it, Jake," I said. "See you soon."

He shook my hand and gave me one of his extraordinary smiles. "Roger, goodbye," he said.

As far as I know, I was the last person who knew him to see him alive. Some time that day or the next day, he went into the river. Tom called me later in the week and told me how worried he was. "He always lets me know where he is," he said. But no word came, and when it became clear what had happened Tom came to see me, and told me, at length, not to blame myself. "This was inevitable," he said. "It's been coming for a long, long time."

John Murray's body reappeared in the spring, and a few days later there was a service for him at St. Thomas More, that trim little church on East 89th Street. Tom spoke and told us how much he'd admired and loved Jake all these years—the older brother who was always smarter in school and a better athlete, and better with girls. He also mentioned the magazine, and said that Jake's experience with *The New Yorker* had been the best news for him in many years. It was springtime and the service was crowded, and there was a sense of joy to it.

A few weeks later, I consulted with Tom Murray, and met with Jake's children, Matt and Jeff, who were still in their teens, and consulted their older sister, Melinda, by telephone, and together we talked about *O'Phelan Drinking* and how he might have made the fixes that the story needed. It came out in October—another smash hit—with no mention of what had happened to the author. This good-sized excerpt arrives about halfway through the story—the flashback of O'Phelan's, mentioned above, which comes to him at a time when he's in residence in the awful rehab center. The children's names, it will be noticed, were not fictionalized.

That night, in my room, I must have dreamed about Nantucket, because I woke up while it was still dark and found that I was thinking about 'Sconset. Years ago, when I was in the advertising business, I lived in a house in Darien, with my first wife and my three children. But my wife divorced me and took the house and got my insurance policies and whatever alimony payments I managed to keep up with. She did not, however, take my children; my children could see me freely, and I could take them on vacations. One summer, I rented a house on Nantucket for two weeks, and I was determined that the children and I would go there and have a good time. I was anxious to be with them, because I had been in a big hospital up in Westchester, from which I escaped and to which I had been returned, and I hadn't seen them in months.

The day came, and I drove to Darien, to my old house, where my kids were waiting for me. Melinda was sixteen then, and Jeff was fourteen, and Matt was nine. Matt was very excited about our vacation. We packed the kids' things into the Volkswagen, and I distributed them inside, and we made for the ferry at Woods Hole. Halfway up the Connecticut Turnpike, I slowed the car and pulled over to the shoulder of the road. Jeff was sick. I let him out, and a state trooper pulled up behind us. I almost started up the car again, because I had been hiding from the police when I escaped from the mental hospital. But the trooper said, Do you need any help, and I said no, just a small emergency, thank you very much. He tipped his hat and drove on. Jeff got back in the car and we drove to Woods Hole in time to pick up our reservation for the afternoon boat to Nantucket.

It was a pleasant trip. We sat in deck chairs on the foredeck listening to a conversation at the rail between two lawyers, one young and one old, who were discussing some mutual friends who had spent part of the summer at Westhampton Beach. The young lawyer was saying that he did not like people who went to Westhampton Beach, and he wondered why his friends had gone there. The old lawyer simply shrugged, but Melinda and I decided that although *he probably felt the same way as the young lawyer did about Westhampton, he did not think it was something you went around saying.*

We arrived in Nantucket as the sun was going down, and drove to 'Sconset, across the island. Our house looked like a boat and lay very near the beach, and when we had unpacked we went outside and played with a Frisbee. We had eaten on the boat and we weren't very hungry for dinner, so we came back inside and I broke open a deck of cards, and I taught my children the game of crazy eights, which I had learned at the hospital in Westchester. They loved it. We played for a long time. Then they got sleepy and went to their rooms.

When I had kissed them good night and closed their doors, I went to the kitchen and suddenly felt very lonely. I missed my girlfriend—my girlfriend then—whose name was Lucinda, and I missed a girl at the hospital named Peggy, and I even missed my first wife, who had come with us on those jaunts in the past. I did not really need a drink, but I made one anyway. I made a rum and Coke. It tasted good but made me nervous, drinking it so soon after the hospital and daily doses of Thorazine. I poured the rest of it down the sink and then I went to bed.

The next day, the kids rode their bikes and swam, and on the following days we visited various beaches, went on picnics, and had a good time. Hummock Pond was our favorite place. Sometimes we cooked out in the evenings and watched the Northeast Airlines

Yellowbirds out over the ocean as they made the turn toward the Nantucket airport. One afternoon, Jeff tried out the Volkswagen and knocked down part of the fence beside the driveway because he got mixed up about the brake and the clutch. I was mad and yelled at all three of the kids, but then we got over it and it was all right again. In the second week, I took out some oil colors and started a painting of our house. Twice, I went to general delivery at the post office to look for mail from Lucinda, but there was none.

One gray afternoon, some people from across the boardwalk dropped in. I knew them all from Connecticut, especially a striking blonde called Isabel Channey—a nice enough woman, I had always thought. Well, there was some sand in my bedroom and in the kids' rooms, and sand in my bed, and all the beds were unmade, and the house had a very casual look about it, and Isabel Channey chewed me out loudly. She told me I was no good and a terrible father. My kids heard her. I took it all, feeling very helpless and ashamed. I had been drunk and crazy, had blown my marriage, and now this. I decided I would not let it ruin the rest of the vacation, but it gnawed at me. When the people finally left, I went in and made myself another rum and Coke and drank all of it, right in front of the kids, and when I was finished I said to them, Don't sweep up and don't make your beds. Then we sat down and played crazy eights.

A few days later, we packed up and left. We felt good. We stopped outside Nantucket town for blueberry pancakes. This had been a farewell breakfast for us for years. The trip back to Darien was easy. I dropped the kids at the house and they helped me unload the stuff. I hugged them goodbye. Then I was off into the night. As I drove down the Hutchinson River Parkway, I had a sudden urge to turn off at the Harrison exit and drive over to the Playland amusement park, where I would buy a bottle of rum and demolish it aboard the roller coaster, screaming wildly and happily with every swoop and turn, and staying aboard until it closed down for the night. But I resisted that temptation and drove on to the city. The next day, I went back to work at the advertising agency, safe and sound.

I think what Jake wanted so badly in those last weeks and days wasn't just publication but the continued risk and adventure of writing, and the orderliness of the editing process. Our brief meetings have stayed firm in my memory, of course, appearing there at times with something like the washed clarity that descends before a sunset. I hope I haven't patronized him by overpraising his work. These are not the best stories ever written. They deal with contemporary forms of suffering—stuff that we all know almost by heart now—but without inflating them to tragedy or explaining them away as case history. The writing has a Hemingway brusqueness, but isn't confessional or self-pitying.

Nor is it particularly intellectual. These are good stories, first-class, and the best that Jake Murray could have done when he wrote them. I have come to the conclusion that he understood this and that he paid us at the magazine a grand compliment by entrusting the rough second manuscript to us, when he saw that it was time at last for him to be moving along.

Hard Lines

ONE of my great-grandfathers, James Shepley, was born in Saco, Maine, in 1826, went to Bowdoin College, graduating in the class of 1846, and set up a law practice in the frontier town of Red Cloud, Minnesota, where he had a hand in the writing of the state constitution. In a small photograph, taken in 1862, he stands with his right foot slightly forward and holds a long horseman's coat in one hand. He has a scruffy beard and is wearing two pistols, military gauntlets, and a dusty tunic and pants perhaps made of canvas. Next to the photograph in its family album, one of my great aunts has written "Father as he appeared in St. Paul after riding two hundred miles through the Indian country to get relief for Fort Abercrombie on the Red River to the North." A bit later, while he was still in his mid-thirties, Shepley won a Civil War commission as an aide to a cousin of his, General George Shepley, but he contracted malaria and was confined for months to a hospital in New Orleans. Back home at last and eager to recover his health, he became a farm manager in Naples, Maine. He and his wife had three children by now, and in 1873, hoping to improve the Shepley fortunes, he bought into a sheep ranch near Fresno, California, and went west with a friend. He planned to bring his family out to join him, once he got settled. One spring night in 1874, while sleeping at a camp at Little Dry Creek, he was murdered—garroted with a piece of wire. Two Portuguese sheepherders were tried for the crime but acquitted; there was no evidence of a robbery or suggestion of some other motive, and the case was dropped. The mystery was never cleared up.

His widow, Mary Barrows Shepley, now abruptly deprived of income, moved to a house in Boston with her children and began taking in boarders. An impoverished gentility was preserved, though just barely, and rescue arrived at last as if from the pages of Jane Austen. One of the boarders, a young businessman named Charles Sergeant, fell in love with the youngest Shepley child—Elizabeth, known as Bessie—and in the spring of 1880, when she turned twenty-three, the two were married. Both of Sergeant's parents had died by the time he was seventeen, and he found himself the sole support for five sisters and a younger brother. A classic self-made man, rising from accountant to a district manager with the Eastern Railroad, he became a vice-president of the West End Street Railway Co.: the Boston El. As the new family prospered, they moved from Winchester, Massachusetts, to suburban Brookline, with their three daughters, the youngest of whom,

Katharine, was my mother. All went well until the spring of 1899, when, on a visit to New York, Bessie Sergeant died of a burst appendix. My mother was six years old when this blow fell, but I never heard her speak of it. Not once. There is a family story, though, that her oldest sister, my Aunt Elsie, who was seventeen at the time, was not permitted to cry at their mother's funeral. Elsie went on to graduate from Bryn Mawr, and to become a bluestocking and a respected author, but nothing came easily for her. In her twenties, she was confined for a time in a mental hospital in Paris, and then in an asylum in Zurich, where she was treated by Carl Jung.

As I've written, my father, Ernest Angell, lost his father at the age of nine, in a marine disaster, the 1898 sinking of the French liner La Bourgogne, in a night collision near Sable Island. He and my mother married young, had two children, and were divorced in 1929, when I was eight. One explanation for the divorce was that my father, who went to France in 1917 with the A.E.F. as a counter-intelligence officer—he spoke French and some German—adopted a Gallic view of marriage and was repeatedly unfaithful to my mother after he came home. Another was that my mother had fallen in love with E. B. White, a colleague of hers at *The New Yorker*, where she was an editor. She always insisted that there was no connection between her divorce and their marriage, which came three months after her return from Reno. Whatever. What can be said for sure is that each of my parents grew up with a critically missing parent—she a mother, he a father—and pretty much had to fake it in these roles with their own kids. They worked at this all their lives, though it sometimes pissed you off or broke your heart (choose one) to watch them.

The day my mother told me about the divorce, she took me for a walk to the waterfall at Snedens Landing, where we went in the summer. The waterfall is still there— a brook splashing down over steep-sided ledges and into a dark pool a few yards west of the gliding Hudson. I loved the narrow woodland path down to the pool—I'd learned how to swim there—and it was a kick to have my mother to myself on that day. On our way back, she summoned her courage and sat us down on the steps of an empty Victorian house, the Lawrence place, to deliver her news. I remember the look of the overgrown lawn and our knees oddly in a row, there on the porch steps. I did pretty well until she told me that Nancy and I would still be living at our house on Ninety-third Street with our father, but she wouldn't. She'd still see us a lot, practically all the time, on weekends and vacations. "No, no, I want to stay with you!" I said indignantly. "I'll come, too. Nancy can stay with Father—I don't mind."

Memory is fiction—an anecdotal version of some scene or past event we need to store away for present or future use. John McCrone, a British science correspondent, writing in a recent issue of the *Times Literary Supplement,* calls memories "cognitive reconstructions," and goes on to say that our brains, though not well evolved for retrospection or contemplation, never give up a reshuffling process in their effort to extract what is general and what is particular about each passing moment of life. Garry Wills, in his book *Saint Augustine's Memory*, writes, "The past...is not an inert structure in which we can deposit a remembered item to remain unchanged until called up again....In fact, what is being recalled is the experience that a person underwent in acquiring anything to be remembered." But when do we get to throw away the piercing announcement, the over-contemplated morsel of bad news? A few weeks after my parents split up, I was with my mother on the echoing main concourse of Grand Central when Father appeared, rushing up to us with a newspaper under his arm and sliding like a boy across the last few feet of the shiny floor. "Sorry I'm late," he said. He was soon grave again, and I went off with him, as arranged. My sister, Nancy, would not have approved of this playful moment, which I had seized upon as a sign that our parents still liked each other after all. She was less forgiving about what had befallen us, and after she got married and had kids of her own she became a serious Episcopalian, of all things. My father never got over Mother going off the way she did, and still woke up brooding about it through his sixties and seventies and eighties, despite his long second marriage and full-house second family. The divorce never grew stale to him.

While I was in my thirties and still in my first marriage, another memory of me with my mother came back repeatedly. In this dream or scene, I am a small child who has awakened in the night with an upset stomach—this is in our first Snedens house—and when Mother appears in response to my cries she snatches me up and carries me to the tiny bathroom under the stairs, to throw up. This came back again and again, haunting me, until a reliable shrink asked, "And how often did your mother hold you in her arms back then?" Then it stopped. Nobody in our family was much of a hugger, to tell the truth, Mother least of all. Instead, she worried about us, and about everything. She became a world-class worrier in the end, and probably even worried about her low hugging marks, along the way.

Loss is the common currency of family tales—who doesn't have a sad ancestor or a stopped child to tell about?—but it isn't talked about much, out of respect for others, whose news, come to think of it, is probably worse than our own. "Get over it!" is the cry I hear lately in conversations about some mopey pal or once happy couple, by which we mean shut up about it, give us a break. My grandfather Charles Sergeant, a stooped, sweetly polite man, painted oil landscapes in his old age, standing before his easel in tweeds, with an incessant ash hovering on the tip of his Chesterfield. He could not have forgotten his early orphaning or the sudden loss of his young wife, but he never got around to such matters at the dinner table. I am his age now, and find myself wondering what he thought about late at night in his bedroom, or in the unexpected moment when his gaze lifted from the sunlit cove or difficult oak he wished to capture on his little canvas. I could also jump back a good deal farther here and speculate in similar fashion about Captain John Sheple (as the name was then spelled), the murdered James Shepley's great-great-great-grandfather, who at seventeen was captured by the Abenaki Indians on July 27, 1694, in a raid on Groton, Massachusetts. He was one survivor of a massacre—it was an early skirmish in the French and Indian Wars—that took twenty-two lives, including those of his parents and his two siblings. After a captivity of more than three years, he returned to his native town, where he married, produced five children, and, in the words of a local historian, "held many offices of trust and responsibility, both civil and ecclesiastical." His memories are not mentioned, and no wonder.

It's my guess that we cling to the harsher bits of the past not just as a warning system to remind us that the next Indian raid or suddenly veering, tower-bound 757 is always waiting but as a passport to connect us to the rest of the world, whose horrors are available each morning and evening on television or in the *Times*. And the cold moment that returns to mind and sticks there, unbidden, may be preferable to the alternative and much longer blank spaces, whole months and years wiped clear of color or conversation. Like it or not, we geezers are not the curators of this unstable repository of trifling or tragic days but only the screenwriters and directors of the latest revival.

Two years ago, I had a telephone call from a woman in her fifties named Cally Field, whose voice I hadn't heard for thirty years. "Sorry to bother you like this, Roger," she said, "but I've forgotten so much about my father. Is there anything that comes to mind?" I said yes, sure, and mentioned his socks—cheap, pinkish-brown athletic socks from Sears, Roebuck that he commonly wore at home in the evening— or at dinner at my house—tucked into a pair of ancient and badly cracked patent-leather dance pumps. Nobody else did this: only Walker Field, my neighbor, my college classmate, my old reliable. I filled in a little more for Cally, who was his oldest child, mentioning his narrow wrists and alert gaze and long fingers, and perhaps the absorbed, delighted way he watched his hands that were tipped down, oddly vertical above the piano keys, as he played: as they played—it was all from within—"Take a Pair of Sparkling Eyes," say, or "Memories of You," or "Do Nothin' Till You Hear from Me," or flashes of Ravel and Schubert. If there was a party and some singing along, he knew the best word or words in a great lyric—giving an enunciating clarity to, say, the "cling" in the bridge of "Makin' Whoopee":

> *Picture a little love nest, down where the*
> *roses* cling;
> *Picture that same sweet love nest: see what*
> *a year can bring.*

The socks, I explained to Cally, were affectation carried to the upper levels of cool. Walker was the most stylish gent I knew, with the possible exception of his older brother, James Field, a celebrated professor of American history at Swarthmore, who was even leaner and longer than he, with a narrow nose that came to a point. Jim—to continue this digression—while on a visit to Walker and his wife, Nancy, in the mid-nineteen-fifties, drew himself a bath, and lying at ease in the tub received an unexpected visit from Cally's two younger brothers. After an extended silent inspection, Sam Field, then perhaps five, said, "Uncle Jim, are all men like you?" Jim was so pleased with his response that he passed it along to me that evening. He said, "Very few."

I spared Cally this riposte, but offered instead a moment

from 1941 or thereabouts. Walker, who had an ongoing pair of subscription tickets to the Boston Symphony, took me along one spring Friday afternoon. We had lunch somewhere off Beacon Street and were back in the sunshine in plenty of time before the overture, when Walker said, "Let's run." And away we went, a couple of twenty-year-old Harvard juniors in jackets and ties and narrow summer pants, leaping like deer across the Commonwealth Avenue traffic, hurdling hydrants, dodging in front of dowagers and startled pedestrians, our feet spattering down the red brick Boston sidewalks, our heads straining like Olympic sprinters. Laughter got the better of us at last and stopped us, wheezing and sweaty, with our hands on our knees, a block or so short of Symphony Hall. There was no point to this, I told Cally: we were young, was all. Talking with her, I suddenly recalled what Walker and I watched for that day, once we got inside and found our seats. Serge Koussevitzky, the Symphony's revered long-term conductor, always halted infinitesimally when he walked out onstage from the right and then made a smart, almost military pivot toward the podium. It was Walker who first spotted the mannerism and named it "Koussey's Pause." Here again, we nudged each other and smiled in the dark when the maestro delivered as promised, then strode across the illuminated and waiting stage.

All my recollections of Walker are playful, which is surprising, because he was a serious man: a talented architect who built himself a brilliant Wright- or Mies-touched house on a steep hillside in Rockland County. He became engrossed in the larger forms of design and served as chairman of the regional planning board during the first explosion of postwar suburban growth. At Harvard, he'd been elected to the Signet, the honorary scholars' society. Reading his senior honors thesis—I'd asked to see it—I encountered the word "eclectic" for the first time: "When the flow of works from the boards of the Grand Eclectics first began to wane," or some such. He'd put me on to a favorite professor of his, Kenneth J. Conant (mentioned in a previous chapter), whose electrifying visits to Cluny and the Tugendhat House, delivered in lectures I took with him on medieval and modern architecture, almost brought about a late shift in my major. Walker had been in the Navy during our World War, but then suddenly we were neighbors, when, in 1950, my wife, Evelyn, and I bought a house in Snedens Landing, my old boyhood place on the Hudson, where Walker and Nancy Field's glass-and-fieldstone home had just risen above the road to the waterfall path. Here my two young daughters (by coincidence, the older one was named Callie) overlapped at school with Eliot and Sam Field. There were five young Fields in the end, and we Fields and Angells became part of the self-entranced Snedens car-pool and kids'-playgroup and grownups'-party set, there in the fifties. Nobody said it, but Walker and the vibrant, dark-haired Nancy were easily our Dick and Nicole Diver, without the doom and boozing. Their parties lit up the best weekends, with Walker at the piano—at night in their cantilevered living room it seemed suspended amid the trees—or, later on, playing his trombone in soft accompaniment with Tricky Sam Nanton and Lawrence Brown on the 78 of "Never No Lament," while we danced. He had all the Ellingtons—a discology he'd begun to collect before his teens.

Walker's tennis game survives within this communal panorama. Each shot of his—his left-handed first serve to my backhand, his volley toward the deep right-hand corner, where there's always a slippery damp spot on the gray clay beyond the baseline to think about—still brings a hurrying response and counter-strategy to mind: slice him crosscourt up the line, or, no, better lob and get your ass back toward the middle. Mostly, he killed me. His first serve was a rocket, and the second—a spin so severe that it appeared to turn the midair ball into a fuzzy lozenge—sometimes jumped up into my face, reducing us both to laughter. And now here we are in September of 1958, playing each other once again in the semifinal singles of our unserious late-summer tournament, with the same audience of kids and dogs and waiting players arrayed on the weedy grass between the old court and the softly arriving cars on River Road. We are tied in the first set, but unexpectedly I break his serve and then hold my own, to win it. I take the second one as well, and more easily, and it's over. I'm elated but a little let down. Sitting next to Nancy, with a towel on one shoulder and his knees drawn up, Walker says, "It's so strange. I keep feeling we're about to start."

A few weeks later, the four of us are bound for a dinner party in Haverstraw when Walker, who is driving, misses a left bend in the road and instead shoots us straight ahead and halfway up a gravel driveway, where we come to a sudden stop. He sits behind the wheel, shaking his head, then murmurs, "Now, why did I do that?"

There have been some questions, as we know by now. Something's been happening to Walker—the doctors can't say what. More tests are coming up. He's going to be O.K., of course, but you have to be sure. There's a missing piece somewhere. Walker talks about it calmly, but soon only Nancy can remember what's been going on. We hear of some other slips and confusions, and now there's a chance of surgery, down the line. Nancy talks to us in private, and sometimes calls back again, late at night. Their kids are told. The operation, at Mount Sinai in March, goes well, but the news couldn't be worse. It's an infiltrating glioblastoma: a killer flower with its snaky tendrils all over the frontal lobes. Nancy makes a date for me, and when I call upon Walker one more time, early in the spring, he is sitting stiffly upright in a hospital chair, in clean green pajamas and white robe. A perky hat sits on his bald head, hiding the scar. He looks at me narrowly—he can't take his eyes off me—but I'm doing all the talking. He follows some of my chatter, but then his gaze fades or clicks off again. He has still said nothing. The nurse comes in, smiling, and says, "This is your friend Roger," and Walker is impatient with her. "We play tennis together," he manages. Then silence. When I get up to leave he's neither sad nor glad. He keeps looking at me, trying to figure it out. We shake hands.

Out on Fifth Avenue again, I am too shocked to cry. A wave of anger slams me and almost knocks me down. How could this have happened? How could Walker let it happen? Weeks or months later, it comes to me that death's dire nature, its publicized awfulness—the Man in the Bright Nightgown, the skeletal dancer with his scythe— has little to do with darkness or the shroud, but lurks within the unreturned gaze. My friend doesn't know me,

and I am an infant again, flailing in the night and yelling
to be picked up and held and whispered to.

He didn't get better. He never quite knew us, and in
time Nancy began to make shorter visits. He died four or
five months later, in another hospital: a friendly pneumo-
nia did the honors. He was thirty-eight. Before this, and
because she didn't want the children to meet his empty
stare, Nancy sometimes arranged for them to visit Mount
Sinai but only to stand across the avenue and look up to
where their father would be waiting at his window, looking
down at this pretty woman and some blond kids waving
their hands. The nurse would come by and say something,
and he would raise his hand, too. What this was like or is
still like for the kids is unimaginable: they're all still around,
middle-aged now, with full lives and a cumulative nine
children of their own, and so is Nancy. She got on with it,
had a long and fulfilling second marriage, and, a widow
once again, is now in Portland, Maine. Eliot Field, a lawyer,
lives in a nearby town and keeps an office in Wiscasset. I
have not asked any of them how much they remember
about their father's or their husband's death. This is my version. Hard lines.

This was a phrase that Walker and I and some friends
of ours said to each other in tough times, starting in college.
"Hard lines!" we murmured if someone complained about
an overdue history paper. "Hard lines!" to your undeserved
hangover or sudden cash shortage. It covered more serious
stuff, too: hard lines about your alcoholic father and your
departed terrific girlfriend. Hard lines about the war coming, and then about what the people in occupied Paris were

suffering, with the Wehrmacht there now. I think the thing had begun with an older college friend of ours, John Brackett, who left law school after Pearl Harbor, and encountered hard lines indeed when the bomber he was piloting in an advanced Navy training exercise crashed one night and killed him. But Walker and I went on saying the same coolly comforting words after we'd become fathers and neighbors together. Hard lines about Levi, your dead bulldog. Hard lines about your mother: I'm so sorry.

Walker's long-widowed mother, Amy Field, a tall and elegant figure with an air of affectionate reserve, if that is possible, lived in the city but came out to Snedens Landing on birthdays and holidays. She always asked what I'd been reading. She grew troubled in her seventies and one day called on my father, a lawyer, whom she'd known years before, to tell him that she was being watched by agents of a foreign power. Her phones had been tapped, and lately secret messages for her were appearing on billboards and in the *Times*. Her sons put her into Roosevelt Hospital, where she had weekend outpatient privileges, and from which she soon took her leave, from a high balcony. In her lucid stretches she'd recognized the dementia that was overtaking her. After she died, Walker and Nancy and Jim and Lila Field realized that she had contrived to say goodbye, at some length, to each of them and to all eight of her grandchildren, before the end. "The last great act of a gallant lady" was the way Walker put it to me.

I've had a life sheltered by privilege and engrossing work, and shot through with good luck, but I don't believe that this accompanying trickle of rotten news is exactly rare. Stuff piles up, and people my age come to understand that what's been happening around them all this time is probably happening all over, in some version or other. It's comforting to conclude that everyday life in olden times was chancier than it is now, but I'm not even sure about this. Other stories creep back, catching us unaware. My young friend Eva coming home from school in Copenhagen one day to find her mother, Korin, a suicide. Jake, a sweet writer but tired of his demons, leaving my office on a January afternoon and, as related, putting himself into the Hudson. A little news item, down at the corner of a page, that caught my eye after the great ice storm that crippled upper New England and parts of Canada in January, 1998. It mentioned an isolated farm couple, both elderly, in East Sullivan, Maine, who'd gone without power for days, then roused themselves and drove down the rink-slippery driveway to collect the mail and newspapers from their roadside box. Coming back, their car slid into a frozen ditch not far from their garage. She fell on the ice, trying to make it home, and he could not get her back on her feet. Leaving her with his jacket folded under her head, he teetered toward the house when he, too, went down, quite close to her, and in turn could not get up. When they were found a day or so later the positions of their frozen bodies told the story, if not their last conversations. Oh, no, we exclaim when such news reaches us, but these tales are part of a classic repertory we recognize as our own. A woman I'd known for years surprised me when she said that her father had died in a fire when she was an infant; he'd saved her life but lost his. More recently, I asked a doctor friend if she'd ever known anyone who was murdered, as I have. She said no, but then called back a few days later and said, "You know, I was wrong. There've been three." What's strange and not so rare about this—it's not rare at all—is the way we press on. We get over it.

I had a visit from Walker Field while I was writing this piece, when he turned up in a dream, nicely dressed and with his freshly combed hair still dark from his shower. He gave me a friendly look, through his horn-rims, and proceeded past, perhaps headed for a party. It was one of those dreams you recognize as dreams while they're happening, and make you a witness and a participant at the same time. And along about then or a little earlier I remembered a photograph of him in another cheerful setting. I couldn't find it in any of my old albums, but then my daughter Callie told me that she still had a print of it. Looking at it, I can name the day and time of day when it was snapped: late afternoon on May 8, 1956. It's our back garden, on Evelyn's thirty-fifth birthday, and here she is, lean and glamorous, with her hair combed back and her favorite party earrings gleaming.

That winter, we'd lost an ancient apple tree that stood in the middle of the scruffy lawn behind the house; we'd hung a swing for our girls from one of the low branches. There was an ice storm, and when I looked down there the next morning the ancient centerpiece was slightly askew, still standing but snapped off clean at its base. Now the group in the family picture is surrounding its replacement, a nymph-thin apple sapling that's just been planted a few yards from where the old one stood. The tree is a surprise present from the Fields, who have brought it up the hill in a truck, with kids and neighbors and shovels and tootings, before the party they've arranged for Ev, at our place. The photograph has the perfection of the moment; Giotto couldn't make it better. Unwrapped and debagged, the tree is already in the ground. One of my neighbors, the pathologist Lewis Thomas, is letting fall a last shovelful of loam, and my old car-pool pal Dick Salmon, a cigarette in his mouth, is kneeling at the right, hand-raking dressing he's taken from a white paper bag labelled "Sheep Manure." The men are in jackets and neckties. Beyond and to the left, my young daughters are side by side, five-year-old Alice in her bathrobe—it's almost her bedtime—and Callie inside an old field jacket of mine, with the sleeves pushed back. Maybe it's been raining. The girls wear an expression of delight—Alice's mouth has fallen open—as they look up at Walker Field, just beyond the slim tree to the right, who seems to be laughing, too, even with his lips pressed to the mouthpiece of his trombone. He is lean and young. The forefinger of his left hand is hooked over the shaft of the trombone, and its long descending slide becomes another elegant angle in the composition. Evelyn is leaning over our girls as she explains that the tune that Walker is playing is the old Joyce Kilmer thing "Trees."

I was not there—maybe this is why the picture means so much now. I was off in London on assignment for *Holiday* magazine, where I worked—I hated being away for this notable birthday—but within a few minutes the phone in our kitchen would ring with my surprise call, and Evelyn would let me know what I'd just missed. She sounded young and lit up with happiness—just the way everyone in the photograph looks now. Across our patchy little property and up the steep hill beyond, our neighbors Rita and Bob Norris have just stepped out onto their terrace—they're coming to the party, too—and they burst out laughing when the faint, globelike notes of the corny old song come floating past them, glowing like summer lanterns.

I am grateful for friends and colleagues at *The New Yorker*, where some of these chapters first appeared, and in particular for my editors: William Maxwell, Gardner Botsford, Charles McGrath, Ann Goldstein, William Shawn, and David Remnick.

—R. A.